Published by Collins
An imprint of HarperCollins Publishers
Westerhill Road
Bishopbriggs
Glasgow G64 2QT
collins.reference@harpercollins.co.uk
www.harpercollins.co.uk

First published 2019

© HarperCollins Publishers

Text © Philip Parker

See page 288 for map and image credits.
Unless stated, all mapping © Geographers' A-Z Map Company Limited
www.az.co.uk
© Crown copyright and database rights 2019 OS 100017302
London 2012 Pictograms © LOCOG 2009. All rights reserved (page 175).

The A-Z logo is registered and used by permission of Geographers' A-Z Map Co Ltd.

Collins® is a registered trademark of HarperCollins Publishers Ltd

A catalogue record for this book is available from the British Library

ISBN 978-0-00-835176-2

10 9 8 7 6 5 4 3 2 1

Printed in China

MIX
Paper from
responsible sources
FSC™ C007454

THE

A to Z

HISTORY OF
LONDON

Philip Parker

contents

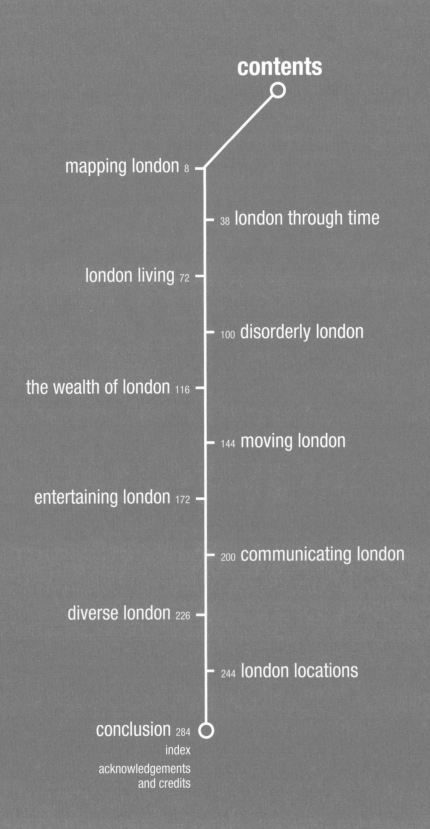

introduction

There are over 60,000 streets in London and that number is changing all the time, as historic alleyways are blocked, new routes cut through and housing estates spring up on the city's fringes. Such a complex urban space has an equally complicated history, as labyrinthine as the medieval maze of streets which lies at its heart.

There have been many Londons throughout the nearly 2,000 years of its existence: from the Roman outpost guarding a strategic crossing of the River Thames to the teeming chaos of Shakespeare's time, the vigour and grime of the Victorian metropolis and today's global financial centre, which is undergoing a cultural and demographic resurgence after decades of decline. There is, though, a certain fascination in the mature city, in its development and ability to adapt to challenges once through the phases of its infancy and youthful vigour, when the response to problems was often simply to grow (more people, more land, more infrastructure).

The period since the 1930s is one which is often overlooked in histories of London, or relegated to a final chapter. Yet it, too, has been a time of massive change: from the Blitz of the Second World War which reduced many districts to rubble, the decisions about how to reconstruct it afterwards, the impact of large-scale immigration on the shape of the city's population from the 1950s, the new cultural phenomena of the 1960s, and the disappearance of traditional industries and the decline of London's port. More recently, the capital has seen a renaissance, with an expanding financial sector colonizing a new district along the river bank and fuelling a crop of architecturally inventive skyscrapers in the traditional City of London, as well as new investment to build new tube and rail lines to bring relief to London's hard-pressed yet stoic commuters.

The 1930s saw another development, too, with the appearance of the first fully-indexed portable street map of London. Perplexed by the effort needed to navigate London's streets, Phyllis Pearsall resolved to find a solution. Herself the daughter of a cartographer, and a woman of unusual determination, the result in 1936 – after years of hard grind walking what was then Central London's 23,000 streets in order to chart them accurately – was the *Geographers' A-Z Street Atlas*. From unpromising beginnings – the first edition was delivered to retailers from a wheelbarrow, and many were suspicious of its novelty – the London A-Z became a cultural icon and shorthand for almost any map of the capital (just like the 'hoover' for vacuum cleaners).

It seems only fitting, therefore, to illustrate this history of London from the 1930s with A-Z's mapping, which has been there from the very start of the period and has guided puzzled Londoners and unwary tourists right up to our present day of the Millennium Bridge, the Shard and the Docklands Light Railway. By looking at mapping from that first 1936 A-Z, and its many successors, we can see, in stark visual form, how much London has changed over the course of the past eight decades: the new suburbs which have bloomed, the transport links which have appeared, and the whole districts which have been utterly transformed (a glance at the 1936 map of the Isle of Dogs and its equivalent today gives the lie to any notion that London is a sclerotic city in which everything remains, in essence, the same).

The last eighty years, of course, do not exist in isolation and the first chapter of this book looks at London before the 1930s, at its growth and setbacks from that tiny Roman outpost in the AD 40s to its almost unrecognizable descendant in Edwardian times. It documents, too, the successive attempts – from mid-Tudor times onwards – to map it (an effort that became ever more necessary, and frantic, once the pace of London's expansion hotted up after the Industrial Revolution). The second chapter deals decade by decade with London's development since 1936, showing how the city has expanded, both physically and in terms of population, and the political and economic changes which it has weathered to reach the third decade of the twenty-first century. The succeeding part of the book follows London through the themes and issues which have preoccupied its citizens in the modern era, whether its markets, such as Covent Garden (which migrated south of the River in the 1970s to leave a new 'must-see' tourist destination on its old site), its fashion (from the austerity wear of the 1940s to the punk wave of the 1970s), its transport (from the death of trams in the 1940s to their rebirth in the twenty-first century), its turbulent history of political turmoil and terrorism, and the challenges and enrichment which migration from East Asia, South Asia, the Caribbean and Europe have brought. The final part of *The A to Z History of London* looks at a selection of London locations and districts which have undergone particular changes during the past eighty years from Covent Garden itself; to Nine Elms, the new home both of Covent Garden Market and the United States Embassy; King's Cross, which has been transformed from a desert of derelict warehouses to a new cultural quarter; and the City of London, which has acquired a rash of new banking palaces with irreverent nicknames such as the Cheesegrater and the Walkie Talkie.

London's recent history has almost as many twists and by-ways as its 60,000 streets. I hope that *The A to Z History of London* will provide as reassuring and enlightening a guide to the multifaceted and almost dizzying changes which it has experienced as the A-Z mapping which accompanies it has given to generations of Londoners and visitors.

Philip Parker

MAPPING LONDON

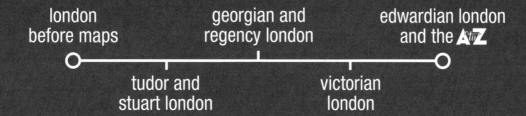

london
before maps

georgian and
regency london

edwardian london
and the A to Z

tudor and
stuart london

victorian
london

london before maps

For the first century and a half of its existence, London went unmapped. The settlement that sprang up at a strategic crossing of the Thames in the early AD 50s, less than a decade after the Roman invasion of Britain, showed little portent of its distant future as capital of a world empire and global financial centre. Clustered against the north bank of the river, with a small outpost to the south in Southwark, early Roman London was little more than a frontier trading post, which suffered an almost fatal setback when it was burnt to the ground by Boudicca's Iceni rebels in AD 60. From the ashes of this early wooden (and so eminently combustible) early settlement, a stone phoenix arose, complete with the full panoply of public buildings to be found in urban centres throughout the Roman Empire.

Centred on the modern City of London, Roman Londinium boasted a stone fort, at Cripplegate in the northwest, a basilica (the centre of the provincial administration) to the east, an amphitheatre to entertain its 50,000 or so citizens, and a series of bath houses (including one at Cheapside) to cleanse them. This burgeoning proto-city – already equipped with a teeming set of wharves to carry the cross-Channel trade in fine pottery, wine, furs and slaves – was laid out on a rectilinear grid which, sometime early in the third century, as the empire's defences became more permeable to barbarian raiders, was equipped with a stone wall.

London would remain penned within this fortification for around a millennium, confined to a space in which its inhabitants found no need of mapping to navigate. The Romans did make maps but they tended to the monumental – a marble one of the empire was erected in Rome on the orders of Emperor Augustus's chief lieutenant, Marcus Agrippa – or practical long-distance itineraries (of which a single example survives in the form of the *Peutinger Table*, a medieval copy of a fourth-century map showing routes across a squashed

50,000
the approximate population of roman london at its height

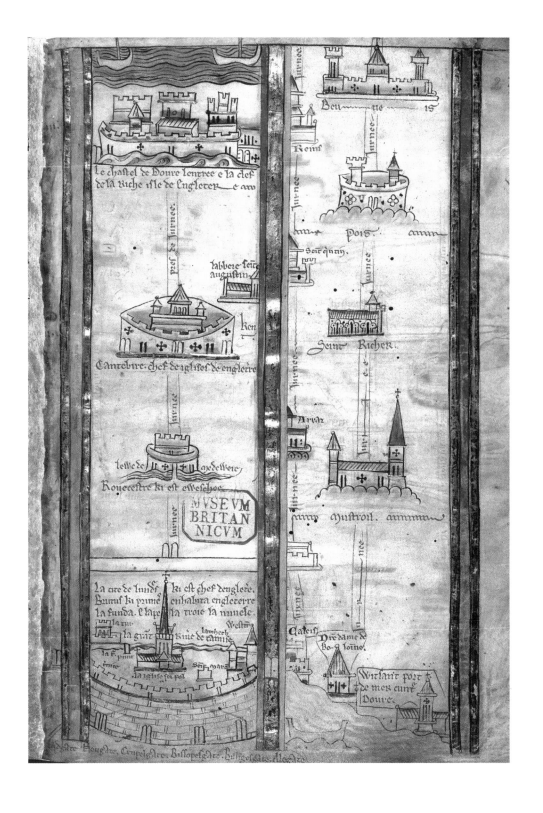

Le chastel de Douvre lentree e la clef
de la Riche isle de engletere. e aw

Pref de iurnee

labbeie seit
augustin

Kent

Cantebire: chef de iglises de engletere

iurnee

lesse de
Roucestre ki est eveschoe

iurnee

La cite de lundr ki est chef denglere
Brutus ki prime enhabita engletere
la funda. lapele la troie la nuvele.

Westm
lambeth
la grant riue de tamise

Seit mars

la ígliſe ſei pol

iurnee

Deu...te 15

Reins

iurnee

iurnee

Pois

Seir enim

iurnee

Seint Richer

iurnee

iurnee

Arraz

iurnee

iurnee

Mustroil

iurnee

Caleis

Notre dame de
Bo-g-loine

Witsant port
de mer cunt
Douvre

and elongated Europe which, unfortunately, only contains a portion of the southeast coast of England).

For an idea of London's appearance, we have to rely on a medallion struck to commemorate its reconquest after the collapse of a breakaway British empire in 296. It depicts the wall, punctured by a gate but, sadly, shows nothing of the city's interior. Within a century-and-a-half that gateway was rendered redundant. When the Romans abandoned the province of Britannia in 411, its cities were left to the uncertain stewardship of native warlords who proved incapable of stemming the relentless advance of Anglo-Saxon invaders crossing the North Sea from Europe. Markets dried up, towers tumbled and farms replaced forums, as urban life all but disappeared.

London, though, somehow survived. The newcomers established a settlement called Lundenwic a little to the west of the old Roman city, near Trafalgar Square and along the Strand. Over four centuries trade recovered, bringing a modest level of prosperity to the city, which became the centre of a bishopric shortly after St Augustine brought Christianity to southern England in 597. London's growing wealth attracted raids by Danish Vikings, who first attacked it in 842, highlighting the city's terrible vulnerability. To protect it, Alfred the Great, king of Wessex, who had just acquired control of the area in 886, moved London's population back inside the Roman walls. Lundenburh, as it was now called, began to develop its medieval street pattern during this late Saxon period, and the construction by Edward the Confessor in the 1060s of a new monastery and cathedral (which became known as the 'west Minster') provided London with a new focus, and a centre for royal government independent of the old city.

When the Normans in turn invaded England in 1066, they built a series of castles to secure their conquests. One, the Tower of London, survived to become the cornerstone of the city's defences; the others, at Baynards' Castle and Montfichet's Tower near St Paul's, were demolished by the thirteenth century. Londoners by then probably needed a map, as the population had grown to 80,000, making it by far England's largest town – until

◁ 11
The thirteenth-century St Albans monk Matthew Paris produced an itinerary map showing towns along the pilgrimage route from London to Jerusalem. In his depiction of London (bottom left on the map), Matthew includes Old St Paul's Cathedral and London Bridge ('Le Punt de Londres').

the Black Death cut it in half again in 1348. Along the riverfront – which had encroached almost a hundred metres into the Thames as land was reclaimed – sat a complex of wharves at which goods were landed for transport into the city. There, a host of trades from ironmongery to weaving provided livelihoods for its inhabitants, who lived in streets lined with timber-framed and plastered buildings. Yet, save for archaeology, we have scant evidence of the city's layout or how it looked, only a handful of drawings such as one of London included by the thirteenth-century monk Matthew Paris in his itinerary map. This has Old St Paul's Cathedral (the predecessor of Wren's magnificent church, and which was destroyed in the Great Fire in 1666) clearly visible. In addition, a poignant illumination of the Poems of Charles, Duke of Orléans – composed while he was imprisoned after the Battle of Agincourt in 1415 – shows the author as a captive in the White Tower of the Tower of London, and the Pool of London and the port's Custom House in the foreground.

By 1500, London stood on the cusp of a new stage in its history, which would transform it from a modest market town to the capital of a growing empire. As well as an era of explorers and merchants, it would be an age of maps.

tudor AND stuart london

Between 1500 and 1700 London underwent a profound change. Transforming from an overblown provincial town of around 80,000 people to a metropolis of half a million, it was at the heart of a nation beginning to assemble an empire and assert itself on the world stage. The city experienced pestilence, fire and constitutional upheavals. The changes to its fabric were no less profound: a metamorphosis that saw the landscape change from a forest of wood to a jungle of brick and stone. Bursting out of its old bounds, the colonization of suburbs began, an expansion that would continue unabated right into the twentieth century.

The first agent of this change was Henry VIII's Dissolution of the Monasteries, which from 1536 released vast tracts of urban property onto the market (the religious houses had owned over half the buildings in certain parts of the city). Some was taken over by local landowners, others by favoured courtiers or royal officials who diverted plum properties their own way. Blackfriars passed to Sir Thomas Cawarden, Master of the Revels, while over time fashionable houses sprung up in former ecclesiastical residences along the Strand, attracted by its proximity to the new centre of royal power at Westminster and by its distance from the overcrowded, stinking alleyways of the old city within the Roman walls.

For the first time London was mapped; the Copperplate Map of 1558 shows the densely packed streets of the city, its skyline dotted with the spires of the many churches that continued to function despite the Dissolution and the plague that periodically culled London's lower orders.

The pace of change was rapid – new royal palaces were built (such as Henry VIII's new residence at Bridewell, constructed between 1515 and 1520), and the city's population became more cosmopolitan. Dutch refugees from the war with Spain began to arrive

3

the number of days it took for three-quarters of the city of london to burn down

from 1568, and French Huguenots fled following the St Bartholomew's Day Massacre of Protestants in 1572. The changes were chronicled by John Stowe, the son of a tallow chandler, who like many of relatively modest means was able to make his way through the guilds of merchants that dominated the commercial life of the city (with over forty-seven company guild halls in place by 1600). His *Survey of London* cast a slightly melancholic eye on the vast changes London had undergone in the preceding decades; the monasteries that had become breweries, and the spread of suburbs eastward and southward into Southwark (which, being exempt from the rule of the city government, became a haven for otherwise forbidden pleasures – including bear-baiting – and the first theatres, such as the Rose – opened on Bankside in 1587 – and the nearby Globe, built in 1599). The city's growing pains were captured in visual form by John Norden, whose 1593 map showed it breaking out of the Roman walls. Its label describes it as 'a guide for cuntrye men in the famous cittey of London', making it perhaps the first cartographic representation of the city that was self-consciously designed as an aide for the perplexed outsider. For the modern viewer its most striking aspect is the large expanse of fields that surround the inner core, with areas such as Marylebone, Islington and Richmond still villages well outside the city bounds.

The turn of the seventeenth century brought a new dynasty – the Stuarts – and a new king. His aspirations for London 'that we found our Citie and suburbs of London of stickes, and left them of bricke' were not quite fulfilled, even though the aristocracy's increasing wealth allowed them to begin that work, as a rush of speculative building on noble estates brought the building of squares such as Lincoln's Inn Fields and Leicester Square (though the Earl of Leicester lost a legal battle with his tenants, which meant that the central part of the fields had to be left open, explaining why it, unlike almost all the surrounding area, was not built upon). The grandest of them all, Covent Garden, which was designed by Inigo Jones and laid out on land belonging to the Duke of Bedford, was modelled on Italian piazzas, but it also pointed the way to the decline of aspirations that such squares would become elite enclaves within the city. Already within decades, however, many of the

16-7 ▷

This woodcut map shows London in the mid-1560s at the beginning of Elizabeth I's reign. Traditionally called the Agas map – after a surveyor who probably in fact had nothing to do with its compilation – it shows the city still largely confined within the old Roman walls.

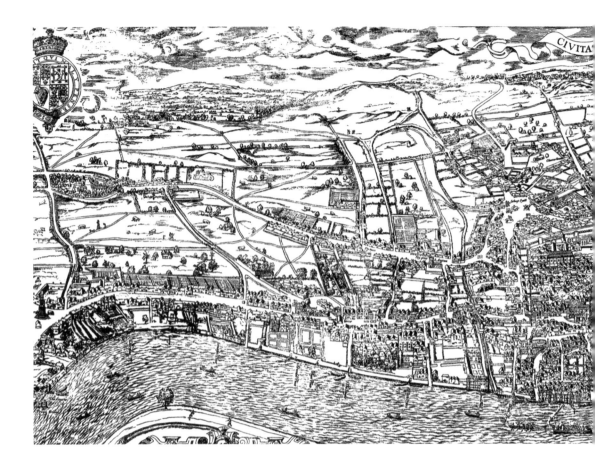

houses initially bought by well-to-do families had become taverns or coffee houses and the nearby development of Seven Dials, begun in 1694, rapidly declined to become a notorious urban slum.

James I's aspirations for a brick-built city were fulfilled in unexpected and catastrophic fashion when a fire that broke out in a baker's shop on 2 September 1666 spread through the combustible wood of the neighbouring streets, a blaze which, by the time it had burned itself out three days later, had consumed almost three-quarters of the City of London's buildings, including St Paul's Cathedral (where the lead of the roof had melted and set fire to a pile of books stored below). As the rubble was cleared, grandiose plans were aired for a reshaped city to emerge from its ashes, but the ambitious schemes of John Evelyn and Christopher Wren for wide boulevards and showpiece squares were never realized (though Wren did get to rebuild fifty-two churches, including St Paul's). Instead the interests of existing property-holders trumped those of rational city planning and inner-city London retained its general contours. The exceptions to this were the cutting through of King Street from the Guildhall to the Wharf, and the continuing development on aristocratic estates,

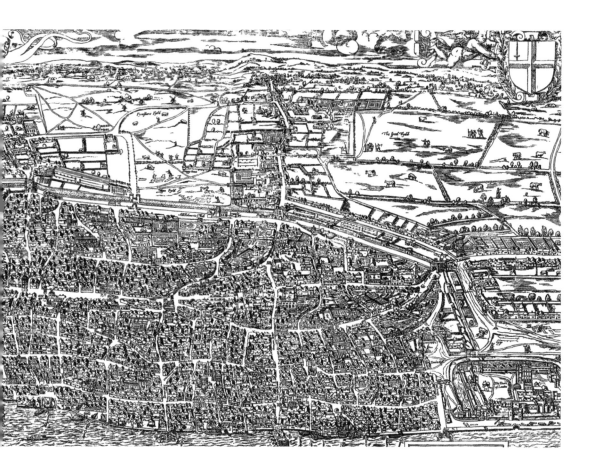

such as the growth of St James's from the 1660s, with the laying out of several new roads, such as Jermyn Street.

The speed of rebuilding was remarkable, and by 1671 around 9,000 properties had been replaced, restoring most of the damage caused by the fire. Meanwhile an Act of 1667 had set down for the first stern controls on additions to the facades of buildings, leading to a uniformity of street fronts, which became one of London's most graceful features. By the time John Ogilby – a former dance master who had turned to cartography after an injury prevented him pursuing his previous career – produced his map of London in 1676, the reconstruction was almost complete. London had weathered the Civil War, the Great Fire and, after the brief excitement of the ousting of James II for his catholic tendencies and replacement by the Protestant Dutch William of Orange, was about to enter a period of relative political stability. The city, though, already pressing at its edges towards Islington and Shoreditch to the east, and nudging past Tyburn towards Mayfair and Marylebone, was poised for further growth.

georgian AND regency london

In 1700, London was in many ways still a medieval city. Despite the rebuilding in the aftermath of the Great Fire, its teeming lanes and great houses still lacked basic services such as public transport, street lighting, basic sanitation or police and fire services. By the dawn of the Victorian Age in 1837, all that had begun to change. With the capital having swallowed up the surrounding fields and absorbed hamlets such as Hampstead and Islington, and with its population swollen to more than a million, London stood on the edge of being the world's first global city.

It was trade that brought this new wealth to London. The acquisition of colonies in the New World and in Asia (most notably India) brought an influx of mercantile money to London (including from the slave trade), which enabled established aristocratic families and a nouveau rich middle class alike to invest in grand London residences. At the start of the period there were still fields in what is now the centre of the city, at Lamb's Conduit Field and Leicester Fields (now Leicester Square), and a periodic hay market took place in the street of that name.

Large estates such as those belonging to the Cavendish-Harley and Portman families were divided up into plots and laid out in grand squares, with high-quality housing surrounding them. Once built, the family retained the freehold of the land but the houses were let out on long 99-year leases that reverted to the freeholder on expiry. John Strype's 1720 edition of Stowe's *Survey of London* still labels Mayfair as 'Pasture Ground' and in the east Stepney is virtually unbuilt on. Yet scarcely a quarter of a century later, John Rocque's magisterial 1746 map of the capital shows how the area between Bond Street and Tiburn Lane (now Park Lane) had developed. Cavendish Square, to the north of Oxford Street and

1 in 8

the proportion of londoners thought to be involved in criminal activity in 1797

laid out in 1717, was one of the first of these new developments, while a further boom in the mid-century led to the development of Piccadilly, Berkeley Square and Portland Place.

London's growth was not all grand houses and opulent squares, no matter the hopes of the developers, and more modest suburbs sprouted at London's margins, such as Pentonville – laid out from the 1770s – and Somers Town, which was developed in the 1790s but rapidly descended down the social scale into a slum. The building of new bridges to supplement London Bridge, which had been London's only river crossing since the time of the Romans, aided the city's spread southwards. Westminster Bridge was completed in 1750, and Blackfriars Bridge opened in 1769; to these the Regency period added Vauxhall Bridge in 1816 and Southwark Bridge in 1819, aiding the development of suburbs in Kennington, Walworth and Camberwell. The construction of crossings further west at Putney Bridge in 1729 and Kew Bridge in 1759 encouraged the westwards spread of London and the incorporation of hamlets such as Richmond into the capital.

By the time Richard Horwood made his huge thirty-two-sheet map of London in 1799, which included the numbering of houses for the first time, the south bank of the Thames had been colonized by a web of streets. Thirty-five years on, Benjamin Davies' map showed that development had reached the open fields around Marylebone and up to St John's Wood, while John Nash's iconic Regency Terraces had brought a grace and uniformity to the environs of the new Marylebone Park (which soon became known as the Regent's Park). This new London was better connected than ever before, as turnpike trusts were established to finance the repair of old roads or the building of new routes, such as the New Road (now Marylebone Road), which cut through what was then the northern edge of the capital between 1756 and 1761 to allow travellers to bypass the increasing congestion of the centre. New coach services took advantage of the improving roads to reduce travel times between London and provincial centres, binding the country closer to London than ever before: the journey from London to Manchester had taken three days in 1760, but consumed a more modest twenty-eight hours by 1788.

20–1 ▷

John Rocque's beautifully engraved twenty-four-sheet map of London took six years of meticulous surveying to compile. The new network of formal squares recently laid out to the west of the City of London, including in Mayfair and Marylebone, is clearly visible.

Inside the city, conditions grew both better and worse. Gas lighting first came to the city in 1814 with its installation on Pall Mall, and within a decade London boasted nearly 40,000 lamps lighting up what until then had been its dangerously dark nocturnal streets. New hospitals such as St George's, the Middlesex, and Westminster were built between 1720 and 1745 to tend to the capital's sick. For those with wealth and the health to enjoy it, pleasure gardens such as Ranelagh (opened in 1742) and smart shopping arcades such as the Burlington (which began business in 1819 off the newly developed Regent's Street), catered to the growing middle classes.

Further down the social scale, however, London remained as desperate and dangerous a place as ever. A rapidly growing population meant that buildings were subdivided and overcrowding of damp, decaying tenements created rookeries such as Seven Dials, Chick Lane, Field Lane and Petticoat Lane that would remain a blight on the capital and its conscience for more than a century. Such areas became paradises for drunks (laid low by an epidemic of gin-drinking that Hogarth brilliantly captured in his *The Rake's Progress* series from 1732 to 1734), prostitutes and thieves. In 1797 Patrick Colquhoun, a Tower Hamlets magistrate, estimated that London's underworld involved some 115,000 people, around an eighth of the entire population.

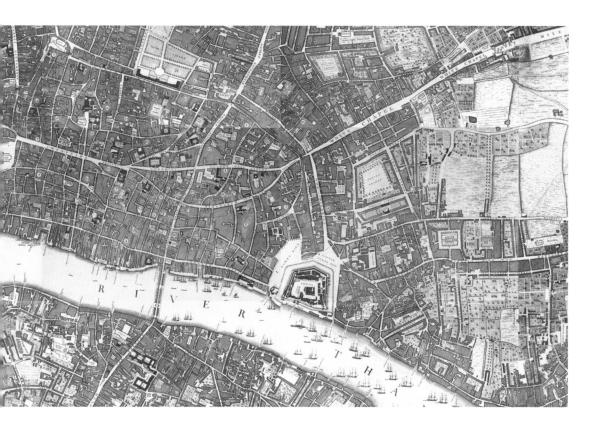

Such a world of thieves bred colourful characters and a volatility that often spiralled into disorder. The Gordon Riots that broke out in 1780, although ostensibly anti-Catholic (sparked by resentment at a 1778 Act reducing legal disability on Catholics), tapped into the anarchy that lay just below London's surface and, during three days of destruction, came perilously close to a Revolution. The reaction of the authorities to these threats was fitful. When they caught notorious criminals, such as the highwayman Jack Sheppard, they would hang them (he swung at Tyburn in November 1724 before a crowd said to have been 200,000 strong), but petty crime was endemic. It was also insoluble until the establishment of the Metropolitan Police in 1829 began the slow process by which the Government reclaimed control of London's streets.

Richer, larger, more chaotic and disorderly than ever, boasting grand squares and squalid slums, it was a vibrant and vigorous London that faced a new reign, with the accession of 18-year-old Queen Victoria in June 1837.

victorian london

The reign of Queen Victoria saw an unprecedented explosion in London's population, which nearly quadrupled from 1.6 million in 1831 (the last census before her accession) to 6.5 million at her death. Those nearly five million additional Londoners strained the ingenuity of Victorian planners, politicians and philanthropists, transforming the capital from a city where there were barely any public services and which was still only just spilling out of its historic geographical bounds into a sprawling metropolis whose fingers extended deep into the surrounding counties and which was provided with the very latest in transport, communication, retailing and sanitary innovations.

A city that cannot move, will die, and it was transport that made Victorian London possible. Until the nineteenth century virtually all transportation had been a matter of private hire, but the introduction of horse buses in 1829, and then the advent of the railways in the 1830s, marked a turning point. These innovations meant that workers could actually get to work without living in the immediate vicinity of their employment, and so were free to move out to further flung suburbs where housing conditions might be better than the squalid rookeries of Holborn or St Giles. The appearance of an army of lower-middle-class accountants and clerks meant, too, that there was now a significant sector of society that could not afford the pretensions of the well-to-do, but had the aspirations, if not always the money, to distance themselves from the living conditions of the working classes.

Between 1836 and 1841, London acquired six railway terminuses, bringing travellers in from the provinces on journeys that took hours, rather than the traditional days. At first they did not quite reach the centre – passengers from the southwest were debouched at Nine Elms, pending the construction of a station at Waterloo in 1848, while during the

76,000
the number of londoners forced from their homes to make way for railway construction between 1855 and 1883

1830s those coming from the north alighted at Camden Town, rather than the as-yet-un-built Euston Station (which opened in 1837).

It took a while for trains to become a practical means of commuting: when the Great Western opened in 1838, the first stop after Paddington was West Drayton, a full thirteen miles away. Train fares, both on the railway and the underground – which first opened in 1863 – were expensive. It was not until 1883 that the train companies were forced to offer concessionary 'workers' fares' in the morning and evening peak hours, in part as compensation for the slum clearances that the building of new lines had involved, and which had forced 76,000 Londoners out of their homes since 1855.

The introduction of electric 'tube' trains on the underground from 1890 and the electrification of trams from 1900 meant that working-class people could also join the middle-classes in the suburbs, with large concentrations settling in East End suburbs such as Bermondsey and Deptford, close to the employment opportunities of the docks. To a small extent their housing needs were met by the philanthropic bodies such as the Peabody Trust, which built estates on land cleared by the Metropolitan Board of Works (which, curiously, was allowed by law to clear slums but not to build replacement housing on them). The process, though, was painfully slow, and by 1900 the seven largest charitable housing trusts had only re-housed around 80,000 people.

In newly fashionable suburbs such as Holloway and Camberwell, the middle classes demanded a superior quality of house, with the luxury of inside toilets or, if they stayed close to the centre, they began to live in flats. The first modern block of flats was built opposite St Pancras Old Church on the Euston Road in 1847, and more soon colonized large parts of districts such as St John's Wood, Bayswater and Knightsbridge (with local authority-built council flats appearing for the first time in the 1890s). They benefitted from improved sanitation, after politicians had finally taken action following the cholera epidemic of 1853–4 and the 'Great Stink' of 1858, when the Thames had become so pungent that MPs could scarcely tolerate the reek in the debating chamber of the House of Commons.

24–5 ▷

Charles Booth produced his *Maps Descriptive of London Poverty* as part of his more general *Inquiry into Life and Labour in London (1886–1903)*. The distinctive colour-coding of streets (and even individual buildings) for the predominant social class made them all the more striking.

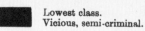
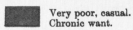

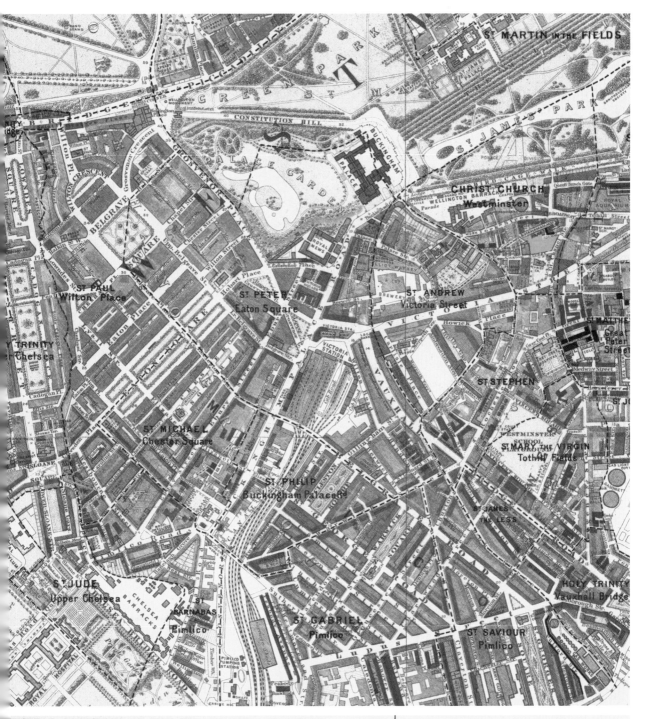

Joseph Bazalgette, the chief engineer of the Metropolitan Board of Works (itself only established in 1855), was given the herculean task of replacing London's leaking and fetid drains with a system fit for a modern, and growing, city. When, in 1875, he completed the task of installing a network of main drains that formed the basis of London's sewage disposal right into the twenty-first century, he became one of London's true (if unsung) heroes.

The capital's capacity to absorb outsiders had always been notable, but Victorian London sucked in an extraordinary host of migrants: from the million who made the trek to the metropolis from East Anglia and the West Country between 1841 and 1871; to the Irish who came in search of casual labour and to escape the after-effects of the Famine back home (and who added 178,000 to the population, mainly in Holborn, St Giles, Whitechapel and Southwark); and the Jews who fled persecutions in Eastern Europe from the 1880s, raising the number of Jewish Londoners to 140,000 by 1914.

Even growing at this breakneck pace, London still had an air of youthful vigour about it. Almost every year brought an innovation, a new service or an improvement as the prevailing ethos that there was no problem that money could not solve, or charitable zeal at least mitigate, brought new specialist hospitals, such as the London Chest Hospital (1848) and the Great Ormond Street Hospital for Children (1852); new road developments, such as the cutting through of Victoria Street to ease congestion around Westminster in 1851; and the establishment of the Metropolitan Fire Brigade in 1866 after a massive warehouse fire on Tooley Street five years earlier had shown the inadequacy of private provision. Those wishing to furnish their new flats could now go to a variety of department stores or specialists such as the Maple's Furniture shop on Tottenham Court Road, which opened its doors in 1841. Leisure opportunities proliferated, from new parks such as Primrose Hill, which opened to the public in 1841; and the Royal Botanic Gardens in Kew, which began to receive visitors in 1840; to galleries, such as the Tate, which opened on Millbank in August 1897; concerts, with the very first night of the Promenade Concerts taking place on 10 August 1895; and sport, with the first men's tennis championship taking place at Wimbledon in 1877.

London, of course, had a darker side. There was practically no welfare provision and much of the population still lived in highly unsatisfactory conditions. The capital was as much the London of Jack the Ripper – who murdered at least five women in the dark, decaying alleys of Whitechapel in 1888 – as it was of the British Empire and the public celebrations for the Diamond Jubilee of Queen Victoria in 1897. One man made it his life's work to chart the social conditions of London. Charles Booth's *Life and Labour of the People of London*, which chronicled the conditions of the capital's most deprived inhabitants, included maps documenting the level of poverty on each street, even individual buildings, with colour coding that ranged from yellow (for 'upper-middle and upper classes. Wealthy') to black (for 'lowest class, vicious semi-criminal'). This black tint spread like an accusing stain in large parts of London such as the East End, and even within a stone's throw of the mansions of Mayfair in certain ill-fated buildings along Broad Street.

Other cartographers struggled with the more mundane task of simply recording a capital that was growing year by year. In 1848 the Ordnance Survey began a two-year project to map the capital at a scale of five feet to the mile, which resulted in an unwieldy 487 different sheets to cover the then extent of the city. A rather more manageable twelve inch to the mile map went on sale at the same time, but it was hardly a very portable gazetteer with which to navigate the city's streets. A series of maps produced by the map publisher Edward Stanford from 1862 ably charted the city's growth, but they were rather more suitable as wall maps than for carrying on a brief journey into an unknown suburb. There was clearly an appetite for something more, and travellers resentful at the depredations of the notoriously rapacious Victorian cab-drivers bought great piles of Mogg's *Ten Thousand Cab Fares Map*, which allowed the calculation of point-to-point fares on a large number of routes and was so popular it went through several editions after 1876. One novel solution to navigating the confusion of London's new roads and ancient alleys came in the form of a 'Hand Guide' in which the map of a section of the capital was printed directly onto a glove, which the owner literally carried on their hand.

The Hand Guide only seems to have reached the prototype stage, and never seems to have been produced in any numbers, but it is an interesting example of Victorian inventiveness and the adaptations Londoners were making to live in a city that was larger, richer, and more populous than it ever had been. What they lacked (as they had done ever since Roman times) was a simple way to find their way around.

edwardian london AND THE A to Z

London had undergone an astonishing transformation during the reign of Queen Victoria, but the dawn of a new reign and a new century did not allow the capital to pause for breath. It was not so much the continued upward curve in the population graph (which spiralled from 6.5 million in 1901 to 8.1 million in 1931, meaning there were more Londoners than ever before) that was so startling, but the new possibilities that changing patterns in work, in housing, in leisure and in transport brought.

Edwardian London remade itself physically. The slum clearances of the Victorian era continued, and new grand schemes were implemented in the centre to help the city compare with continental rivals such as Paris or Berlin. At the top end of the Strand, a hotpotch of old housing was cleared out – though Christopher Wren's church of St Clement Danes was retained – and a new wide-curving thoroughfare was cut through in 1905 and christened with the suitably antique-sounding name of Aldwych. At the junction between Whitehall and The Mall a new ceremonial gateway, Admiralty Arch, was built in 1910. This further enhanced the set-piece of Trafalgar Square, though the effect was rather marred by the increasing levels of traffic that clogged up the square until it was partially pedestrianized in 2003 and its famed, if rather unhealthy, pigeons were evicted.

The process continued in the 1920s, as Regent Street metamorphosed from an ugly duckling ill-assorted collection of buildings into a swan of an avenue with imposing stone facades, fittingly opened by King George V in 1927. Its high-end shops enticed even more shoppers into the West End, already a destination for the newly wealthy middle classes who shopped at Harry Gordon Selfridge's new retail emporium on Oxford Street (which opened in 1909). For those more workaday purchases, shoppers could stay closer to home, at a new breed of supermarket such as Tesco, whose first store appeared in Burnt Oak in 1929.

23,000
the number of streets phyllis pearsall walked in order to create the first street atlas of london

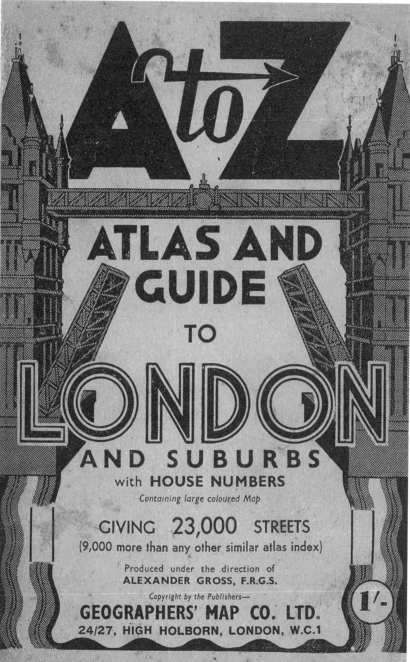

A to Z

ATLAS AND GUIDE

TO

LONDON

AND SUBURBS

with HOUSE NUMBERS

Containing large coloured Map

GIVING 23,000 STREETS

(9,000 more than any other similar atlas index)

Produced under the direction of
ALEXANDER GROSS, F.R.G.S.

Copyright by the Publishers—

GEOGRAPHERS' MAP CO. LTD.

24/27, HIGH HOLBORN, LONDON, W.C.1

1/-

THE ONLY QUICK MAP REFERENCE SUPPLEMENT
TO ALL OLD AND NEW STREET NAMES

The cover of the very first A-Z Street Atlas from 1936 proudly proclaims the 23,000 streets that are mapped within (and does not fail to mention that this is 9,000 more than its competitors). It was only at the last-minute insistence of Phyllis Pearsall that it did not begin life as the 'OK Atlas'.

The Edwardian era and the 1920s were the heyday of the suburbs, as the Metropolitan Line ploughed further to the north and west of London, making journeys into the centre from districts such as Harrow, Pinner and Wembley a practical proposition for clerks and shop assistants. There was plenty of work, too, in the suburbs. New factories opened, even during the Great Depression of the 1930s, to which London proved itself largely immune. Between 1932 and 1936, some 1,573 factories opened in the capital, around half the national total. London's industrial quarter burst its traditional bounds on the fringes of the City and around the docks to colonize Hayes, Enfield, Croydon and Dagenham (where the Ford Motors factory began production in 1931). As a result, the population there boomed, with Dagenham ballooning from a modest parish of around 9,000 people in 1921 to a mini-city of over 100,000 inhabitants a decade later. As well as the Ford factory, West London received new works such as the H. Bronnley & Co. soap factory; the T. Wall & Sons factory, which opened in Acton in 1922, as the company made an eclectic sideways diversification from sausages into ice-cream; and Hoover, who opened up production in an art-deco palace in Perivale in 1932. Some areas did not fare so well, and the docks, which had long been the engine of East London's prosperity, began decades of long, slow decline (and ultimate closure in the 1970s).

As it approached its 1,900th birthday, London entered the 1930s in expansive mode, building for a future that just nine years later was to be brutally ripped away. The First World War had revealed the shocking state of much of Britain's (and the capital's) housing, as rank after rank of conscripts exhibited the poor physical condition that had arisen from the straitened circumstances of their upbringings.

Conditions, though, were improving. London County Council (LCC) engaged in wholesale clearances: in Clerkenwell it had swept away the old Union Buildings by 1907, pushing 1,414 people out of their old slum dwellings and erecting replacement blocks and homes on the Bourne Estate. New 'cottage estates' were built with small houses, each with their own garden, in an effort to bring a sense of arcadia into the smoky metropolis. Many, such as Totterdown Fields in Tooting or Old Oak in Hammersmith, were at the end of LCC-built tramlines, further extending the areas from within which Londoners could comfortably travel to work.

The 1919 Housing and Town Planning Act laid down that half a million houses were to be built across the country. Progress was initially very slow, but with a fevered burst of activity from 1924 onwards the numbers reached a million by 1939. The LCC demolished over 125,000 slum houses in the 1920s; to replace them it opened up new areas to housing, and also remodelled old ones. As a result, London pushed out through Middlesex to the north, Surrey to the south, and southeast to the leafy fringes of Kent. The largest of all the new developments was the Becontree Estate in Barking, where some 27,000 houses were erected by 1938. Its cottage-style houses and ample gardens, parks and green spaces offered the prospect of an Elysian future which never quite materialized.

New estates south of the Thames – at Roehampton, Norbury in Croydon and Bellingham in Lewisham – housed a quarter of a million people between 1919 and 1939, while improved transport links, such as the Dartford Loop Line and stations at Albany Park and Upminster Bridge, made more areas of London accessible to an easy commute. To the north, London Transport enthusiastically advertised the virtues of living in 'Metro Land' (estates adjacent to the new Metropolitan Line stations) and Pinner exploded from being a tiny village in the 1920s to a small town of 23,000 a decade later. So concerned was the Government that this expansion might entirely swallow up the countryside around London, the 1935 Restriction of Ribbon Development Act was passed to try to stop the urban sprawl from snaking up the main road arteries out of the capital. In 1938 the Green Belt Act put a near total halt on development within a green ring around London, holding fast even into the twenty-first century.

Although the appearance of these new estates had a certain identikit similarity that later became the object of mockery (no less than the more prosperous suburbs, where mile upon mile of semi-detached houses with faux-Tudor frontages appeared), Londoners who lived in these new developments enjoyed amenities that had been unavailable to their parents. In Becontree, most properties boasted the unheard-of luxury of an indoor toilet and fitted bath, and by 1939 three-quarters of houses had a gas cooker (and an adventurous eight per cent an electric one), while more and more houses boasted their own telephones. Closer to the centre of the city, the old private mansions that had been such a feature of the streetscape started to disappear, to be replaced by blocks of flats. Large developments such as Dolphin Square in Pimlico, Dorset House in Baker Street and Du Cane Court in Balham owed their existence to the 1930s town planners.

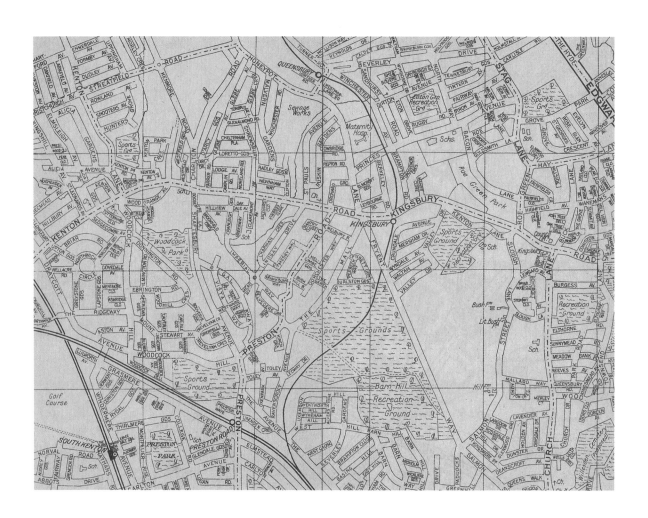

△

Kingsbury and Queensbury were among the suburbs that saw extensive development with the coming of the Metropolitan Line in the 1930s. Kingsbury was an old established village (the novelist Oliver Goldsmith lived there from 1771 to 1774), while Queensbury was a newly developed suburb, its name – intended to mimic its near neighbour – the result of a newspaper competition.

As cars became affordable for the middle classes, new roads were needed to cope with the increase in traffic. In 1936 the Ministry of Transport proposed a massive programme of road-building, with flyovers soaring over much of Central London, and the demolition of large parts of the inner suburbs. Perhaps mercifully, the war would intervene before this plan could be carried out, and so the worst motoring indignity to which Londoners were subjected was the installation of the first automatic traffic lights at Trafalgar Square in April 1933, only marginally slowing their journeys down.

As well as working, Londoners played, and the opportunities for them to do so extended vastly. The lifting in 1921 of restrictions on clubs, which had been imposed during the First World War, led to an explosion of dance venues. The largest of these was the Kit-Kat Club, which opened its doors in 1925 and had seating for 1,500 late-night patrons, many of whom flocked there after a night at the theatre. Cheaper entertainment could be had at one of the 266 cinemas that had opened up in the LCC area by 1929, or at the new Lyons Corner Houses (which offered the capital a taste of casual dining at an affordable price), or at a football match. The newly built Wembley Stadium was first used for the FA Cup Final in 1923, before becoming the venue for the 1924–5 British Empire Exhibition, which pulled in over twenty-seven million people over its two-year opening period.

London politics, though, could be turbulent. The suffragettes of the Women's Political and Social Union, founded by Emmeline and Christabel Pankhurst in 1903, moved their focus to London in 1905, and held a massive meeting in Hyde Park before 300,000 supporters in 1908. Four years later, they began a series of attacks on property, including a mass window-smashing campaign in London's retail districts.

During the First World War, London was the first major European city to suffer aerial bombardment, as German Zeppelin airships dropped nearly 200 tons of bombs from 1915, and then the long-range heavy Gotha bombers started raids in 1917, killing between them over 600 Londoners. The damage was nothing like as severe as the capital would suffer during the Blitz in the Second World War, but with anti-German feeling spiking during the air raids – and after the sinking of the liner *Lusitania* by a German U-boat in May 1917, in which nearly 1,200 people died – there were violent attacks on some of the 40,000 Germans who lived in London, especially around Charlotte Street, Aldgate and Poplar.

The 1920s saw tensions arising from the deteriorating economic situation, when London joined in the General Strike in May 1926 in support of mineworkers. Part of the capital became an armed camp as the authorities sought to protect the nerve-centres of government and to secure the passage of vital supplies to keep London fed and working. A darker side of London showed its face, too, as some were attracted by the authoritarianism becoming rampant in Europe as Mussolini's Fascists and Hitler's Nazis took power in Italy and Germany. Anti-immigrant feeling rose, and in July 1920 the LCC bowed to public pressure and banned all foreigners from council jobs. Violence broke out in the East End, where Oswald Mosley's British Union of Fascists made a series of provocative marches through districts with heavy concentrations of Jewish residents. They were seen off by an alliance of locals and socialist sympathisers in an epic battle along Cable Street in October 1936, but the episode showed that deprivation breeds jealousy of others and particularly of those perceived as newcomers, a phenomenon that has blighted London for centuries.

London politics, always a testing ground for those whose ambitions extended to making the short hop to central government in Westminster, became more contested as the 1929 Local Government Act gave county boroughs more power. In London, the LCC became responsible for hospitals and schools and when Labour took over the LCC after winning over 50 per cent of the vote in 1934, it began a programme of investment (and made several other reforms, including the removal of the ban on married women teachers in 1935).

London was becoming an increasingly complex place, the contradictions that had built up over the ages in its layout, governance and tastes ever more apparent as the twentieth century progressed. And it was becoming increasingly difficult to navigate. The capital had last been mapped by the Ordnance Survey in 1919, and by the early 1930s the information was over a decade out of date at a time when London's outer suburbs had been expanding helter-skelter. What maps were available were hardly practical affairs, designed more as tributes to the sheer grandeur of the metropolis than as practical aids to navigate its streets. The seventy six-inch-scale sheets that made up the whole Ordnance Survey map of London would have taxed even the most herculean traveller's carrying capacity.

◁34-5
A-Z's Pictorial Map provided a colourful and accessible guide to the centre of London in the mid-1930s, with key transport links marked, as well as such useful locations as the British Museum and the Coram's Field playground.

One extraordinary woman saw a business opportunity in all of this muddle. Phyllis Pearsall, the daughter of a rather picaresque Hungarian businessman-turned-cartographer Sandor Gross, had not initially followed in her father's footsteps. Sandor had started a mapping company, Geographia Ltd, close to the Strand in 1908, whose fruits included the production of a world atlas in 1920. Yet the vicissitudes of finance left him losing his original business and he ended up stranded in the United States for most of the 1920s. Finally, in 1936, he began another British cartographic venture, the Geographers' Map Company. Its second publication was to be Phyllis's brainchild.

Having taken note of friends' comments about how difficult it was to get around London, she had looked at existing publications and seen the problem. They were simply not designed with getting around in mind – and did not have simple aids such as house numbers to help the traveller on foot. She resolved to put that right and – according to her own rather colourful account (the product of an undeniably artistic temperament) – she spent the next eighteen months pounding London's 23,000 streets for up to eighteen hours a day, faithfully documenting each road, each junction, each alley and each house number (blocks without labelled numbers particularly vexed her) until she had it all in a dozen bound notebooks. It was at that point she realized she would need an index and once it was complete, the simple list of London's streets in alphabetical order appealed to her. Instead of calling the publication the *OK Atlas of London* as had been originally intended, she christened it the *A to Z Street Atlas*, in the face of some choice invective from her equally strong-minded father.

London, then, reached the dawn of the Second World War with a map that Londoners could carry around with them (and of which even those long-distant Roman centurions might have been jealous). But as soon as it had begun, this happy era ended, when the outbreak of hostilities caused the Government to forbid the retailing of any detailed maps of British cities (lest German bombers use them for better targeting). The lights had gone out, the television of the newly established BBC was turned off, and the maps were put away. War was coming.

LONDON
THROUGH TIME

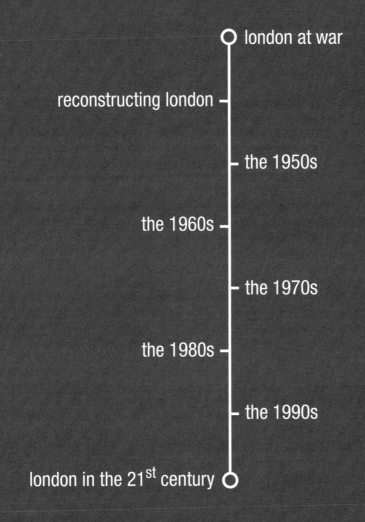

london at war

reconstructing london

the 1950s

the 1960s

the 1970s

the 1980s

the 1990s

london in the 21st century

london AT war

Even before 1939, London had bitter experience of the destruction that total war could inflict. German air raids had struck the city during the First World War, carried out by Zeppelin airships and then Gotha bombers. Between them, they killed 667 Londoners and instilled a fear among the British political classes that 'the bomber would always get through'.

As a result, when a second war with Germany broke out in September 1939, the Government, expecting a new wave of air raids, ordered the immediate evacuation of the capital's children. Around 600,000 of them assembled at schools throughout London, clutching suitcases, with cardboard name labels tied to their coats. This exodus of the young surged out of London in coaches and on trains, to arrive in bemused rural areas, mainly in the West Country.

There was no immediate air assault on London, however, nor even any serious fighting involving British troops. During this 'Phoney War', a false sense of euphoria took hold that the war might not be quite as bad as expected. Two hundred thousand evacuees returned to the capital, surprising the authorities who had closed their schools and converted the classrooms to offices for war work. The children came back to find darkened streets, since the Government was still enforcing a blackout, and sandbags, which were used to strengthen strategic buildings against bomb blasts and presented a constant hazard as Londoners stumbled through the gloom.

Despite the Air Raid Precaution wardens who enforced the blackout, and the growing visibility of men and women in military uniform, much carried on as before. The theatres, which had temporarily closed, reopened and nightlife thrived. Actors were exempt from call-up and so companies still had a full complement (although male ballet dancers,

5 years hard labour
the penalty for looting during german bombing raids

LEAVE THIS TO US SONNY — <u>YOU</u> OUGHT TO BE OUT OF LONDON

WAR MAP No. 8

THE

MEDITERRANEAN

NORTH AND EAST

AFRICA

SHOWING ALL THE TERRITORY OF

ITALIAN EAST AFRICA

INCLUDING INSET of the WORLD SHOWING
BRITISH AND FRENCH POSSESSIONS
AND A LARGE SCALE INSET OF ITALY

BY FAR THE LARGEST, MOST UP-TO-DATE AND
DETAILED MAP PUBLISHED AT THE PRICE

PRICE **6**^{D.} EACH

Produced under the direction of
ALEXANDER GROSS, F.R.G.S.

GEOGRAPHERS' MAP CO., LTD.

24-27, HIGH HOLBORN, LONDON, W.C.1

curiously, were not exempt and so Sadler's Wells lost a good part of its troupe). The major
casualties were animals at the zoo, where the poisonous snakes and black widow spiders
were gassed in case they escaped during an air raid and the manatees were shot when the
aquarium was drained.

Food was an exception, as strict rationing on butter, bacon and cheese was introduced in
January 1940. Even tinned meat and breakfast cereals were subject to a points system that
limited the amounts an individual could buy. As the war progressed, Londoners acclimatized
to the new conditions. A 'Dig for Victory' campaign had some success in getting people
to grow food on allotments, although the piggery which Hyde Park acquired was not an
innovation that most could emulate in their back gardens.

Then on the night of 7 September 1940, everything changed. With the Luftwaffe largely
defeated in the Battle of Britain, thwarting Hitler's ambitions to invade Britain by denying
German command of the British skies, the German air force turned its ire against Britain's
cities. That night London suffered the first air raid of the Blitz, beginning four days of
bombing which left the capital reeling. The East End suffered the most, as it would do in
so many of the seventy-one raids that London had to endure over the next six months.
West Ham and Bermondsey, with their strategic docks, were set ablaze, and Stepney,
Whitechapel, Poplar and Bow were reduced to fields of rubble. The next morning, rescuers
found 430 bodies.

The atmosphere in the capital changed. Fearful of the raids and with a desperate
shortage of bomb shelters, over a hundred thousand people repaired to the comparative
shelter of tube platforms. Although the Government at first discouraged this, in October
it relented and made formal provision to install makeshift kitchens and first-aid stations
underground. Up above on London's streets, a feverish pseudo-normality prevailed.
Restaurants remained open, 90,000 people attended matches at Lord's cricket ground in

1941 and queues snaked round Leicester Square to see *Gone with the Wind*. Yet the toll, particularly at night after the Luftwaffe switched from daytime bombing in November, was terrible. London was hit almost every evening. Incendiary bombs struck particular fear into Londoners. On 7 September the largest fire London had seen since the Great Fire of 1666 reduced St Katharine Docks to ashes. The large quantity of oil and wax that was stored there poured into the Thames, setting the river ablaze. Even worse was to come. On 29 December a massive air raid produced a firestorm around St Paul's as the flames united to create an inferno. Miraculously the cathedral survived, and the photograph of its silhouette, outlined against the blaze, became a talisman of London's resistance.

The docks and railway stations were pounded and even the House of Commons was hit. After a raid damaged Buckingham Palace on 13 September, the Queen remarked that 'now I feel we can look the East End in the face'. Remarkably, social cohesion survived, as communities pulled together to help those whose houses had been destroyed or families killed. Yet there were strains: by the end of September it was recorded that one in three Londoners was getting fewer than four hours' sleep a night, and the police struggled against waves of looting that broke out in the aftermath of the larger raids. Some of this looting was simply carried out by desperate people who felt they had little to lose, though sentences of five years' hard labour did provide a deterrent.

The Blitz's final massive air raid took place on 10–11 May 1941, launched by the Luftwaffe before its planes were pulled back to take part in the Operation Barbarossa offensive against the Soviet Union. As it became clear that the air offensive had abated, London breathed a sigh of relief and slowly, as the rubble was cleared, life began to return to normal. The shock, therefore, was even more profound when Hitler unleashed one last spasm of destruction on the capital during 1944. Firstly, the 'Baby Blitz' was delivered by conventional bombers in January, and then the German V-1 weapons began to rain down on London. Nicknamed doodlebugs, the rockets made a characteristic whining sound that cut out seconds before impact, giving the briefest opportunity to take shelter. The first landed on London on 13 June 1944, striking Grove Road in Bow, and a few days later one hit the Guards' Chapel at

▷

A-Z's All in One War Map No. 5 gave an overview of Europe with an enlargement of the Franco-German border. It was an area in which the First World War combatants fought for years in almost static trench lines. During the Second World War, the German blitzkrieg overran the area in a matter of days.

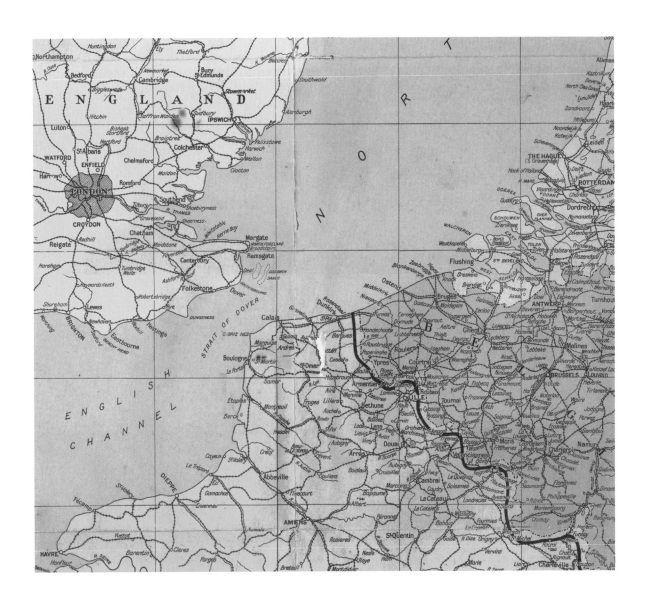

Wellington Barracks, killing 119 people. By the time their launch sites were overrun, when British troops pushed into the Pas de Calais after the Normandy landings, some 2,340 V-1 bombs had reached the capital, killing nearly 5,000 people.

The final terrible blow came in the form of the V-2 rockets, ballistic missiles developed by German scientists late in the war. They made no sound and could not be stopped by anti-aircraft fire or London's defensive fighter screen. The first hit Chiswick on 8 September 1944, and because there was so little that could be done, the British government concealed the true nature of the attacks until November. But the attacks damaged morale terribly; one rocket killed 168 people, including many children, when it hit a packed Woolworths in Deptford just before Christmas.

The V-weapons caused another exodus from London, with more than 200,000 children flooding out by July 1944. The capital's streets emptied once more. Had the V-2 offensive not ended on 27 March 1945 – as the last of its launch sites in the Netherlands were captured by the Allies – or had the war carried on even longer, the patience of its citizens may finally have snapped. Ironically, though, when the air offensive did end, people complained about the silence, and pharmacists reported an increase in demands for sleeping pills to help Londoners get through the eerily quiet nights.

Peace, when it finally came on 8 May 1945, was anything but quiet. London's streets erupted with a pandemonium of flag-waving crowds, singing, dancing and drinking well into the night. At Buckingham Palace, where the royal family acceded to constant demands that they appear on the balcony to wave to the ecstatic well-wishers thronging around the railings, the jazz trumpeter Humphry Lyttleton, then a relative unknown, performed an impromptu concert accompanied by a scratch orchestra that had somehow spontaneously emerged.

London had survived. But the 18,000 tons of high explosives that had been dropped on the city had destroyed 50,000 houses and left 288,000 in need of major repairs. The Docklands were devastated, and many public buildings had been shattered. London lay badly in need of rebuilding.

▷

From September 1940, local authorities were tasked with assembling records of the damage caused by air raids. In the capital, surveyors from the London County Council attended after each attack and their records were used to assemble colour-coded bomb-damage maps (with black indicating total destruction and blue buildings damaged beyond repair). This map of Farringdon and the City of London shows St Paul's Cathedral surrounded by a sea of devastation.

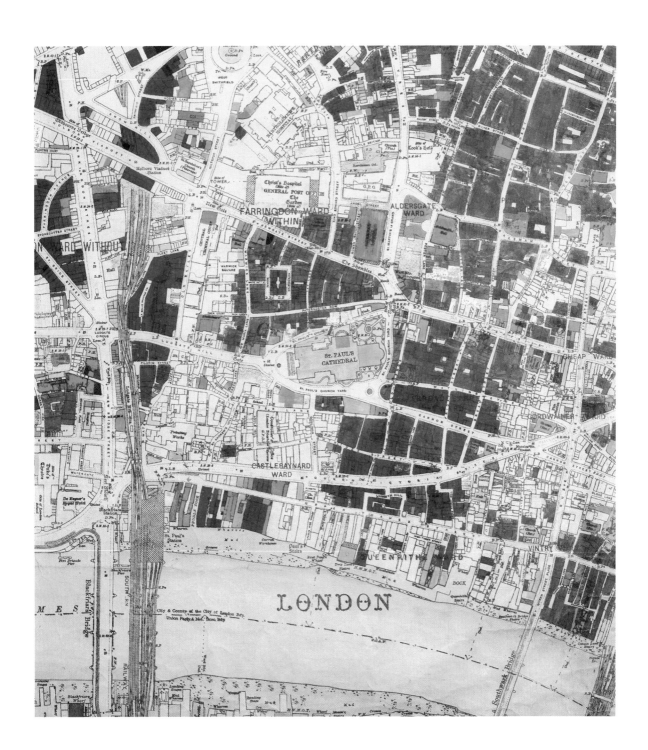

LONDON

reconstructing london

For London, the celebrations of VE Day on 8 May 1945 marked a pyrrhic victory. Thirty thousand Londoners had died in the Blitz and large parts of the city lay in ruins. Around a million buildings had been damaged and 1.2 million people rendered homeless, while two million had moved out of the city, reducing the population of the inner suburbs by over 40 per cent. Many children who had been evacuated in 1939 could barely remember their old homes.

The Government regarded the clearing of the rubble and the rehabilitation of damaged properties as one of its most urgent priorities. In 1944 it established a London Repair Executive, which by May 1945 had overseen the repair of 800,000 homes. By 1947, the process was largely complete, but long before then planners had set in place measures intended to radically reshape the city and its relationship to its rural hinterland. In 1943, the eminent architect Sir Patrick Abercrombie produced the County of London Plan, followed up a year later with the Greater London Plan. The two proposals were premised on the dispersal of growth outside London. The inner city was not to be replenished, but its displaced population instead diverted to a series of New Towns on a ring outside London, where better and more spacious housing could be provided to accommodate them. At the same time, a reinforced Green Belt was thrown around London, beginning where the city's expansion had halted in 1939 at the start of the war.

Abercrombie's plans called for the building of three concentric ring roads around London, obliterating large parts of inner suburbs such as Camden (although bomb damage had already done much of the work for him), and the construction of a parallel system of ring railways (of which the section from Paddington to Liverpool Street was revived decades later

1.2 million
the number of londoners rendered homeless in 1945

as Crossrail). There was no special planning authority to enforce his plan, however, and a separate proposal by the City of London authorities in 1947, together with the tendency of piecemeal muddling along to take the place of strategic vision, meant that much of it never came to pass. Only part of Abercrombie's C Ring was built, as the South Circular Road.

The New Towns plan was another survivor of Abercrombie's vision, and an Act in 1946 designated eight new settlements on the borders of the metropolis. Stevenage was the first to be established that same year, followed by Crawley, Hemel Hempstead and Harlow. Work began rapidly and by 1953 over 17,500 new homes had been built in the fledgling towns. Within the larger area of Greater London, however, work proceeded more slowly and only 37,000 new homes had been built by the end of 1948, still leaving a terrible shortfall.

Some high-profile buildings were never repaired, and some areas were beyond saving. The Cripplegate ward of the City of London was so badly damaged that only forty-eight people were recorded as still living there in 1951. It was razed in the 1960s and replaced with the modern Barbican Development (with only the church of St Giles in Cripplegate being preserved). The church of St Dunstan in the East, which had stood since 1100, was destroyed in the last great attack of the Blitz on 10 May 1941 and was turned into a public garden, while St Mary Aldermanbury Gardens, gutted in a bombing in 1940, was dismantled and its remaining stones transported to Fulton, Missouri, where a replica was built in 1966. Other buildings were too iconic to lose, and the House of Commons debating chamber was lovingly restored and reopened in 1950 (during the interregnum MPs had to endure a kind of timeshare with the aristocrats in the House of Lords).

London began a slow return to normality in other ways, too. Adversarial politics, which had largely been suspended during the course of the war, was resumed. The Conservatives suffered a crushing defeat in the 1945 election, as returning servicemen voted en masse for change. Labour's Clement Attlee used his powerful mandate to establish the National Health Service in 1948 but the party's management of London's local government went less smoothly. The city had to repair hundreds of schools damaged during the Blitz, and

50 ▷

The map in 1948 shows a complex of streets in Cripplegate, north of the Guildhall, which were so badly damaged that the decision was taken to demolish the whole area and redevelop it as the Barbican complex.

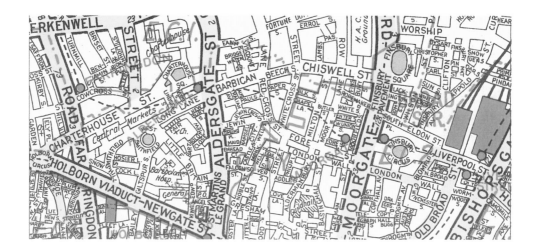

struggled to cope with larger numbers of older pupils after the 1944 Education Act raised the school leaving age to 15. As a result, Labour very nearly lost control of London County Council in 1949.

There were lighter moments. The treasures of the British Museum and National Gallery were restored to their homes in 1946, allowing museum-goers to enjoy artefacts that had remained hidden for seven years, and the first big post-war musical came to the capital when *Oklahoma* had its London première in April 1947 at Drury Lane, marking the rebirth of the West End theatre scene. More spectacularly, the Olympic Games opened at the Empire stadium on 29 July 1948, a bold statement that Britain had completed its recovery from the war (though the rubble that remained just outside the stadium said otherwise). Even with home advantage, Britain won a disappointing three gold medals (all in rowing or sailing), easily surpassed by her wartime Allies the United States, who scooped thirty-eight, and the French, who won ten. For those pining for the glories of pre-war shopping, John Lewis finally reopened its bomb-damaged store on Oxford Street in 1950, while new ways of escaping London opened up in May 1946 when Heathrow Airport officially superseded Croydon as the capital's air gateway.

Much had been achieved, but in some ways London had lost its heart. By mid-1945 the population of the city centre and inner suburbs had only climbed back to 2.6 million, still more than a third less than its pre-war total, and even in 1951, when it had recovered to 3.6 million, this meant the core of London had lost 400,000 citizens. Despite all the optimism of May 1945, the reconstruction of London and the recovery of its self-confidence still had a long way to go.

THE 1950s

1950s London was a Janus-like city, one face turned towards the past, nostalgically intent on recreating its pre-war glories. The other, uncertain, looked to a future affected by new currents in planning, politics, immigration and culture, which together would ultimately reshape it.

By 1950 the Second World War was long over and the immediate problems of demobilization, readjusting to a peace-time economy and clearing away bomb debris had been overcome. After all the relentless struggle, the nation – and London in particular – was in need of a fillip. The required boost was provided in 1951 by the Festival of Britain, held to mark the centenary of the Great Exhibition, though unlike its predecessor it was intended as a purely British celebration of the nation's industry, technology and communal values.

No sooner was the Festival's iconic Skylon, a giant needle-like obelisk, dismantled from the festival site (to make way for the building of the Royal Festival Hall, London's first large post-war public building), than the nation found itself entering a new era. The accession of Elizabeth II to the throne, following her father's death in February 1952, was followed by Britain's first post-war coronation, with seating for 100,000 people erected in the streets around Westminster and the delivery of tens of thousands of television sets to allow royal pomp into the capital's living rooms for the first time.

Hopes for a 'New Elizabethan' age masked serious problems in the city. Although industry continued to flourish, with de Havilland manufacturing the Comet, Britain's first jet airliner, being made at Colindale, and Ford producing 250,00 vehicles a year at its Dagenham factory, London's population was in decline. At first it fell only slightly from its 1931 level of 8.3 million to 8.1 million in 1951, but the establishment of a series of satellite towns by the New Towns Act of 1946 was beginning to suck people, and hope, out from the centre of the city. In recompense the long campaign for a Green Belt around London, which finally succeeded in 1959, ensured that London would not become a hollowed-out core in the centre with an ever-spreading creep of new suburbs pushing out from its margins.

Those Londoners who remained had to suffer choking smogs like the one that killed up to 12,000 people on 5 December 1952, when a pea-green miasma settled on the city's streets and even crept into its theatres, causing the abandonment of a production of *La Traviata* at Sadler's Wells. The Clean Air Act that was passed in 1956 began to provide some respite for Londoners' lungs, but 750 of them still died in a smog even six years after that.

As the clouds of pollution cleared, Londoners could see new housing estates springing up as pre-war slums were cleared. Not all were as well appointed or planned as the Lansbury Estate in Poplar, which formed a kind of architectural outreach programme of the Festival of Britain, and much was carried out by private developers, such as the construction of the Castrol House office block (now Marathon House) in Marylebone. However, the spread of estates, which promised better housing, ended up accelerating the segregation of working-class Londoners from their more prosperous former neighbours.

Some of the decaying urban terraces that survived the developers were occupied by newcomers – migrants who gratefully rented space from slum landlords such as Peter Rachmann, when no one else would have them. Large-scale migration from the New Commonwealth had begun with the arrival of nearly 500 Jamaicans aboard the *Empire Windrush* in 1948, but it accelerated in the 1950s. Communities from the Caribbean became established, particularly in South London where 10,000 West-Indian born people settled. Parts of North London, such as Neasden and Wembley, became host to large numbers from India and Pakistan. London, as a consequence, became more diverse, but the change also brought new tensions, with the capital's first race riot in modern times erupting in Notting Hill in 1958.

London was in flux in other ways, too. Although many clung to tradition, with audiences flocking to see Noel Coward plays and the opening in 1952 of Agatha Christie's *The Mousetrap* – which would still be drawing in theatregoers almost seventy years later – attacks on the Establishment such as John Osborne's *Look Back in Anger* (first performed in 1956), and the emergence of youth sub-cultures like the Teddy Boys suggested that whatever direction London was heading by the late 1950s, it was not going to be a recreation of its pre-war persona.

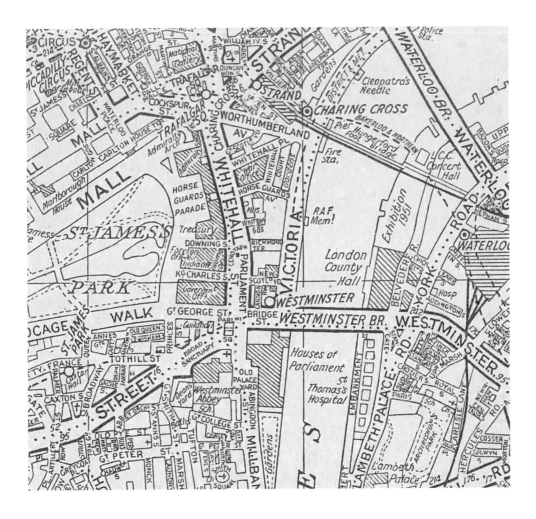

△

The choice of a derelict site on the South Bank for the holding of the 1951 Festival of Britain, and its subsequent redevelopment to provide cultural venues such as the Royal Festival Hall, showed a commitment to the regeneration of the city centre after the damage caused by the Second World War.

THE 1960s

London finally seemed to be breaking from its past in the 1960s. New roads, new buildings, a new administrative structure and a new-found global reputation for cultural innovation as 'Swinging London' seemed to herald a bright future for the city. Yet there were warning signs and old problems resurfaced, as jobs ebbed from the centre and political reform and the repair of crumbling infrastructure could not come fast enough to satisfy deep-seated discontent.

The most striking change was the way in which London was governed. It was London County Council (LCC) that provided an overarching body for the motley collection of ancient medieval boroughs and new suburbs that constituted the London of the early 1960s. Yet the veteran institution – established in 1889 – was proving woefully inadequate for the strategic planning and cross-borough co-ordination that such a complex city required. In 1965 the old system was abolished and a new hierarchy of thirty-two local authorities instituted under the umbrella of the Greater London Council (GLC). Within this, many of the smaller boroughs were engulfed by larger neighbours (so that St Marylebone was absorbed by Westminster and Battersea swallowed up by Wandsworth). Only the City of London, with its powerful financial and political backers, managed to retain a Lilliputian independence with around only 10,000 residents (and triple that number of businessmen allowed to select its council).

It was expected that the Conservatives would dominate the new body, but social changes, and the flight of some of the traditional working classes from the centre, meant that their hold on traditional suburban electoral strongholds was slipping. In the first GLC elections,

320,000
the number of mourners who paid their repects to winston churchill while his body laid in state

Labour won sixty-four of the 100 seats and a new political power base, glowering at the Houses of Parliament from across the Thames at City Hall, was born.

Among the GLC's key new responsibilities were planning and roads. There was a clear need to get a grip on the piecemeal development that had seen the destruction of key parts of London's historic fabric, such as the Doric Arch at Euston, demolished when the station was redeveloped in 1962. There had to be a middle way between the insistence on conserving every last existing building and the architectural brutalism that gifted South London the Elephant and Castle shopping centre, which opened in 1965, amid a concrete spaghetti of walkways and underpasses. The idea that the tower block would resolve London's housing problems took a stumble in 1968, when the recently completed Ronan Point tower in Canning Town partially collapsed after a gas explosion, near-miraculously only killing four people. The era of the tower block was not quite over – by the time the last of these residential leviathans was constructed in 1974, London had over 380 of them – but, plagued by safety problems, social ills and vandalism, they were now seen as part of the problem and not the solution.

Parking meters had made their first appearance on London's streets in 1958, with traffic wardens policing them from 1960, though these measures did little to divert the growing streams of cars that were trying to navigate their way through the labyrinth of Central London. Previous schemes to provide a system of ring roads had foundered in the 1950s, but the GLC, undeterred, tried again with a proposal in 1969 to construct three concentric ring roads around the capital, involving a spend of £2 billion and the demolition of 30,000 houses. In the end, the idea of turning much of London into an urban motorway proved too much to stomach and the sole survivor of the grandiose scheme was the M25 London orbital motorway, only finally completed in 1986.

As well as clogging the roads, Londoners were increasingly travelling by tube. The solitary 1960s addition to the system was the Victoria Line, initially from King's Cross to Victoria, which was completed in 1969 to ease congestion in Central London. Its official opening in March 1969 saw Queen Elizabeth II become the first British monarch to travel on the system, although the publicity stunt of having her purchase her own ticket with a sixpence almost backfired when the coin jammed in the ticket machine. Many of the Queen's subjects were now travelling further, or out of the capital completely as, despite an era of

generally plentiful employment, old industries began to wither away in the urban core. Pears shut down its soap factory in Isleworth in 1962 and the Beckton Gasworks closed in 1969, but the worst losses were in the docks. As Britain's colonies gained independence, the flow of trade from them began to dry up, and the 1960s saw an almost 50 per cent decline in imports and exports from Commonwealth countries. The docks became uneconomic, and the need to modernize and containerize made things worse: the East India Docks were the first to close in 1967, followed by London Dock and St Katharine Docks in 1968–9 (though the long-term project to turn the latter into a marina ultimately did rejuvenate the area).

As London's old fabric began to fray it acquired a new set of social problems. London's communities of Caribbean and South Asian migrants had grown, and begun to prosper, finding niches in public transport, hospitals and the catering business. However, resentment at their presence was fanned by nationalist politicians, creating the need for the passing of a first Race Relations Act in 1965 – the year before the first Notting Hill Carnival – legally barring discrimination. Even so, a strike broke out in April 1968 among London's meat porters and remaining dockers, calling for an end to immigration. A more sinister side of London surfaced after the liberalization of gambling legislation enabled organized criminal groups, such as those led by the Richardson family and the Kray brothers, to rake off huge sums from the 12,000 licensed clubs that sprang up in the course of the decade. Parts of the East End acquired a reputation as a gangland, until the Krays were finally arrested in 1968 following the brutal murder of a rival at a Whitechapel pub.

For many, and perhaps for most outside Britain, London's image was not as a place of racial tension, crime, planning blight or unemployment, but as the centre of a new youth culture that brought a bright and buzzy feeling to a city with a reputation for haughty stuffiness. Fashionable boutiques proliferated, such as Barbara Hulanicki's Biba in Fulham (opened in 1964), which became a mecca for young style seekers. At the same time a new music scene burgeoned, fuelled by the appearances of the Beatles at the Abbey Road Studios in North London, where they recorded most of their hits between 1962 and 1970.

Winston Churchill's funeral in 1965, after his body had lain in state and been viewed by 320,000 mourners filing by, was a symbolic passing of an age for London, his coffin carried by figures from the past, such as Earl Mountbatten and Viscount Slim. The 'Swinging London' of the Beatles was the perfect counterpoint to this, proving that the capital could once again reinvent itself.

◁

The opening of a number of boutiques along the Kings Road, which attracted the new youth market, made the area the epitome of fashion during London's 'Swinging Sixties'.

THE 1970s

London in the 1970s seemed to lose its stride, the enormous creative energies of the 1960s dissipating as the city failed to cope with adverse economic conditions and the final winding down of industries that had sustained it for centuries. The capital was becoming, simply put, a less attractive place to live and its population declined from 7.4 million to 6.6 million over the decade, reaching a point below its 1911 level. More of this, and London might lose its coveted role as one of the premier international cities.

There was still creative force, although it was of a spikier sort, as the Punk movement arose after Malcolm Maclaren (the manager of the band the Sex Pistols) opened a boutique on the King's Road, making it a magnet for leather-clad and Mohican-sporting punks to parade up and down at weekends. London, too, saw an opening out to previously marginalized groups as the first Gay Pride march was organized in 1972 (a mere five years after the 1967 Sexual Offences Bill decriminalized homosexuality). However, immigrants from the New Commonwealth, whose numbers had increased steadily throughout the 1960s, found their rights to enter the United Kingdom severely curtailed by the Commonwealth Immigration Act in 1971. Even so, a large new influx arrived after the expulsion of Ugandans of Asian origin by the Idi Amin regime in August 1972. Minority communities faced further antagonism with the rise of far-right politics, notably through the actions of the National Front (founded in 1967), which in August 1977 carried out a provocative march through New Cross and Deptford, both areas with large migrant communities. Their anger boiled over into rioting at the Notting Hill Carnival in 1976, in which 100 police and sixty members of the public were injured.

The mid-1970s saw the arrival of Irish nationalist terrorism on the mainland, with a campaign of IRA attacks on targets in the capital beginning in 1974, including the forced

800,000
london's population decline during this decade

evacuation of 10,000 visitors from the Earls Court Ideal Homes Show in January and a bomb that killed a woman at the Tower of London. In 1979 an MP, Airey Neave, was assassinated when IRA terrorists detonated a bomb in the House of Commons car park. London, as a consequence, remained in a high state of vigilance until the final IRA ceasefire in 1997.

London's authorities continued to try to plan for the city, even though wrestling with the accumulated problems of such a huge metropolis was next to impossible. The Greater London Council's (GLC's) Greater London Development Plan in 1976 foresaw the building of new urban motorways – an obsession that London planners could never quite shake off – and more rigid zoning of retail, commercial and recreation spaces. London's weakening economy prevented the plan being carried out, and only the Westway, slicing through Paddington and North Kensington, which opened in 1970, survived from the original scheme. Budget problems made advances in other areas of transport slow, although the capital did benefit from improvements to the Tube, when Heathrow finally acquired a direct link in 1977, and the Jubilee Line (which had originally been proposed as the Fleet Line) opened in 1979.

The idea for the new name came from the celebrations for the Queen's Silver Jubilee in 1977, which brought Londoners out onto the streets for parties to commemorate the occasion and revived an attenuating sense of community that some feared had been permanently lost. Losses, though, there were, as slices of London's industry closed forever. The Bryant and May match factory in Bow finally shut in 1979. As the site of the famous 'match girls' strike' of 1888, its disappearance was a sad blow to those with a sense of the history of Britain's labour movement. The docks, too, were now in terminal decline; the Surrey Commercial Docks shut down in 1970, and the Queenhithe Dock, the last in the city, was demolished in 1971 to make way for hotels. By the end of the decade, there was almost no commercial cargo being handled in London's traditional docks, with most business having transferred to the container port of Tilbury in Essex.

60 ▷
The projected path for the Westway is shown, just before its completion in 1970. The road was the last surviving part of a series of grand projects for urban motorways striking through the heart of London.

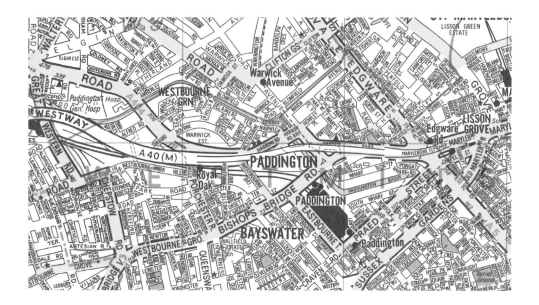

In all the gloom, however, there were bright spots, as the historic Covent Garden market buildings were saved from demolition in 1971, to be converted to a tourist-friendly emporium; the fine Victorian cemeteries at Nunhead and Abney Park were rescued from a bramble-choked decline when Southwark and Hackney Councils took them over in 1977, beginning a long-term process of restoration; and the National Theatre opened in 1976 after a decade-long planning battle. There may have been be fewer Londoners than before, but they were determined to fight for the soul of their city.

THE 1980s

By the late 1970s, it seemed almost as if the decades following the Second World War had been about managing the decline of a once great metropolis and accustoming it to a reduced international role that matched the straitened circumstances of the country as a whole. The 1980s was the decade when London turned a corner, and began its re-creation as a global city, the narrative that would occupy centre stage for the next forty years.

London's population began to recover, too, from 6.6 million people in 1981 to 6.9 million at the time of the census a decade later. It was a modest increase, but it stemmed decades of decline, and that most of the rise took place in the inner boroughs indicated that a profound change was taking place. Gradually, London was becoming a fashionable place once more. Boroughs such as Islington, Camden and Westminster were beginning to act as magnets for young urban professionals – the social class derided by mid-1980s commentators as 'yuppies'.

Changes in the City accelerated this trend. The 'Big Bang' reforms in 1986, which ended fixed commissions and introduced electronic trading, enabled a massive expansion in the London Stock Exchange's business and a large increase in jobs in banking. The sector expanded to employ 600,000 Londoners by the end of the decade. The regeneration of the Docklands, which took off after the creation of the London Docklands Development Corporation in 1981, and the designation of the Isle of Dogs as an enterprise zone, reached a critical point with the beginning of work on the Canary Wharf Development. In subsequent decades this would refocus London's economic heart to the east of the City in reversal of a centuries-long trend for its western suburbs to be more prosperous.

London's transition was not untroubled, however. The election of the first of Margaret Thatcher's Conservative governments in 1979 set up a power struggle with the Greater

300,000
london's population increase during this decade

London Council (GLC), which came under the leadership of the radical socialist firebrand Ken Livingstone in 1981. His 'Fare's Fair' policy, intended to reduce the cost of commuting for Londoners, led to a stand-off with the Government, which objected to the level of subsidies given to London Transport. In the end the GLC capitulated, although the long-term result was the introduction of zonal fares on the Tube in 1983, which finally did give some relief to long-suffering Londoners (who continued to swelter in ever more crowded carriages as travel on the underground at peak hours grew by almost 30 per cent between 1983 and 1990). The episode showed that Westminster was unable to tolerate a strong rival in County Hall and the Local Government Act of 1986 abolished the GLC altogether, leaving the capital without a city-wide administration for the first time since 1855.

London needed that sense of directing purpose. The 1980s saw the outbreak of very serious race riots, beginning in Brixton in 1981, and flaring up again on the Broadwater Farm estate in Tottenham in 1985. Chronic tensions between local black communities and the police were laid bare and the Scarman Inquiry that followed the Brixton riots did very little to resolve the underlying causes: poor quality housing, lack of educational and employment opportunities, endemic racism in society as a whole, and heavy-handed policing. The rising population in the Central London boroughs did not help, either, as property prices began to push even modest houses and flats out of the reach of working families, either to rent or to buy. The disparities in wealth in parts of London yawned ever wider.

London faced other challenges, too. Sieges at the Iranian embassy in Knightsbridge – where Arab separatists took over the building in 1980 – and at the Libyan People's Bureau on St James's Square – where a policewoman was shot by a gunman operating from inside the building in 1984 – showed that the capital was frighteningly vulnerable to the backwash from international political developments. A long-standing political problem closer to home reappeared in the 1980s, as the IRA launched a new campaign of violence on the British mainland, with bomb attacks against British servicemen in Hyde Park and Regent's Park that killed eleven soldiers.

The 1980s saw the loss of some old London traditions and landmarks: Billingsgate Market transferred to a new site on the Isle of Dogs in 1982, and newspaper publishers began to desert Fleet Street when Rupert Murdoch moved publication of *The Times* and *The Sun* to new premises in Wapping in 1986 (sparking a prolonged industrial dispute that ultimately fizzled out). London pulsated to the vibrant sound of a new trend in inner city night clubs, while at the weekend, more sedate (or exhausted) residents could enjoy new shopping centres such as the Broadway in Bexleyheath (opened in 1983). Alternatively, they could

top ▷
The 1980s saw the beginning of a new phase of building in the City, including the completion, in 1980, of the NatWest Tower on Old Broad Street.

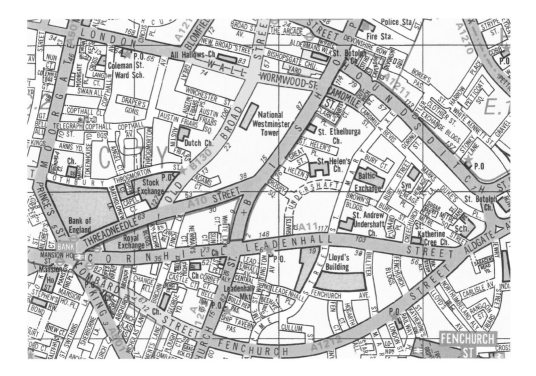

gaze up at the City's new Leviathan, the NatWest Tower (now Tower 42), which formally opened in 1981, or enjoy a leisurely Test Match at the new Mound Stand at Lords, which welcomed spectators for the first time in 1987. For those wishing to escape the capital, Heathrow continued its expansion, until it received sixty-two million passengers in 1999. Meanwhile the opening of City Airport in 1987 offered a rival to the east, and the completion of the M25 ring motorway around London in 1986 proved in the end to have done little to banish the capital's chronic traffic jams.

The decade saw tragedies, such as the fire at King's Cross underground station that killed thirty-one people when a fireball erupted after discarded cigarettes ignited combustible material under an escalator in November 1987, or the *Marchioness* disaster in 1989 when a pleasure cruiser was accidentally rammed by a Thames dredger and fifty-one passengers drowned. But it also saw triumphs, such as the public outpouring of support for the monarchy at the wedding of Prince Charles and Lady Diana Spencer in July 1981, when crowds lined the streets of the capital to cheer the royal couple on.

It was an echo of a simpler past. Another hint at the unbroken thread that makes up the capital's history came in 1988, when archaeologists discovered the remains of London's Roman amphitheatre – for which they had long searched in vain – near the Guildhall. It was a reminder that even in the newly vibrant city of the 1980s, Londoners were just a few footsteps away from the world of their distant ancestors.

THE **1990s**

In the 1990s, London seemed unstoppable. Its population continued to climb, increasing by almost five per cent over the decade to hit 7.2 million (which, even so, was still below its level in 1971). Londoners had new opportunities, but faced a sharper-edged, brasher capital, where money talked and those less prosperous continued to struggle.

The symbol of London's new riches was the Canary Wharf development, where the largest financial tower, at One Canada Square, opened in August 1991 as part of the wave of construction that gave London's latest financial district ten million square feet of office space. It nearly foundered early on, however, as the recession that hit the United Kingdom in the early 1990s led to a contraction in the financial sector, leaving many of the new buildings briefly redundant. Britain recovered, though, and the advent of the European Union's Single Market in 1993 meant that it was easier for British banks to do business in Europe (and for European banks to set up in the United Kingdom), providing a powerful boost for the renewed growth in the later 1990s.

New transport links were needed to avoid the growth of Docklands being choked off. The Jubilee Line extension, which passed through Canary Wharf before it looped back north to Stratford, opened in 1999, and in November 1994 Eurostar services began (at first at Waterloo, pending the building of an entirely new terminal at St Pancras), offering direct rail links to Europe for the first time in history. Britain was no longer an island and London's ties to the continent grew with an increase in young Europeans taking advantage of their new rights to live and work in the capital.

Not everyone was content with London's (or Britain's) new face. In 1990 a mass protest against the Government's imposition of a new local tax (which became known as the 'poll tax', as it was a per capita charge) brought 200,000 demonstrators into Trafalgar Square and

£150,000,000
the cost of the damage caused by the IRA bomb at canary wharf in 1996

degenerated into rioting in which over 100 people were injured. London's black community, too, still faced chronic difficulties in their relationships with the police, highlighted by the failure to find the perpetrators of the racially motivated murder of the black teenager, Stephen Lawrence, in 1990. This ultimately led to the findings of the Macpherson Inquiry in 1999 that the Metropolitan Police had been 'institutionally racist'.

The police faced other challenges, as the IRA continued to threaten the capital, with the devastating bombings in April 1992 that killed three people and so damaged the Baltic Exchange that it had to be demolished; an explosion near South Quay station in Canary Wharf in February 1996, which caused two fatalities and over £150 million-worth of damage; and an attack on Harrods in December 1996 that caused several injuries. Only the signing of the Good Friday Agreement in 1998, which brought the cessation of the Troubles in Northern Ireland, finally removed the threat of Irish nationalist terrorism on London's streets after more than a century.

All growing cities need new buildings, and 1990s' London saw some bitter planning battles, most notably over a large-scale development proposed at Paternoster Square near St Paul's Cathedral, which was only finally completed in 2003 after the original plans were scaled down; also around the Limehouse Link, which opened in 1993 as London's most expensive stretch of road; and over County Hall, long the symbol of London's democracy, which was sold off to a leisure company that then opened an aquarium there.

That democracy, though, took on a new lease of life when a referendum in 1998 returned a 72 per cent vote in favour of establishing a Greater London Authority consisting of a London Assembly and a directly elected mayor. Although between them they would have fewer powers than the Greater London Council (or the London County Council) had possessed, there was now at least once more a voice to speak for London.

Londoners had other reasons to be grateful as the end of the 1990s approached. London Zoo, which had announced its impending closure of 1992, was saved by a wave of nostalgic remorse that brought its ticket receipts back to a level that made it viable, while

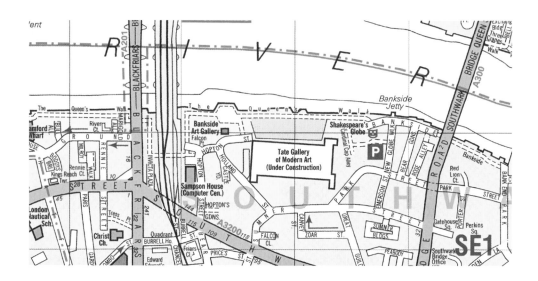

St Bartholomew's Hospital, another stalwart of the London scene, was also reprieved. London even acquired a new version of its own past, when the New Globe Theatre, a reconstruction of Shakespeare's original, opened in the traditional Elizabeth theatre district of Southwark in 1997. And the capital celebrated the end of the decade – and of the millennium – with a vengeance. A spectacular new venue, the Millennium Dome, was built on the Greenwich Peninsula. The city also acquired the London Eye, a huge Ferris Wheel, which was floated up the Thames in sections and erected on the South Bank in December 1999. Those who rose on one of its thirty-two observational capsules (one for each of London's thirty-two boroughs) were treated to an unparalleled view of their home city. Stretching out far into the distance, as it approached a new millennium (and almost the third millennium of its own existence), London presented a glorious sight.

△ ▷
London acquired a number of new landmark buildings to celebrate the new Millennium in 2000, including the Millennium Dome (opposite), where a year-long exhibition of British culture and technology was held, and the Tate Modern (above), in the former Bankside Power Station, a rather more enduring tribute to British artistic prowess.

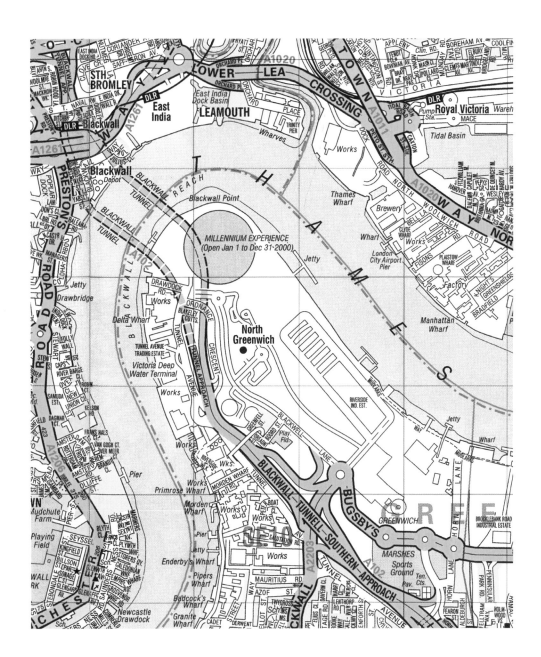

london IN THE 21st century

As London approaches the third decade of the twenty-first century it is larger than ever before, both in size – as the tendrils of its urban sprawl creep ever further into the countryside of Kent, Surrey, Hertfordshire and Essex – and in its population. In 2015 the number of Londoners reached 8.6 million, surpassing the previous peak in 1939, just before the Second World War.

For a city that was supposedly withering away, a victim of its sheer size, sclerotic transport arteries and the nimbleness of its competitors, London has recovered its vigour with surprising aplomb. In 2000, it regained its sense of unity, too, when the Greater London Authority was established, restoring some form of city-wide government for the first time since the abolition of the Greater London Council in 1986. It acquired an elected mayor, too, first in Ken Livingstone, the nemesis of Conservative governments in the 1980s, then the rumbustious figurehead of Boris Johnson, followed by Sadiq Khan, who came into office in 2016 as Britain's most senior Muslim politician. Each of them pursued their own political initiatives, although in 2003 the introduction of the congestion charge, a daily fee for entering London's central zone, and it subsequent strengthening, notably by the imposition of an Ultra-Low Emission Zone (ULEZ) in April 2019 to keep the most polluting vehicles out of the inner city, looked likely to have the most long-term effects.

The capital's twenty-first-century struggles mirrored those of the previous decades, although with a more vibrant economy it was easier to find funds to establish new transport links, such as the opening of the Croydon Tramlink in 2000, and the extension of the Docklands Light Railway, first to City Airport in 2005, and then to Lewisham in 2009. The opening of the new St Pancras terminal for the Eurostar in 2007 was an affirmation of London's status as a cosmopolitan city. It made rapid access to Europe much easier at a

22
the percentage of londoners whose mother-tongue is not english (2011)

time when the capital's community of EU-born citizens was growing after the accession of eight Central and Eastern European countries – most notably Poland – in 2004 provided a much-needed pool of labour to feed the city's voracious appetite for workers in finance, retailing and the healthcare sectors. By the 2011 census, around 22 per cent of London's population had a mother tongue other than English, creating challenges in education, but also affirming the capital's status as the international city par excellence.

London continued to acquire new buildings. Some of these were re-creations of much-loved favourites, such as the redeveloped Wembley Stadium, which reopened in 2007; others were at the cutting-edge of the architectural imagination, like 30 St Mary Axe – popularly known as the Gherkin – which was finished in 2004, the Shard, inaugurated in 2012, or the Gherkin's near-neighbour, 70 St Mary Axe, unkindly nicknamed 'the Can of Ham', which was completed in 2019. Attempts, though, were made to mitigate the effect of the city's growing population and soaring skyline on its environment. As well as the ULEZ, continuing efforts were made to clean up the Thames, long the repository of pollution from London's industrial zone. The decline of riverside factories and concerted conservation initiatives such as the Biodiversity Strategy for London, published in 2002, led to the recovery of fish populations in the Thames to the extent that over 120 species can now be found swimming in the river – including the notoriously pollution-sensitive salmon – while waterfowl such as heron and cormorant can be found wading along its banks for the first time in many decades.

The twenty-first century has not been without its tragedies. Bomb attacks in 2001 by the Real IRA, a dissident Irish nationalist faction, against the BBC Television Centre in White City and an Ealing pub did not result in any fatalities or the feared re-igniting of the bomb campaigns of the 1970s, but terrorism reared its head from another direction. On 7 July 2005, Islamist terrorists inspired by al-Qaeda detonated a series of bombs on the Tube and on a London bus, killing fifty-two people and raising the capital to a heightened level of security it had not known for thirty years. Further attacks in 2017, when vehicles rammed pedestrians at Westminster and on London Bridge killing some victims, while the Islamist terrorists stabbed others to death, reminded London that the backwash of international political events can never be wholly avoided in a city of such size.

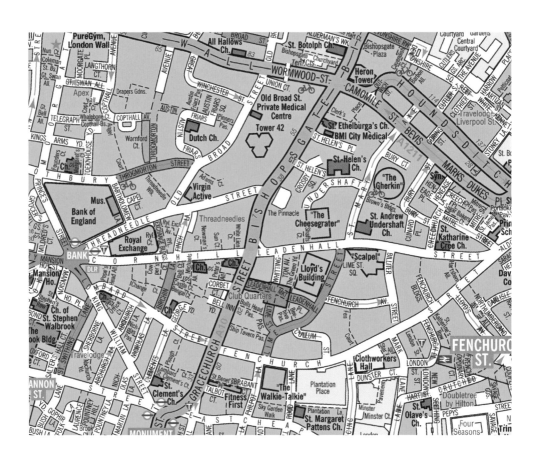

The death of more than seventy people in June 2017 in a fire in the Grenfell Tower block of flats in North Kensington – caused by external cladding accelerating the blaze rather than retarding it – raised questions of social justice for the predominantly poor and migrant community that had lived there. The huge demonstrations that took place in the twenty-first century – in 2003 against Britain's participation in the Iraq War and in 2019, when a million people marched to demand a confirmatory Referendum before the United Kingdom left the European Community – were warnings to politicians that a city such as London has the size and capacity to demand action outside the confines of traditional politics. Ever growing, ever changing and ever more challenging to manage, the one certainty about London in 2020 is that it has the ability to challenge and surprise those who rule over it and to provide a complex sea of struggle and opportunity for those who live there.

◁
The streetscape of the City was transformed in the early twenty-first century with the construction of a series of architecturally arresting buildings, including the Shard, the Cheesegrater and the Walkie Talkie.

LONDON LIVING

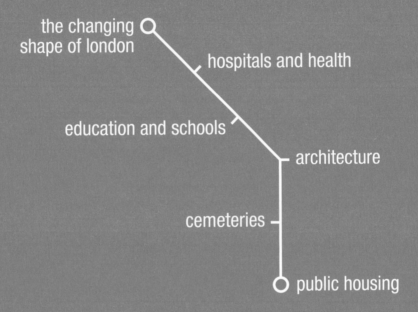

the changing shape of london

hospitals and health

education and schools

architecture

cemeteries

public housing

THE **changing shape** OF **london**

London's historical progress seems like that of a person, from its infancy in Roman times, through its medieval and Tudor youth, to the self-confident adulthood of Victorian times and the middle age of the post-war city (though whether it is now experiencing a final decay into old age or a renewed flush of youth it is hard to say). And, like any person, the shape and size of London have changed over time.

The first of these many Londons, under the Roman occupation, was tiny compared to today's metropolis, occupying just part of the area of the capital's modern-day financial district. Its successors in Anglo-Saxon and medieval London, although they infiltrated along the river towards Westminster, remained largely confined within the old Roman walls. It took hundreds of years for what is now modern London to fill up, as elegant squares colonized the land between Piccadilly and Marylebone in the eighteenth century, while in the late nineteenth and early twentieth centuries, the railway and then the Tube made it possible for workers to travel from ever more far-flung suburbs into the centre.

The London that developed was governed in a piecemeal fashion by a patchwork of small boroughs and authorities which had grown up unplanned throughout the ages. There was no city-wide government to engage in rational planning for the increasingly complex needs of the capital. Finally, in 1889, London County Council (LCC) was created – immediately attempting to address the problems of slum housing in Central London – and in 1900 the maze of tiny authorities in the centre was swept away with the creation of twenty-eight metropolitan boroughs.

The LCC, though, only had sway over the inner area of today's Greater London. Many growing areas, such as West Ham, were excluded from it, while some of the LCC's highest-profile housing schemes, such as the Becontree estate in Dagenham, begun in 1921, lay

1972
the year the whole of london finally adopts the new postcode system

outside its boundaries. The LCC responded with recommendations that those boundaries be vastly extended right up to the margins of the Home Counties, but the proposal was too grandiose, and alienated many of those who would have been subsumed within the larger authority. As a result, serious reform of London's borders had to wait until the Royal Commission on Local Government, headed by Sir Edwin Herbert, published its report in 1960.

Historical and local sensibilities were outraged by his findings, which proposed absorbing significant parts of Kent, Essex, Hertfordshire and Surrey into a new Greater London Authority. A 'Save our Surrey' campaign was launched, but failed to stop Richmond and Twickenham being amalgamated into a new London Borough of Richmond. Elsewhere, almost all of the new thirty-two boroughs (plus the City of London) found themselves formed by an uneasy union of existing, smaller boroughs, or, in outer London, by land-grabs into other counties. Barnet came into being through the joining together of Hendon, Finchley and Friern Barnet (which had been within the LCC) with East Barnet and Barnet (which had been in Hertfordshire), while Bromley was formed by combining together Beckenham, Bromley, Orpington, Penge and Sidcup & Chislehurst, which had all been in Kent (though confusingly Penge had been in Surrey prior to 1889). The area around Knockholt revolted against the new arrangements and was transferred back to Kent in 1969. In the inner city, the smaller metropolitan councils disappeared, as minnows such as St Marylebone and Paddington were bolted together to form the City of Westminster.

The new boroughs and the Greater London Council (GLC) which sat above them in the local government hierarchy came into being in 1965. Covering a region of about 600 square miles, it constitutes what most people now think of as London, although the city's urban sprawl spreads out further into Kent, Surrey, Hertfordshire and Essex. The GLC, though, offered a powerful alternative power base to Westminster, and central governments chafed at its pretensions. This was particularly so during a prolonged and bad-tempered cohabitation between its radical socialist leader Ken Livingstone and the Conservative government of Margaret Thatcher, which led to its abolition in 1986. City-wide government

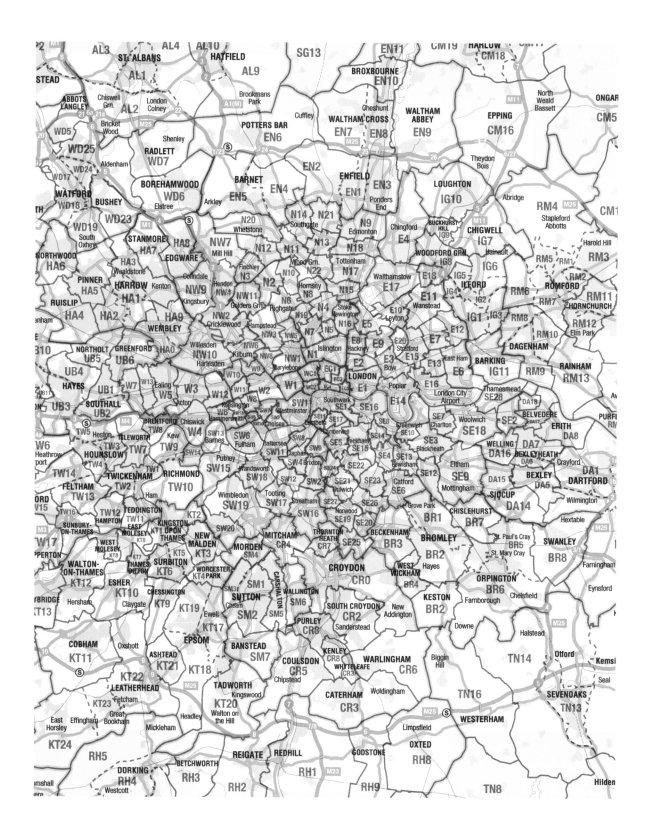

of a sort was restored in 2000, with the installation of a directly elected mayor and a London Assembly, though their powers fell far short of those of the GLC.

London has an alternative set of boundaries, and a far less controversial one, in the form of postcodes. The division of the city into postal areas began in 1857, after the introduction of the Penny Post by Rowland Hill led to an explosion in the number of letters being handled by the Post Office. The city was divided into lettered areas according to the points of the compass (with EC and WC for the most central districts, and N, NE, E, SE, S, SW, W and NW for the rest). All of these have survived until today, with the exception of S and NE which were abolished after a report undertaken by the novelist Anthony Trollope in 1866. Numbered subdistricts (such as W1 or NW8) were added in 1917, and in 1958 the full six-digit alphanumeric codes were first trialled in Norwich. Their introduction to the rest of the United Kingdom was slow, and Croydon was the first district in London to receive postcodes in 1966 (albeit as CR codes, not one of the compass designations for Central London).

It was not until 1972 that the whole of London was covered by the new system (after a government campaign to 'Remember the Postcode'), but its completion revived old geographical rivalries. The Central London postcodes only covered 40 per cent of the GLC area, and large parts of the city had postcodes associated with the old counties from which they had been sundered in 1965 (so, much of Harrow remains HA, while Twickenham is resolutely TW and Bromley proudly BR). While inside London, whether one lives in Westminster or Camden, or in the parts of Richmond covered by SW14 postcodes or TW1, is a very serious matter indeed.

It all goes to prove that boundaries do matter, even in a city that might, to outsiders, seem a homogenous urban sprawl.

◁

As well as boroughs, historic districts and informal designations such as 'Marylebone Village' (some of them dreamed up by estate agents or local businesses to promote their area), Londoners also identify by postcode, with the difference between W1 and NW1 – scarcely discernible on the ground – a matter of fierce pride.

hospitals AND health

L ondon has a continuous tradition of healthcare in hospitals that stretches back deep into the Middle Ages, making it one of the oldest systems in the world. St Bartholomew's Hospital in the City was founded in 1123 by Rahere, an Augustinian canon and favourite of Henry I, putting it close to its ninth centenary of caring for patients. In common with most of London's early hospitals, it was run by a religious order and, like many of them, it survived the Dissolution of the Monasteries between 1536 and 1540 to re-emerge as a secular institution run by the Corporation of London.

By the early twentieth century, the piecemeal development of London's health services – all in private hands – had resulted in a patchwork of provision and a multiplicity of hospitals catering to all diseases, social ranks and nationalities. There was a hospital for seamen at Greenwich (the Dreadnought), a hospital for nervous diseases in Maida Vale (founded in 1867), a German hospital in Dalton (1845), an Italian hospital on Queen Square (established in 1884, where a group of Italian Fascists undiplomatically dedicated a bed to Mussolini in 1933) and a French Protestant hospital (opened in 1718). The Great Ormond Street Hospital for Children began treating patients in 1852, and received an enormous fillip when J.M. Barrie bequeathed it the royalties from the copyright of Peter Pan in 1929. The often lethal conditions for patients improved with the introduction of anaesthesia in surgery from the 1850s and antiseptics from the 1860s, while the establishment of the Nightingale Training School for Nurses in 1860 provided a professionally trained corps of nurses for the first time, immeasurably enhancing the level of patient care.

Although medical advances continued, the hospitals struggled to provide universal provision and could not do so without charge, hampering efforts to improve the health

royalties
j.m. barrie granted the royalties from the copyright of peter pan to great ormond street hospital for children in 1929

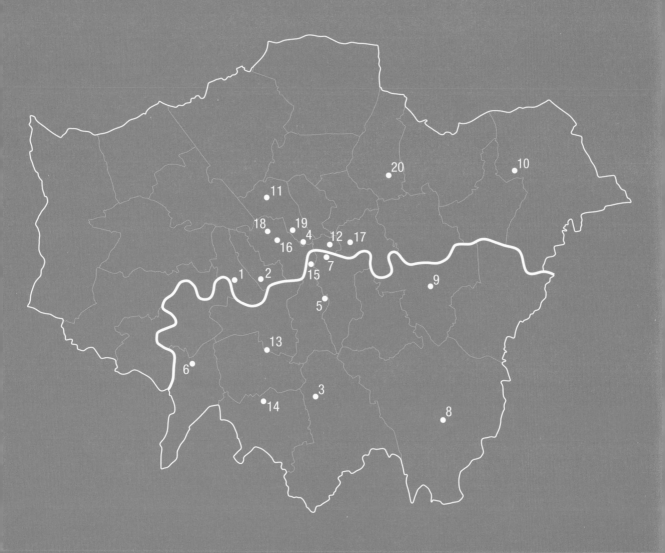

1. Charing Cross Hospital
2. Chelsea and Westminster Hospital
3. Croydon University Hospital
4. Great Ormond Street Hospital
5. King's College Hospital
6. Kingston Hospital
7. London Bridge Hospital
8. Princess Royal University Hospital
9. Queen Elizabeth Hospital
10. Queen's Hospital
11. Royal Free Hospital
12. St Bartholomew's Hospital
13. St George's Hospital
14. St Helier Hospital
15. St Thomas' Hospital
16. The Princess Grace Hospital
17. The Royal London Hospital
18. The Wellington Hospital
19. University College Hospital
20. Whipps Cross University Hospital

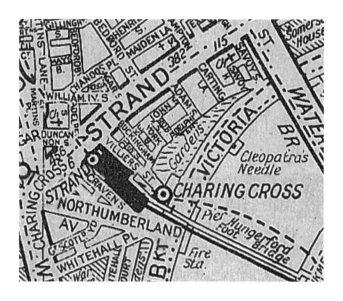

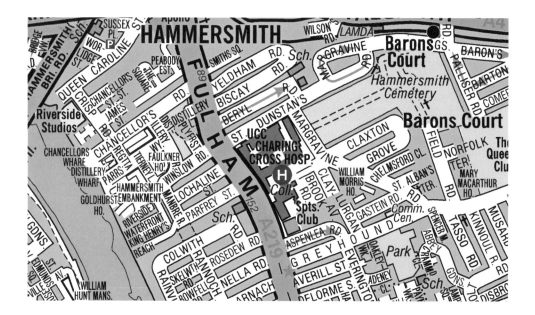

△
The Charing Cross Hospital was established on a small site on Villiers Street by Charing Cross in 1818 (preceding the railway station by forty-six years). It remained there – apart from a few years in exile in Hertfordshire during the Second World War – until advances in medicine meant its building became too cramped, and the Charing Cross was transferred to Fulham (name and all) in 1973.

of the poor. The Second World War was a difficult time for London's hospitals, many of them suffering attacks during the Blitz (on 9 September 1940 a bomb struck St Thomas's, killing two nurses and four physiotherapists when a floor collapsed, and many patients were evacuated to Hydestile near Godalming in Surrey). However, the war also changed opinions about government involvement in the health service, as it had shown the vast benefits national planning could achieve in the face of apparently insuperable problems. In 1942 the Beveridge Report, as part of an all-embracing series of recommendations that laid the basis for the modern British Welfare State, proposed the establishment of a National Health Service offering universal care, which would be free at the point of treatment.

When Labour unexpectedly won the 1945 General Election by a landslide, Beveridge's proposals were rapidly implemented, resulting in the 1946 National Health Service Act. On 1 January 1948, against the bitter opposition of many Conservative hospital doctors who feared for their incomes, the National Health Service was established. At a stroke, institutions such as St Thomas's, which had already been labelled as 'old' by 1215, became part of a national, government-led system. Many hospitals did not make the transition in the long term as amalgamations, funding cuts, and changing needs (with the discovery of antibiotics in 1928 gradually abolishing the age-old blight of infectious diseases) made them unviable. The Italian Hospital had gone by 1990 (despite a reputation for the best hospital food in London) and the London Jewish Hospital, founded in 1919 to serve the Yiddish community in the East End, closed in 1979. Other hospitals transferred to less cramped conditions, while retaining their historic names, such as the Charing Cross Hospital, which since 1818 had been squashed on a site behind the Haymarket Theatre, but in 1973 made the move to new premises in Fulham. Others have had to fight for their survival, particularly after the Tomlinson Report in 1992 concluded that Central London had an over-provision of hospitals and some must close. St Bartholomew's only survived after a high-profile public campaign forced its reprieve (a result of which Sherlock Holmes, whose assistant Dr Watson was trained there, would have approved).

Today, London has fourteen teaching hospitals among its plethora of Foundation Trusts, Acute Trusts, Clinical Commissioning Groups and clinics into which the capital's healthcare has been reorganised. In them medical advances continue to be made, such as the discovery in 1964 at University College Medical School of the Epstein-Barr virus that causes glandular fever. The city as a whole has around 20,000 hospital beds, which receive around 700,000 admissions each year. It faces challenges that are peculiar to such a large urban environment, including a younger population profile than the nation as a whole and where issues such as HIV are more pressing than elsewhere (with the capital having around half the country's recorded cases). Yet despite this, today's Londoners can be thankful for health care provision that is vastly better than what was offered to the Victorian unwell.

education AND schools

Just as elsewhere in Britain, the education of children in London had its origins in the need to train clergymen who were at least passably literate in Latin, the liturgical language of the Christian Church. It is therefore little surprise that London's very oldest educational establishment, St Paul's Cathedral School (founded in 1123) had as its mission the raising of choristers for the cathedral choir.

Over time, the education provided in the capital became more diverse, with public schools such as Eton and Westminster catering to the children of the political and economic elite, a selection of grammar schools for professionals and the upper middle classes, and a vast range of establishments aimed at those of more modest means, run by the church, local authorities, charitable trusts and private organisations. By the mid-Victorian era, it was clear that elementary education for children of the poor had reached a state of crisis, with large numbers of them receiving little or inadequate education. The 1870 Elementary Education Act set up a London School Board, which began a campaign of building schools. By 1876 it had added 100,000 school places for the capital's infants, and appointed superintendents and visitors to inspect the new establishments. It also set in place a curriculum to guide the children's education, in which Bible Study and the 'Principles of Religion and Morality' came a definite first, before Reading, Writing and Arithmetic. Its highly prescriptive nature led to concerns in an 1884 report by Dr Crichton-Browne that the expansion of public education was pushing children into a state of physical and mental breakdown.

London County Council took over all the capital's primary schools in 1904, beginning a programme of renovation of the 'voluntary' schools that had previously not been under central control (and in 314 of which the drains were so putrid that they had to be replaced) and coping with the expansion in numbers that was caused by the raising of the school

1,235,000
the number of children london schools expects to educate annually by 2025

leaving age to 14 by the 1918 Education Act. More serious challenges were raised by the Second World War, at whose outbreak in 1939 some 49 per cent of London schoolchildren were evacuated to the countryside to protect them from the expected German bombs. Around 200,000 had drifted back within a month, leading to chaos, as many schools had been requisitioned for military purposes and emergency classrooms had to be scraped together. For those who stayed outside London, education became a distinctly ad hoc matter, as although pupils of secondary school age were formally attached to a school in the locality to which they had been sent, primary school children were not kept track of.

Concern was already rising that the division of secondary education into grammar schools, 'central schools' (giving a general education to non-grammar pupils) and 'technical schools' (which provided a vocational education) was not adequate for a changing society.

△

Although it was not the first comprehensive school, Holland Park – which opened its gates to pupils in 1958 – soon became the flagship of the movement and was so popular with the families of Labour politicians, that for a time it was dubbed 'the Socialist Eton'.

The 1943 White Paper on Education recommended a national system of comprehensive schools in which all pupils would be educated, but the notion was slow to catch on. The first purpose-built comprehensive, Kidbrooke, a girls' school in Eltham in southeast London, was not built until 1954, while Holland Park School, which became a flagship for the comprehensive education movement, only opened its doors in 1958.

A steady stream of schools did convert (or were established as comprehensives) and the numbers of children staying on in school until 16 rose from 13 per cent in 1952 to 25 per cent in 1960, before the school-leaving age was definitively raised to 16 in 1972. By then, the campaign for comprehensive education had become irresistible, aided by the election of a Labour government in 1974, which was opposed to the system by which many children underwent a selection process at eleven years old to determine whether they went to grammar schools or attended non-selective secondary moderns. In 1977, selection ended in most London boroughs, with thirty-seven grammar schools becoming comprehensives and four opting to convert themselves into independent schools.

The changeover was supervised by the Inner London Education Authority (ILEA), which had taken over the responsibilities for London's education provision at the time the Greater London Council was set up in 1963. It acquired a reputation for educational reform of a sort that Conservative governments found inimical and in 1990 was abolished, its position weakened by the comparatively poor results of London schools in school-leaving examinations. Local boroughs instead took over responsibility for educating their young people (a few boroughs, such as Barnet and Richmond, had managed to retain a small number of grammar schools), marshalling budgets that became ever tighter as the decades passed.

A series of initiatives in the early twenty-first century began to change London's educational scene once more. The Teach First scheme launched in London in 2002 aimed at attracting new graduates into teaching, particularly in subjects such as Science, where shortages were most severe. Its success in raising attainment was such that, from the initial pilot across forty-five secondary schools, it was extended nationwide. In 2000 the Learning and Skills Act mandated the establishment of academies – schools outside the control of the local education authority – which would report directly to the Department for Education. In 2010 a further reform sanctioned the establishment of Free Schools, a form of academy established on the initiative of local groups.

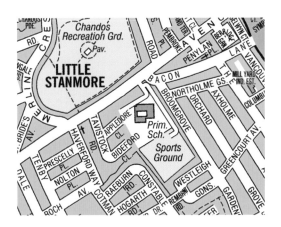

To add to this diversity, London has a large number of faith schools, both those long-run by the Roman Catholic and Anglican churches as Voluntary Aided Schools (which, while receiving partial state funding, retain their religious ethos), and Jewish-run schools such as JFS (which had its origins in a school founded for Jewish orphans in 1732). To these were added Muslim schools, with Islamiyah primary school in Queen's Park becoming the first state-funded Islamic school in 1998; Sikh schools, with the Guru Nanakh Singh academy joining the state-maintained sector in 1999; and Hindu schools, when the Krishna Avanti primary school in Edgware opened in 2008.

The education budget for London schools is now around £7.2 billion and the more than 3,000 schools in the capital are projected to educate 737,000 primary and 498,000 secondary pupils by 2025, their numbers swelled by the unexpected increases in London's population since the 1990s. Their curriculum is far more diverse than that of their great-great-grandparents, including computer coding as well as languages such as Mandarin, and the buildings in which they learn are – on the whole – better equipped, but the education of the next generation remains, just as it was a century ago, one of London's greatest challenges.

△

The Krishnan Avanti school in Edgware became the first state-funded Hindu primary school in 2008. The school has its own purpose-built Hindu temple, built with marble imported from Rajasthan in India.

architecture

London's streetscape and the architecture of its principal buildings has undergone enormous transformations in the course of the city's life. Through the building style that characterized each period, the capital gradually ascended the architectural scale: the stone buildings that graced the late Roman city, to the more modest wooden structures that made up its Anglo-Saxon successor, through the jostle of wooden hovels and stone palaces of the Middle Ages, to the grace of the new Georgian squares of the eighteenth century, the neo-Gothic imperial splendour of the Victorians and finally the technological wizardry of early twenty-first-century offices.

The inter-war period gifted London many of its most beautiful and striking buildings, as the Art Deco style took hold of the capital's architectural imagination. The Daily Express building on Fleet Street, designed in 1932 by Ellis, Clarke and Atkinson, combines horizontal stripes of clear glass and black tiles, making the palace of news seems incongruously like a liquorice allsort. Close to Mornington Crescent station, the Carreras building, built by a cigarette company between 1926 and 1928, combines the exuberant modernity of Art Deco and a backwards historical glance. With Egyptian-style columns on the main façade and two enormous felines standing guard by the entrance it gives a nod both to the Egyptian cat goddess Bubastis, and the company's 'Black Cat Brand'. The Hoover building in Perivale, constructed by the vacuum cleaner company as a factory in 1933, mixes more eclectic influences. Its flattened main section evokes the peristyle columns of Egyptian temples such as Karnak and Luxor, superimposed with Bauhaus-style glazing redolent of 1920s Vienna, and a touch of Aztec patterning and colours. Closed down in the 1980s, it became a supermarket and has now been converted into luxury flats, a fate it shares with many iconic London landmarks.

50

the number of office blocks built in croydon between the mid-1950s and 70s

The austerity that followed the Second World War brooked no such extravagant flourishes and the ethos which informed the Lansbury Estate in Poplar – the 'Living Architecture' section of the Festival of Britain in 1951, with its low-rise dwellings and generous open spaces – was soon forgotten. In its place came a somewhat brutalist and functional approach, as concrete high-rise buildings sprouted all over London, both for offices and as residential towers. Satellite town centres such as Croydon became concrete jungles: between the 1950s and mid-1970s more than fifty office blocks were built there. Residential tower blocks were seen as the solution to a growing housing crisis, but the gas explosion that partially collapsed the Ronan Point tower in Canning Town, in May 1968, just two months after its completion, highlighted the hazards of such structures. That too little thought had been given to their social consequences soon became clear, as the massive blocks failed to replicate the type of social cohesion for which the slums they had replaced had been known. By the 1980s they were a byword for crime, alienation and urban squalor. Paradoxically, though, when a new craze for high-rise building was finally sparked in the late twentieth century in areas of regeneration such as Docklands, the structures were mainly aimed at buyers at the luxury end of the market.

By then, London had escaped from the architectural paralysis that had gifted it the hulk of the thirty-three-storey Centre Point tower on the outskirts of Soho in 1966. The financial district continued to need offices of heroic proportions and the City reached for the sky, with the construction of the 193-metre-high NatWest Tower (now Tower 42) in 1971, a record easily surpassed by the 236 metres of the fifty-storey One Canada Square building, completed in 1991 as the City acquired a satellite quarter in Canary Wharf. There were more innovative architectural projects, too, as London tried to show the world that it could match the modernizing aspirations of its newer and more thrusting rivals. The Tate Modern opened in 2000 as an artful remodelling of an old power station, showing that the new could wear an inspirational older face. Meanwhile the Millennium Dome, designed by Richard Rogers and opened in 2000 (with the Government subsidizing it to the tune of over £600 million) demonstrated that the city was still capable of bringing grand architectural

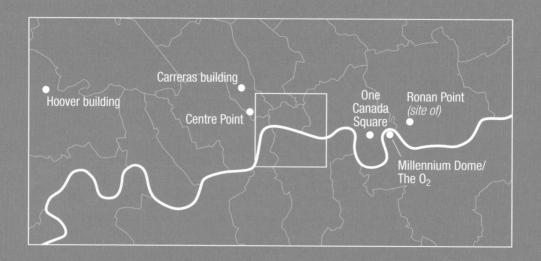

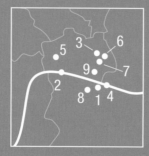

1. Greater London Authority building ('the Onion')
2. Millennium Bridge
3. Tower 42
4. Tower Bridge
5. The Daily Express Building
6. The Gherkin
7. The Leadenhall Building ('the Cheesegrater')
8. The Shard
9. The Walkie-Talkie Building

left ▷

The Carreras building, just north of Mornington Crescent tube station, is one of London's most striking surviving Art Deco buildings, its faintly disturbing Egyptian cats providing divine surveillance of the road north into Camden.

right ▷

Ronan Point, off Butcher's Road in Canning Town, was supposed to be the height of modernity. In fact its explosion marked the death knell of the tower block movement. The building was retained even after the accident, however, and was only finally demolished by Newham Council in 1986.

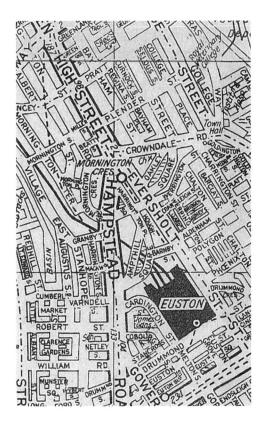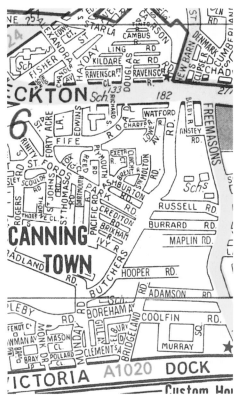

ideas to fruition. The bulbous glass ziggurat of the Greater London Authority (GLA) building (designed by Norman Foster) opened in 2002, showing that London's most modern architecture has not lost its taste for glass.

Londoners meanwhile have retained irreverent humour and have given the GLA building the rather unkind nickname, 'the Onion', from its unusual silhouette, and have labelled a similar string of grand buildings with faintly mocking pet names, so that London now has a Shard, a Cheesegrater, a Gherkin and a Walkie-Talkie. In architecture, as in politics, pretension is likely to be shot down with a dose of barbed London wit.

cemeteries

The twentieth century was not a good time for the burial business in London. The heyday of the cemetery had been the mid-Victorian era, when concern over the squalid conditions of current churchyards (described by Dickens as 'so entirely pressed upon by houses, so small, so rank, so silent, so forgotten except by the few people who ever look down into them from their smokey windows'), led to the establishment of a series of private companies that oversaw the building and operation of new, grander cemeteries. Kensal Green opened in 1833 and was soon joined by others such as West Norwood (1836), Highgate (1839), Brompton (1840) and Nunhead (1840). For those destined for eternal life outside the hustle-bustle of the city, there was even a London Necropolis railway line, with a terminus at Waterloo, that carried corpses and mourners to a mega-cemetery at Brookwood in Surrey until the station's destruction in a German air raid in 1941.

In time, the fatal flaw in the cemetery companies' business plans became evident. Their customers remained resolutely dead, and if their burial plots had been sold freehold, their mortal remains could not be removed. Gradually, the burial grounds became full. Abney Park, London's leading cemetery for nonconformists, was already closed to new graves by 1900. As income dropped, expenditure on maintenance did not and the companies all eventually became insolvent. The last, United Cemeteries, which became a burial behemoth when it absorbed smaller strugglers in the 1960s, finally declared bankruptcy in 1969.

As the means to maintain them dried up, the cemeteries crumbled. Marble angels fell and grand mausoleums cracked open. Once-splendid monuments to the Victorian art of death such as Abney Park, Highgate and Nunhead became impenetrable jungles of ground elder, laurel and ivy. At Nunhead, by 1980, the nonconformist chapel was demolished, the

120
the total number of cemeteries in london

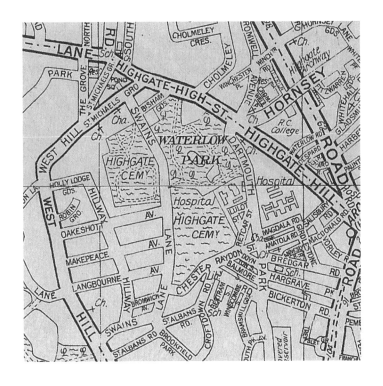

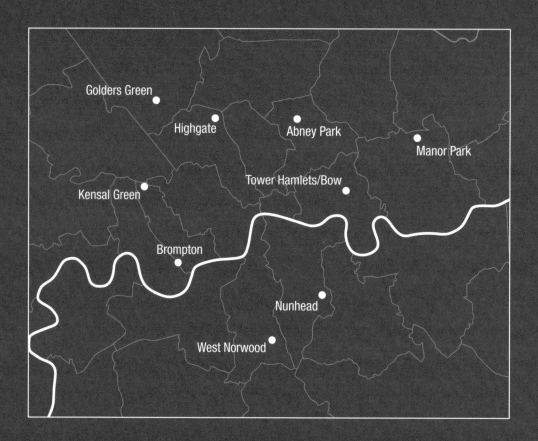

Golders Green ●

Highgate ●

Abney Park ●

Manor Park ●

Kensal Green ●

Tower Hamlets/Bow ●

Brompton ●

Nunhead ●

West Norwood ●

◁ 91 top

Highgate Cemetery was opened in 1839 and proved London's most 'successful', so that by 1975 it contained 51,000 graves. The overcrowding meant that after the Second World War there was little space for new burials and the last interments in the 1960s were paupers' graves marked only by wooden crosses.

◁ 91 bottom

City of London was one of the last of the great Victorian cemeteries to be built, in 1856 – its designer William Haywood is, appropriately, buried in a large Gothic mausoleum near its gates. It was the site of London's second crematorium, built in 1902 and was also used to reinter corpses from many disused City churchyards, as well as the remains of prisoners (including those who had been hung) from the burial ground at Newgate prison.

Anglican chapel burnt out, the lodge in ruins, and the underground burial vaults stripped of lead by vandals. In a desperate bid to save them, some cemeteries were sold to local boroughs, or taken over by them, but even this did not always provide the hoped-for panacea. In 1987 the City of Westminster sold its three cemeteries to a private company for fifteen pence, only to have to compulsorily repurchase them a year later for £10 million following protests (and then, to its relief, obtained a ruling that the original sale had been illegal and got them back, minus some acres at Mill Hill that had been bought by developers).

The rise of crematoria provided some relief for those tasked with disposing of twentieth-century London's 40,000 dead each year. The first, at Golders Green, in 1902, was followed by a sprinkling of others until in 1967 the rate of cremations overtook that of burials. By 2008 Greater London could boast of twenty-five crematoria to complement its 120 cemeteries. The situation of the cemeteries themselves was vastly improved by the foundation of 'Friends' groups. These raised money for the stabilization and restoration of monuments and pathways and made them accessible to the general public for the first time in decades by funding the clearing away of some of the most intractable undergrowth.

Organizations such as the Friends of Highgate, begun in 1975, have brought new life to their kingdom of the dead, in which the last burials had been paupers' graves marked with simple crosses in the 1960s. Although nothing so exciting is likely to occur again as on the night in 1869 when Dante Gabriel Rossetti broke open the coffin of his muse Elizabeth Siddall by the light of a bonfire to retrieve a manuscript of poems he regretted interring with her, the curious can at least now visit the graves of luminaries such as Karl Marx without paying a heavy price in scratched legs, or worse. At Nunhead, similarly, the Friends (founded in 1981) have restored one of the magnificent lodges that was in danger of collapse. Meanwhile a variety of innovative schemes, such as one to deepen graves by lifting up existing remains, digging down further, replacing them, and then carrying out new burials on top, mean that London's cemeteries will welcome new residents for some decades yet.

Whether as unlikely bird sanctuaries – Nunhead has eight-five species recorded – tourist attractions or repositories of architectural wealth, London's cemeteries now have a future that the hard-nosed Victorian businessmen and pious clerics who established them could never have imagined.

John Snow (*d. 1858*),
pioneer in the use of ether,
the earliest anaesthetic
(Brompton)

John Swan (*d. 1860*),
inventor of the
steamship screw
propeller
(Abney Park)

John McDouall Stuart
(*d. 1866*), explorer and
first to cross Australia from
south to north
(Kensal Green)

Charles Babbage
(*d. 1871*), mathematician
(Kensal Green)

Isambard Kingdom Brunel
(*d. 1859*), engineer
(Kensal Green)

Isabella Beeton
(*d. 1865*), author of
*The Book of Household
Management*
(West Norwood)

Catherine Dickens (*d. 1870*),
wife of Charles Dickens
(Highgate)

George El
(*d. 1880*), novel
(Highga

Karl Marx (*d. 1883*), philosopher and father of Communism (Highgate)

Harriet Tebbut (*d. 1893*), nurse, superintendent of the Scutari hospital under Florence Nightingale (Nunhead)

Sir Henry Bessemer (*d. 1898*), inventor of a process that revolutionized steel production (West Norwood)

Emmeline Pankhurst (*d. 1928*), suffragette (Brompton)

John Wisden (*d. 1884*), founder of *Wisden's Cricketers' Almanack* (Brompton)

Emile Blondin (*d. 1897*), first tightrope walker to cross Niagara Falls (Kensal Green)

Hiram Maxim (*d. 1916*), inventor of the Maxim gun (West Norwood)

Freddie Mercury (*d. 1991*), rock star (cremated at Kensal Green)

public housing

Although there had been attempts to make some form of housing provision for the poor since the Middle Ages, with the appearance of almshouses in the tenth century and the development of the workhouse system in the seventeenth, the authorities in London generally did not themselves build houses for those in need. Instead, they left their construction to private developers.

The formation of the London County Council and the provisions of the Housing of the Working Classes Act in 1890 gradually led to a change, as it enjoined local authorities to improve housing in their boroughs. A start was made by identifying around a dozen areas of the inner city that needed urgent clearance, such as the Union Buildings district of Clerkenwell, which was demolished by 1907 to allow the building of the Bourne Estate, housing 2,600 people. A number of other 'cottage estates' were built, such as Totterdown Fields in Tooting, Norbury in Croydon and Old Oak in Hammersmith, with terraces of small houses aimed at working men, often at the end of a tram line to allow for an easy commute.

The discovery that many conscripts called up for service in the First World War were in poor health – because of the terrible state of the houses in which they had been brought up – led to demands for 'Homes fit for Heroes' to provide them with better conditions once they returned home. The 1930 Housing Act further required local authorities to develop slum-clearance plans, and as a result, huge developments such as the Becontree Estate in Dagenham were built. Planned to provide 26,000 new houses, 18,000 were complete by 1930, in time to house the thousands of people displaced by simultaneous slum clearances in the East End.

8,500
the number of dwellings with three or more households in islington, 1965

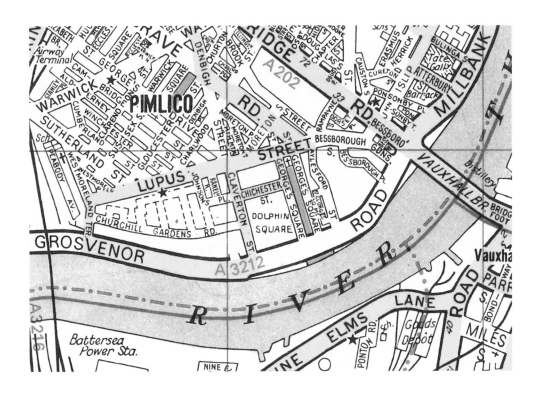

Churchill Gardens in Pimlico, built between 1946 and 1962, was one of the most ambitious of the inner-city regeneration projects carried out according to the Abercrombie Plan. Its complex of mixed-development blocks and maisonettes, intended to provide housing for all social classes, was designed by Philip Powell and Hidalgo Moya, two architects then still in their mid-20s, and won a 2000 Civic Trust award for the most outstanding development of the past forty years.

The Labour government, elected by a landslide in 1945, delivered further improvements to social housing. Estates such as the Lansbury in Poplar, designed as an architectural counterpart to the Festival of Britain in 1948, and the Churchill Gardens Estate in Pimlico, with 1,600 homes in its thirty-two blocks, became showcases for the state of London council housing. However, many of London's less well-off residents were still dependent on renting from the private sector and the activities of slum landlords such as Peter Rachmann, who operated in Notting Hill in the early 1960s, led to calls for change. The 1965 Milner Holland Report on London's housing found that the city needed half a million new homes in the next decade if housing poverty were to be banished. It identified thousands of dwellings with three or more households (8,500 in Islington alone), a key indicator of poverty, and found that Paddington was London's most overcrowded borough, with one-seventh of households crammed in with an average of more than 1.5 people per room.

The solution was to reach for the skies. Between 1961 and 1981 over 400 high-rise blocks were built (125 in the borough of Newham alone) and huge concrete jungles such as Tottenham's Broadwater Farm Estate or the North Peckham Estate in Southwark mushroomed to answer the desperate need for social housing. It was also part of a trend away from private renting, which saw the proportion of Londoners housed by the local authority more than double, from around 19 per cent in 1961 to a peak of 35 per cent in 1981.

At first the experiment seemed a success. Living conditions were better than in the old slums – the new flats virtually all had their own bathrooms – but gradually problems became apparent: transplanting old established communities into high-rises meant that it was harder to get to know the neighbours, and the new blocks had void spaces in communal areas and walkways well away from public roads, where crime could fester. The disaster in May 1968 at Ronan Point in Canning Town, where a gas explosion demolished part of a newly built high-rise, turned local planners away from building many more.

London councils were still left with large estates of the blocks, which within a decade of their building were in urgent need of regeneration. Much of the more desirable housing stock was sold off under Right to Buy Legislation in the 1980s, leaving councils with even less income from their housing account to fund the maintenance of crumbling high-rises. A series of initiatives were set in train, such as the Urban Programme (1978), Estates Action (1985), City Challenge areas (1991) and the New Deal for Communities (2001), though often the answer was the partial or complete demolition of troubled estates and building of lower-rise replacements, in a return to the ethos of the cottage estates of nearly a century beforehand.

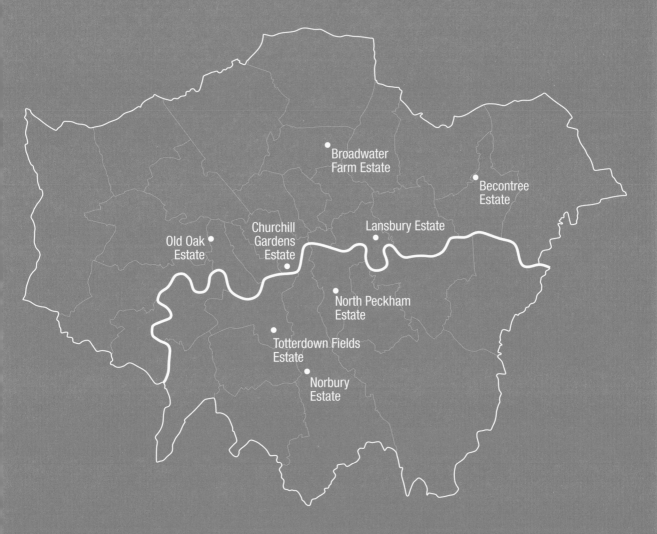

In 2000, local councils were forced to consider devolving their housing stock to ALMOs (Arm's Length Management Organizations), removing them from day-to-day involvement in the running of estates. Much council housing was transferred to housing associations (with Bromley having done so to all its 12,000 properties in 1992). Ironically, this came at a period when London's population was beginning to rise again. New pressures were placed on social housing by the need to find accommodation for large numbers of refugees from conflicts in the Middle East and for economic migrants, many of them originally from sub-Saharan Africa and the former Soviet Union. As London moved into the twenty-first century, it seemed to face a public housing crisis every bit as serious as those of the late Victorian or Edwardian capital, and with less apparent political will to resolve it.

DISORDERLY LONDON

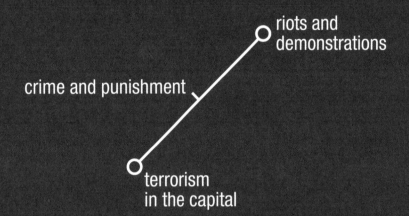

riots AND demonstrations

London's creative ferment, in which deprivation and opportunity sit side by side, has long had a darker face. Although the past eighty years has seen nothing like the tumults and disorders that had characterized previous centuries – most notably the Peasants' Revolt of 1381, which nearly toppled Richard II – the capital has still experienced riots and demonstrations, some of them on an unprecedented scale.

Change has often been the midwife of dissent and throughout the twentieth century, groups that felt they were being left behind – or could be persuaded that they were – turned that alienation into sometimes violent protest. In the 1930s, the lure of Fascism, particularly to traditional white working-class communities, made life difficult for Jewish communities in the East End of London, where they were targeted by movements such as Oswald Mosley's British Union of Fascists (BUF). On 4 October 1936, Mosley's followers, who wore black shirts in homage to their German National Socialist models, tried to march through an area of Stepney that had a strong Jewish and socialist tradition. Three thousand BUF marchers, accompanied by twice that number of policemen, tried to make their way from the Tower of London along Whitechapel's Cable Street. They were met by up to 300,000 anti-fascist demonstrators, who erected barricades to prevent the marchers' progress. Amidst a hail of missiles including chair legs and marbles, and despite charges by mounted police to clear the protestors, Mosley's march ground to a halt and had to be abandoned.

Not all riots and protests in the post-war era had as clear cut a political agenda as the 'Battle of Cable Street' even if they were just as touched by racial politics. As immigration from the Caribbean rose in the 1950s, from 15,000 in 1951 to around 238,000 by early 1962, so tensions rose with those who resented the newcomers. In 1958, targeting of Caribbean migrants by local gangs and more organized right-wing groups flared up into

750,000–1,000,000
the estimated number of people who protested against the iraq war in 2003

rioting in Notting Hill, and there were occasional outbreaks at the margins of the Notting Hill Carnival (notably in 1976, when 400 police officers were injured). Distrust of the police, often aggravated by heavy-handed tactics, finally exploded in Brixton in April 1981 after a misunderstanding over police treatment of a wounded black youth – whom they were in fact trying to help – sparked disorder that rapidly spread into rioting and looting over several nights. Nearly 280 police officers were injured during the first night and 145 buildings damaged, twenty-eight of them by fire, in episodes that saw the first use of petrol bombs on mainland Britain.

Despite a government inquiry led by Lord Scarman, mutual distrust between the police and Caribbean communities festered on estates such as Broadwater Farm, which had been considered a model of modernity when it was completed in 1973, but had declined into a sink estate, troubled by deprivation and crime. On 5 October 1985 the death of an elderly local black woman during a police search of her house sparked fury and a riot in which the police completely lost control of the estate while being bombarded with missiles and petrol bombs from a maze of overhead walkways. At the height of the disorder, PC Keith Blakelock was brutally hacked to death, the first police officer to die in a riot for 150 years.

A further race riot broke out in Brixton in 1995. More extensive rioting in deprived areas erupted in 2011, which touched areas as far apart as Croydon and Wood Green and caused over £100 million of damage (though among those arrested by the police, equal numbers were black as were white). The late twentieth century, however, brought a new political edge to disorder in London, as anti-capitalist groups and right-wing organizations such as the British National Party coalesced to revive the little-lamented tradition of mass agitation and political street fighting. In 1990 a huge march – some 200,000 people – gathered on Kennington Common and marched to Trafalgar Square to protest against the Conservative government's introduction of a 'poll tax' that was charged according to the number of adults living in a property rather than its value. In an effort to contain the crowd, mounted

◁103
The Grunwick Film processing plant in Dollis Hill was the scene of a long-running industrial dispute between 1976 and 1978, during which extensive picketing sought to prevent the management bringing in an alternative workforce. Over 500 arrests were made as violence flared up between strikers and the police.

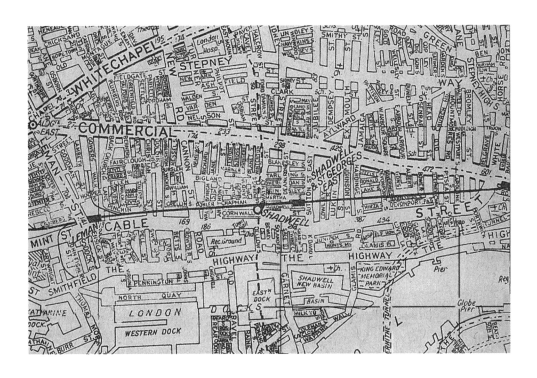

△

Huge numbers of anti-Fascist demonstrators assembled on 4 October 1936 at Gardiner's Corner near Aldgate to block Oswald Mosley's planned march down Commercial Road into the Jewish East End. Mosley then diverted his followers down Cable Street where they ran into barricades erected by protestors. Blocked at every turn, he abandoned the march.

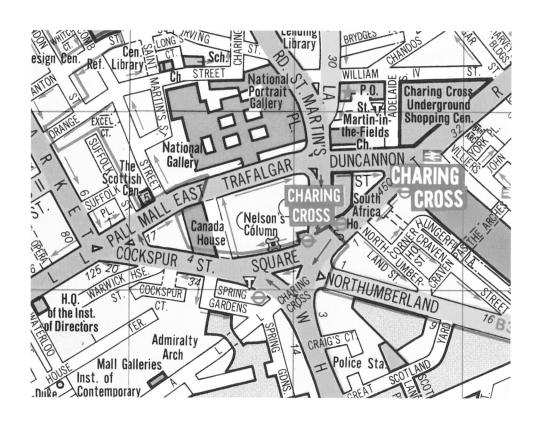

police charged several times, fuelling an atmosphere that spilled over into rioting in parts of the square, and looting as rioters moved north into the West End shopping district, resulting in over 300 arrests.

There was no shortage of commentators who pointed out that the Peasants' Revolt, too, had been sparked by a poll tax, and they were vindicated in assuming that the discontent that had sparked the 1990 riot had not gone away – there were anti-capitalist riots on May Day in 2000 and 2001 and large-scale protests against the holding of the G-20 summit of leading industrialized nations in London in 2009. Yet in the twenty-first century demonstrations in London became more diverse, across a wider range of causes, and, though growing ever larger, they have largely been peaceful. On 22 September 2002, the country came to the city, as the Countryside Alliance organized a march attended by over 300,000 people protesting against perceived central government neglect of rural interests on issues as diverse as fox hunting, lack of internet access in the countryside and the need to buy locally grown produce. In February 2003, this record was broken when between 750,000 and a million people gathered in London to protest against the participation of the government of Tony Blair in the impending Iraq War, making it the largest demonstration in political history. Those numbers were only next approached by the People's Vote March on 23 March 2019, called to exert pressure on the Government to hold a confirmatory referendum on Britain's exit from the European Union.

London has always been a turbulent place – the riot that erupted around the coronation of William the Conqueror in 1066 was probably its first, and the 2011 rioting will not be its last – and disorder bubbles away just below the surface of such a complex city. The challenge for London's twenty-first-century rulers will be, just as it was for their predecessors, to find ways to allow that dissent to express itself peacefully and to ensure that even marginalized communities feel that they can be heard without the need to resort to violence.

◄

Since its opening in 1840, Trafalgar Square has been the scene of frequent political protests and rallies, from the Chartists in 1843, Oswald Mosley's Fascist BUF in 1937, to the anti-poll tax demonstration that ended in a riot in 1990.

crime AND punishment

Unsurprisingly, a city as large and complex as London has always struggled to contain a criminal element seething away beneath its surface, with miscreants ranging from the impoverished and desperate, to the opportunists, the organized gangs, the politically motivated and the truly insane. Over time it has evolved a professional force to capture criminals, and places to incarcerate (or formerly to execute) those who were apprehended.

Crime festered in the slums of Victorian London: rookeries with overcrowded and dangerous tenement buildings bred a casual attitude to life and property in impoverished areas from the notorious Seven Dials (where 'misery clings to misery for a little warmth', as the poet John Keats described it) to the teeming lanes of Whitechapel and the East End. The foundation of the Metropolitan Police in 1829 had made a little difference – at least there was now a formal body tasked with keeping a lid on crime – but a cunning, a brutal or a lucky criminal still managed to thrive.

The culture of suspicion of outsiders kept the police largely at bay in London's most troubled districts, and the partial breakdown of social order during the Second World War led to a surge in crime and the emergence of organized criminal enterprises, led by gangsters such as Jack Spot and Billy Hill in the 1950s. Their successors were even more brutal: the Kray brothers, Reggie and Ronnie, established a virtual criminal fiefdom in the East End in the early 1960s, their protection rackets siphoning money from cab firms, cafés and pubs. Only the shooting of a rival villain at the Blind Beggar Pub in Whitechapel in March 1966 brought the brothers down, and in 1969 they were both sentenced to life imprisonment.

The 1970s brought new crime challenges for London, as drug smugglers established routes from South America and Asia into Europe and the IRA's renewed campaign of violence claimed dozens of victims. 1985 saw the start of a series of race riots, which began in Brixton. As crime in London continued to reflect social and economic changes in wider society, police in the twenty-first century had to deal with new threats from people smugglers and cybercriminals.

The Metropolitan Police (Met) changed over time, too. From a handful of officers, with almost no forensic tools, dependent on witness accounts and confessions to gain

1998

the last year it was still technically possible to receive the death penalty for piracy and high treason

convictions, it had grown to a service employing 16,000 officers by 1900. A fingerprint bureau was established in 1901 as a new aid to catching the complacent criminal. Other new units were set up to respond to the changing patterns of crime. In 1932 the 'Met' acquired a vice squad to tackle the problems associated with prostitution in Central London. This eventually merged with the Human Trafficking Unit in 2010. In 1961 the Special Patrol Group was set up to cope with public order situations, and in 1971 the Bomb Squad was established after a number of attacks by the anarchist group the Angry Brigade. It eventually became a formal anti-terrorist branch, and in 2006 reorganized as Counter Terrorism Command. To house this growing force, which today has more than 43,000 officers and civilian staff, the Metropolitan Police has migrated through a series of buildings, beginning with a set of houses arranged around Scotland Yard in Whitehall and transferring to a new building at Victoria in 1890 (which was dubbed 'New Scotland Yard'). In 1967 the branch moved to a new building on Broadway, before settling into new premises in the Curtis Green Building on Victoria Embankment in 2017.

The fate for those caught by the police is today far better than that which lay in wait for Victorian criminals, when prisons were little better than the slums they had offended to escape in the first place. Philanthropists and prison reformers such as Elizabeth Fry did their best, and new modern prisons such as Pentonville (opened in 1842) and Wormwood Scrubs, built between 1874 and 1890, gradually provided more humane accommodation for prisoners. Holloway Prison was built in 1852 for female prisoners who had previously had to share space with the men at Newgate, London's oldest and most notorious main prison. Conditions gradually improved in other ways, too. The Criminal Justice Act of 1948 ended penal servitude, hard labour and flogging for inmates, and after the Second World War greater efforts were made at the rehabilitation and education of prisoners (many of whom suffered from limited education and learning difficulties).

Nonetheless, overcrowding in prisons has remained a serious problem and successive reports have warned that conditions were unsatisfactory and liable to lead to prisoner unrest. In 2018, an independent report labelled Pentonville as overcrowded and crumbling, rife with gang activity and vermin. Periodic riots have erupted in London's prisons although some, like the 1979 IRA rooftop protest at Wormwood Scrubs, were politically motivated. Other prisoners have adopted a more direct approach and made their escape. The most high-profile of these escapes took place in 1965 when Ronnie Biggs, who had taken part in the Great Train Robbery in 1963 (the theft of £2.6 million of cash from the Glasgow-to-

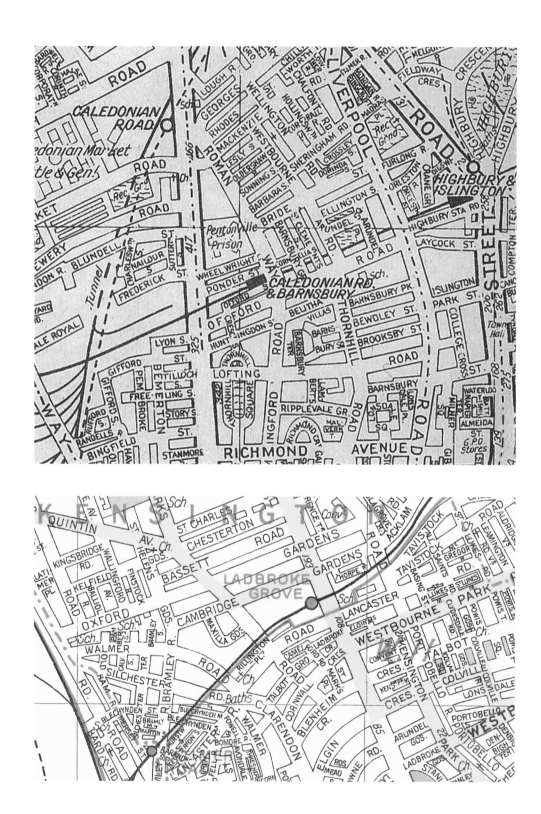

London mail train) broke out of Wandsworth Prison and fled to Brazil, and in 1966, when George Blake, an MI6 officer who had been convicted of working as a double agent for the Soviets, scrambled up a rope ladder provided by accomplices to escape Wormwood Scrubs and make his way back to his paymasters in Moscow.

Blake had not faced the death sentence, unlike previous traitors such as William Joyce ('Lord Haw-Haw') who had made pro-Nazi broadcasts from Berlin during the Second World War and was hanged at Wandsworth Prison in January 1946. Hanging had been the common sentence for a range of crimes (including modest thefts) right up to the nineteenth century, and until 1868 it was often carried out in public in front of baying crowds. Gradually, hanging came to be confined to convictions for murder, and its use for under 18s was outlawed in 1933. A campaign to have it abolished completely stalled – despite a recommendation in 1930 that it be suspended – and it took a series of high-profile cases to bring it back on the public agenda. Derek Bentley, a 19-year-old with epilepsy and severe learning difficulties was hanged in 1953 for the murder of a police officer during a bungled burglary. Bentley had not even pulled the trigger. The outcry over this, together with the hanging the same year of the serial killer John Christie for a murder for which another man had previously been executed, and the publicity surrounding the execution in 1955 of Ruth Ellis (the last woman to be hanged in Britain) caused the campaign for reform to step up a pace. The Homicide Act of 1957 restricted the use of capital punishment to the murder of a police officer, homicide by shooting or homicide while resisting arrest. Albert Pierrepoint, the official hangman, who had carried out over 500 executions during a thirty-year career retired in 1956, and London's last hanging took place in 1961 in Pentonville Prison. The death penalty was suspended in 1965 and finally abolished in 1969, although technically it remained available as a sentence for piracy and high treason until 1998.

Even so the gallows at Wandsworth prison remained in place, tested every six months in case the death penalty was restored, until it was finally dismantled in 1993. London remains a city preoccupied with crime, most lately with an epidemic of fatal knife attacks in 2018 and 2019, but its approach to punishing those caught is far more humane than the floggings, brandings, back-breaking hard labour, transportation or hanging faced by Victorian criminals.

◁ top
Pentonville, built between 1840 and 1842, was intended as a model prison based on a penitentiary in Philadelphia. When Newgate closed in 1902, Pentonville became London's main site for executions, many of the hanged criminals being buried there in unmarked graves.

◁ bottom
Rillington Place was the site of murders carried out by John Christie in the early 1950s. The execution of another, innocent man, Timothy Evans for some of these helped fuel the campaign for the abolition of the death penalty.

terrorism IN THE capital

Although London, as is the case for any large metropolis, has struggled from the beginning to contain crime on its teeming streets, terrorism – the politically motivated criminal activity designed to strike fear into its people, and to force its government to change policies (or even to step down) – is a relatively new phenomenon. It perhaps has its origins with Guy Fawkes and his co-conspirators, who on the night of 4–5 November 1605 tried to lay explosives in a cellar beneath the Palace of Westminster in a bid to assassinate James I, who was due to open Parliament the next day. Their hope was that he would be replaced with a sovereign who would remove penal legislation against Catholicism., This strain of terror, or imagined terror, continued to fester in London, breaking cover in 1678–81 as the Popish Plot, an almost entirely fictitious conspiracy to assassinate Charles II, which owed its existence to the fertile mind of Titus Oates, a former Anglican priest.

Terrorism re-emerged during the nineteenth century, when the British government found itself the subject of attacks by Irish nationalists, who chafed at British rule in Ireland and sought to accelerate the establishment of home rule there. A campaign by the Irish Republican Brotherhood (the 'Fenians') most spectacularly involved a bomb attack on Clerkenwell Prison in December 1867 in which twelve people were killed.

After the South of Ireland achieved independence from Britain in 1922, nationalist campaigners continued to call for the remaining counties of Ireland to join them. In January 1939, the Irish Republican Army's (IRA's) war council publicly declared war against Britain and began its S-Plan of sabotage against Britain's civil and military infrastructure. The attacks included bombs left on 4 February in luggage stores at Tottenham Court Road and Leicester Square underground stations (starting a sequence of terrorist bombings at tube and railway stations that would stretch into the twenty-first century). On 29 March they

1605

the year london experienced its first attempted terrorist attack

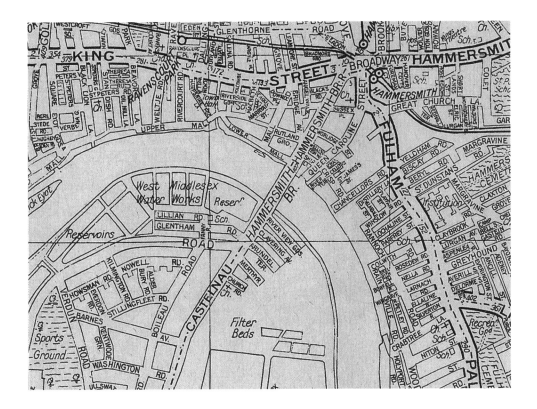

△

Hammersmith Bridge in southwest London has been the scene of a number of IRA attacks, as the organization planted bombs there in 1939, 1996 and 2000. The 2000 explosion caused the bridge to be closed for two years while repairs were undertaken.

115 ▷

Westminster Bridge, close to the politically sensitive Houses of Parliament, saw an attack in 2017 by Islamist terrorists on civilians using a vehicle driven into a crowd, with a follow-up assault using knives. The incident raised fears about how to detect and prevent this type of low-tech terrorist attack.

attacked Hammersmith Bridge – which would also become a favourite target for terrorists, and between then and the end of the campaign in March 1940, banks and cinemas were also added to the list of targets.

London was free of Irish terrorist activity until 1969, when the start of the Troubles in Northern Ireland renewed the threat of attacks on mainland Britain. In March 1973 the Provisional IRA planted four car bombs in London, beginning a campaign that lasted until the late 1990s. Just as in the 1930s campaign, the Irish nationalists targeted civilian and military settings, exploding bombs at Victoria, King's Cross and Euston stations in the first year, and in 1974 attacking Madame Tussauds, the Boat Show, the Houses of Parliament and Oxford Street. Although the Metropolitan Police captured four IRA terrorists who had held two civilians hostage in a house in Balcombe Street in Marylebone, the attacks continued and became bloodier. In October 1981 a bombing at Chelsea Barracks caused two fatalities, and explosives set under bandstands in Hyde Park and Regents Park in July 1982 killed eleven members of the Household Cavalry and Green Jackets. Economic destruction mounted, too, with attacks on the Baltic Exchange in 1992 and Bishopsgate in January 1993 resulting in nearly £2 billion pounds-worth of damage.

The IRA campaign finally subsided after ceasefires in 1994 and 1997 and the signing of the Good Friday Agreement in 1998, which brought an uneasy peace to Northern Ireland. Yet London still faced terrorist challenges, at first closely tied to the Arab-Israeli conflict, in which Britain, as the former colonial power, had to tread a delicate path and was accused of bad faith by both sides. A few bombs had been detonated by the Stern Gang in the late 1940s, in a bid to get Britain to grant independence to a Jewish state, which included an attack on a servicemen's club off St Martin's Lane in March 1947. Middle East-related violence, though, only really mounted from the early 1970s after the attempted hijack of an El Al aeroplane by Palestinian terrorists in September 1970. Assassination attempts were made on the Israeli and Jordanian ambassadors to London.

Shock-waves from conflicts elsewhere sometimes reached the capital and on 30 April 1980, Arab-speaking Iranian campaigners seeking independence for Khuzestan in the south of the country occupied the Iranian Embassy in Knightsbridge and took twenty-six people hostage. They held them for six days before the SAS stormed the building, killing all but one terrorist (and one of the hostages). Almost exactly four years later, PC Yvonne Fletcher was shot by a gunman from inside the Libyan People's Bureau in St James's Square while on guard duty during a protest against the Libyan dictator Colonel Gaddafi. As diplomats, those inside the People's Bureau had to be permitted to leave and the killer has never been tried.

The rise of the Islamist terror groups Al-Qaeda and ISIS in the early twenty-first century brought a new wave of terrorism to London's streets. On 7 July 2004 Islamist suicide bombers detonated bombs on tube trains near Aldgate, Russell Square and Edgware

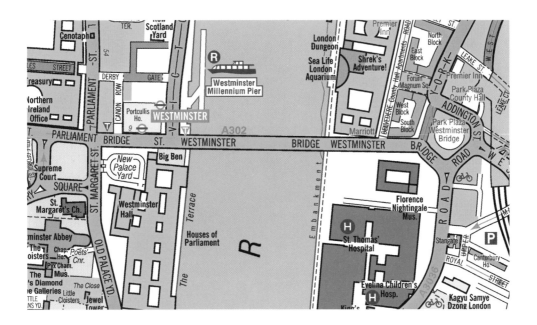

Road Stations, while a fourth bomber set off his explosive device on a number 30 bus near Tavistock Square, badly damaging the back of the vehicle. In all, fifty-two people were killed and around 700 injured. The carnage was nearly repeated when a second terrorist cell tried to set off devices at Shepherd's Bush, Warren Street, Oval and Shoreditch stations, but the bombs proved faulty and none of them detonated.

More recent attacks have proved more diverse, employing means more difficult for the security services to detect or prevent. In May 2013 Lee Rigby, a drummer in the Royal Regiment of Fusiliers, was killed by two Islamists who hacked him to death with a cleaver. In March 2017 an attacker drove a car into crowds on Westminster Bridge, and then killed others with a knife, causing five fatalities, while two months later a van was rammed into pedestrians on London Bridge, killing three of them after which the terrorists stabbed five others to death. More lately intelligence services, already stretched by the monitoring of home-grown terrorists and jihadists returning from conflicts such as the Syrian Civil War, have had to cope with a surge of right-wing nationalist terrorist groups which, while they have not reached the same scale of active operations as Islamist organisations, in June 2016 inspired the first assassination of a sitting MP since 1990 when Jo Cox was shot and stabbed by a white supremacist at a constituency surgery in West Yorkshire.

Throughout it all, Londoners have remained sanguine. From Guy Fawkes, to the IRA bombings and the large-scale casualties of the 7/7 attack, they have responded to the emergency services, treated the casualties, and then continued about their business. Terrorism, in London at least, has not inflicted a long-term feeling of terror.

THE WEALTH
OF LONDON

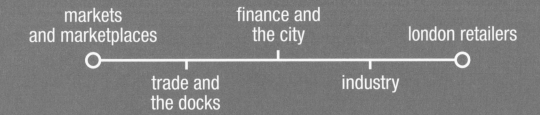

markets
and marketplaces

finance and
the city

london retailers

trade and
the docks

industry

markets AND marketplaces

Since medieval times, London's markets, with their labyrinthine warrens of stalls, byzantine regulations and dazzling array of goods, have added colour to the life of the capital, as well as fulfilling the more mundane task of provisioning its citizens.

The medieval custom of craftsmen and vendors clustering together in quarters that reflected their specialties resulted in London developing a wide variety of markets, each dedicated to a particular sector. It is a tradition that has survived today, with Smithfield still specializing in meat – as it has done for over 750 years – Billingsgate in fish and Covent Garden in fruit, vegetables and flowers (albeit both of them transferred from their original sites). There is also a host of smaller markets, such as Columbia Road for flowers, Portobello Road and Camden Passage for vintage goods and antiques, Camden Lock for fashion, Borough Market for food and a rejuvenated Covent Garden for gifts and collectibles. The result is the most vibrant street market scene anywhere in Europe.

After a late flowering in the Victorian era, which saw the building of new market halls for Smithfield (1877) and Leadenhall (1881) – whose poultry market dated back to 1309 – it seemed as though the twentieth century might sound the death-knell for the great Central London markets. The Second World War took its toll; in 1930 there had been 10,000 licensed pitches in London's street markets, but the exigencies of war forced Caledonian Market (which accounted for a quarter of those) to shut up shop and move in 1950 to a humbler site in Bermondsey. A part of Smithfield was destroyed in 1945 by a German V-2 rocket that struck late morning while the market was busy and killed 110 people. After the war, the hold of old traditions became less tenacious and the porters, pitching gangs and staffmen of Covent Garden – who had all jealously guarded their segmented roles in the movement of

one fish a year
the rent paid by billingsgate market to the local council

goods around the market – or the bumarees – self-employed licensed porters at Smithfield Market – began to seem like quaint survivals in an ever-more competitive age.

It was traffic, though, that seemed most likely to kill the old markets. Covent Garden, situated in the heart of the busy West End and with theatres and the Opera House adding to the congestion, became a choked-up jam of vans, clogging its narrow lanes and making deliveries and collections almost impossible. It had not been designed for the modern age, springing up on the lands of the Duke of Bedford in vestigial form in the 1630s, where it became a formal market in 1670. Its aristocratic owners had sold on their market rights to a private company in 1918, but even this struggled to maintain it as a going concern. A 1921 Ministry of Food Committee report found that it was 'altogether inadequate to the necessities of trade' and a variety of proposals were put forward to rationalize the site, including the drastic steps of re-siting the magnificent St Paul's Church (designed by Inigo Jones) and the Opera House, both of which bordered the market perimeter.

By 1962 the market had been taken back into public ownership and its future looked bleak. Finally, the decision was made to abandon the original site and, after an abortive suggestion that it transfer to Beckton, a New Covent Garden market opened in 1974 on the site of a former locomotive works at Nine Elms in Battersea. There the business of fruit, vegetable and flower selling continues, bringing a medieval tradition to the suburbs. The old market site, meanwhile, became the subject of a bitter planning dispute, with proposals for a series of new roads cutting through the area, and the building of new sports and conference centres that would have radically changed the nature of the district. Good sense in the end prevailed and the old buildings were redeveloped – in the case of the central hall by excavating a deep central well into its former basements and rationalizing the hodge-podge of stalls that had grown up over the years – and in 1980 it reopened as a market for gifts and antiques. Retaining its former guise as a market, Covent Garden is now one of London's most famous tourist attractions.

120–1 ▷

Covent Garden Market weathered all the changes in Central London from the 1670s, when it was first chartered, right into the twentieth century. Still thriving before the Second World War, in 1936, the narrow lanes that surrounded it finally led to its transfer to Nine Elms in 1974. Even so, the site and its historic buildings, despite planners' designs on cutting it through with new roads, survived to become a tourist market.

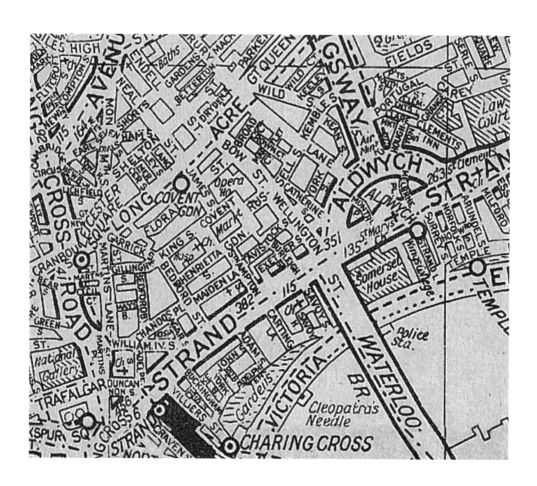

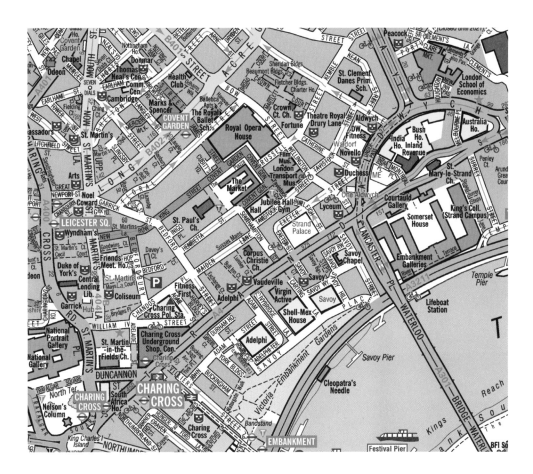

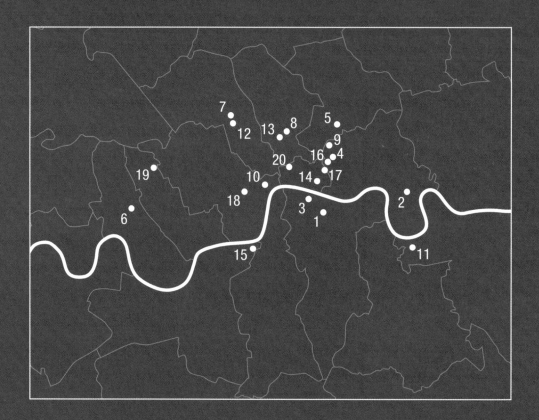

1. Bermondsey Market
2. Billingsgate Market
3. Borough Market
4. Brick Lane Market
5. Broadway Market, Hackney
6. Brook Green Market and Kitchen
7. Camden Lock Market
8. Camden Passage Market
9. Columbia Road market
10. Covent Garden Market
11. Greenwich Market
12. Inverness Street Market
13. Islington Farmers' Market
14. Leadenhall Market
15. New Covent Garden Market
16. Old Spitalfields Market
17. Petticoat Lane Market
18. Piccadilly Market
19. Portobello Road Market
20. Smithfield Market

Billingsgate, London's fish market, joined the flight to the suburbs in 1982, when it transferred to a new site on the Isle of Dogs, for which the City of London, which still operates it, pays a symbolic ground rent of one fish a year to Tower Hamlets, the new landlords. The foul language for which its merchants were once known (even Shakespeare's comment in *King Lear* 'on as bad a tongue, if it be set on, as any oyster-wife at Billingsgate hath') seems to have abated, and the conditions for workers there, described by George Orwell who did a stint as a porter in the 1930s, have considerably improved.

One great London market has resolutely held out in the centre of the City. Smithfield meat market, which was described as early as 1174 as a place where Londoners could buy 'swine with their deep flanks and cows and oxen of immense bulk', has a colourful history. Events that stand out include the joust organized by Geoffrey Chaucer for Richard II in 1390, and the hundreds of heretics who were burnt at the stake there in the 1550s. Even so it gradually became pared down, with the hay market that had been held on Saturdays finally closing in 1914, and the market's main focus, which had been live animals, turning to the purveying of dead meat. During the Second World War, when trading was slack, part of the cold storage at the market was converted into a giant laboratory where the Nobel prize-winning chemist Max Perutz conducted experiments to retard the melting of ice. The Allies needed an airbase in the mid-Atlantic to counter the growing threat of German U-boats and came up with the idea of a gigantic 2.2-million-ton iceberg, fifteen stories high that would be floated down from Newfoundland and – if Perutz's experiments bore fruit – would act as an unmeltable aircraft carrier. Perutz did come up with pykrete, a mixture of ice and wood pulp that melted less easily and was more malleable, but the whole project was grotesquely ambitious, and so Smithfield's most fantastic export never did come bobbing down the North Atlantic.

Still operating from its grand Victorian central hall (called by its designer Horace Jones 'a cathedral of meat'), Smithfield is the largest wholesale meat market in Britain, and one of the biggest in Europe. It is a sign that London's market scene in the twenty-first century can encompass both centuries-old tradition and the innovation that transformed Borough Market from a fading fruit and vegetable market into an astonishingly successful foodie nirvana.

trade AND THE docks

London has always been a trading city, its prosperity in large part dependent on the import and export of goods to a global market. And for trade it needed riverside facilities, beginning with the wharves of Roman London and the docks that King Alfred the Great established at Queenhithe (south of Mansion House) in 889. Throughout the Middle Ages, these docks expanded and migrated eastwards into districts such as Stepney, receiving cargoes of wool, timber, grain and wine to sate Britain's thirst and supply its nascent industries with raw materials.

At the beginning of the Victorian era the docks underwent a boom, as larger ships and the needs of Britain's expanding empire rendered the former rather ad hoc arrangements inadequate. A great building campaign from 1801 resulted in the opening of a string of docks in the East End, from St Katharine Docks hard by the Tower of London to East India, West India and Millwall Docks, which converted the Isle of Dogs into a huge series of shipping basins. Then, as ships grew bigger, the even more monumental Royal, Victoria and Albert Docks were constructed to the east (the latter opening in 1880).

Even though the First World War led to a pause in trade, it prompted the development of the King George V Dock in North Woolwich, opened by the king himself in July 1921 before a crowd of 8,000 invited guests. It seemed as though the docks' heyday would last forever. Yet although some new buildings were erected, and some seven million tons of grain were arriving annually at the port, there were wanting signs. The Port of London Authority, established in 1908 to unify the previously fragmented administration of the dock area, was slow to invest money, and facilities were not upgraded as much as was needed.

300 of 900
the proportion of riverside factories and wharves in the docklands damaged or destroyed during the second world war

The Second World War dealt a terrible blow to the docks. As strategic targets, they were hit in the very first German air raid on 7 September 1940, when timber stored at the Surrey Docks went up in flames and a bomb destroyed the entrance lock of the George V Dock. A second attack the next day on St Katharine Docks ignited coconut oil and paraffin that burnt for several days. Trade through the docks was crippled, and although the West India Docks gained some business in building Mulberry artificial harbours for the Normandy landings, it was clear that the damage caused by the 900 high-explosive bombs that had fallen on the port area would take years to repair.

Of the 900 riverside factories and wharves in the Docklands, 300 had been damaged or destroyed and some would never be rebuilt. The port enjoyed a false dawn in the immediate post-war period and early 1950s, as its competitors in Europe had suffered as badly or worse and so London's creaking facilities were full to bursting: the trade handled at the port rose from thirty-three million tons in 1947 to sixty-one million in 1964. Investment, though, was patchy and it was not until 1958 that the redevelopment of the quays at Millwall docks was begun in an effort to convert the Fred Olsen terminal there to cope with the mechanized pallet loading that was by then becoming the norm in modern ports.

The modernization proved too difficult in the end and poor industrial relations accelerated the decline of the docks. The port was closed for a month from May to July 1966 during a seamen's strike, only one of the twenty-three stoppages that had broken out during the previous two years. Business leaked away and the general cargo trade from Australia relocated to Antwerp. The management struggled to reform antiquated working practices, but they lost the battle and faced a national dock strike in July 1970 and further national stoppages in 1980 and 1984.

The port was now losing money in an unsustainable fashion, its losses mounting steadily from 1969/70 when they amounted to £2 million, to £5 million five years later. The container port at Tilbury, opened in 1967, was siphoning off traffic to a facility that could cope with modern loading methods and the larger ships in which the bulk of trade was now transported.

(continues on page 130)

126-9 ▷
The 1938 A-Z shows a complex of active docks running the length of the riverbank from Wapping to the Isle of Dogs. Its modern counterpart on pages 128-9 shows they have all gone, converted into housing, leisure facilities and the new financial district of Canary Wharf.

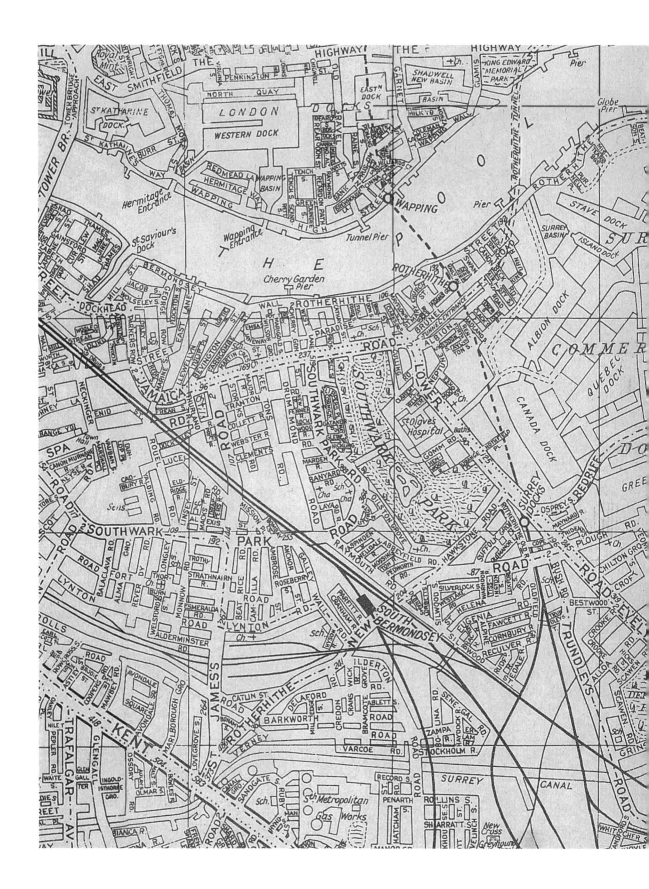

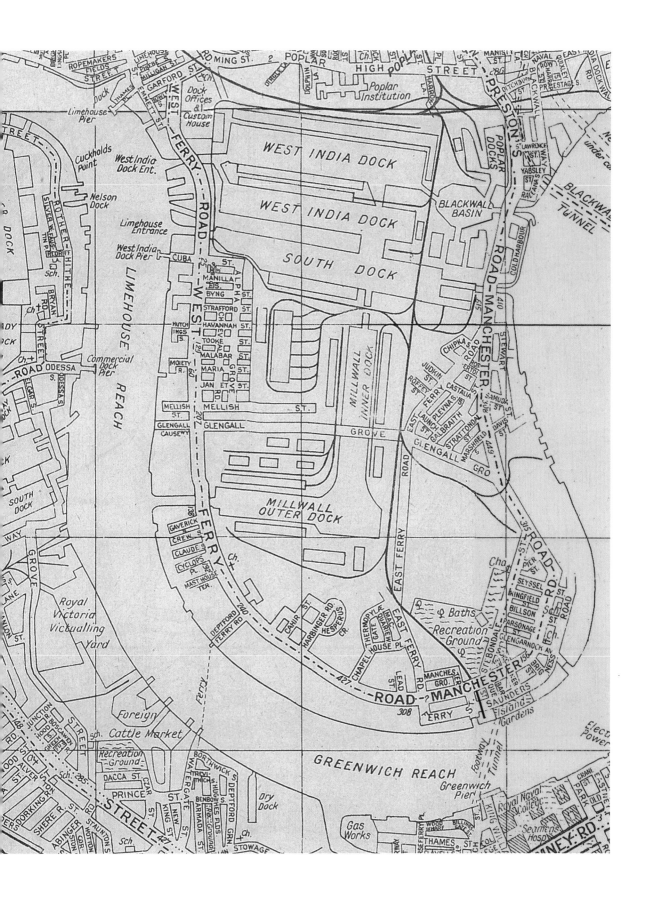

There was little option but to cut back. East India Dock was the first to close, followed by St Katharine Docks and Surrey Dock between 1968 and 1971. West India followed soon after, until finally only Millwall Dock was left of the traditional facilities of the Upper Port. In January 1976, the Port of London Authority announced that it too would have to close and, despite valiant efforts to save it, a strike in 1980 sounded its death knell. Within three years, the larger docks to the east had shut down, too, and the last ship left the Royal Dock in December 1981.

The decline had been devastating for the East End, with the number of registered dockers falling from 24,000 to 9,000 between 1966 and 1989 and then declining to almost nothing. Communities which had depended on the employment that the port had offered faced destitution. Awareness of this had led to early efforts to rehabilitate some areas, with St Katharine Docks being sold in 1969 for redevelopment as a marina. A more comprehensive London Docklands Strategic Plan, developed in 1976, stalled, and parts of the dock area that had been sold to Tower Hamlets Council were not developed.

The pace of regeneration quickened, however, after 1981 with the establishment of the London Docklands Development Corporation (LDDC), whose planning powers circumvented the traditional procedure, kickstarting a process which has seen a mass of new residential developments colonize the riverside and an entirely new financial district open up in Canary Wharf. New transport links have revitalized the area, with the Docklands Light Railway and the Jubilee Line extension through Canary Wharf carrying thousands of residents and commuters to and from the areas each day. Although the Docklands may no longer have working docks and the trade that flows through it is financial rather than physical, the port area of London is now probably busier than it has been at any time in its history.

finance AND THE city

London has been a financial hub since it became the headquarters of the Procurator, the chief financial officer of the Roman province, in the first century AD. The city's later status as the centre of the royal court – with the unquenchable desire of kings for cash to fund wars and to lavish rewards on their followers – meant that, when modern banking began to appear in the fifteenth century, London became its main English centre.

The financial district that grew up acquired the name 'the City' from the cluster of banks inside the old Roman City, the roughly square mile enclosed within the ancient walls that had been London's core until its heady expansion began in earnest in the seventeenth century. Goldsmiths, with their ready access to an easily convertible commodity, established many of the early banking firms, such as Barclays, which owed its origins to a collaboration between John Freame and Thomas Gould at an office in Lombard Street around 1690. The Bank of England was established soon after, in 1694, as a means of funding Britain's burgeoning national debt and ensuring the Government had enough revenue to cover its commitments.

The eighteenth and nineteenth centuries saw the growth of merchant banks such as Barings (1762) and Schroders (1804), set up to finance Britain's growing commercial interests in its expanding empire. By 1914, the City of London was the undoubted master of international finance, a dominant position that its cosy club of the financial elite assumed would continue indefinitely. But by the 1950s London's great rival New York was snapping at its heels, threatening to overtake its less nimble Old World competitor. The enormous cost of the First World War and the damage caused by the Second both financially – in the huge debts incurred to the United States to keep the British war effort afloat – and physically – a bomb fell on the Bank of England building on Threadneedle Street on the second night of the Blitz on 8 September 1940 – were taking their toll.

£827,000,000
the losses sustained by the rogue trader nick leason in 1986

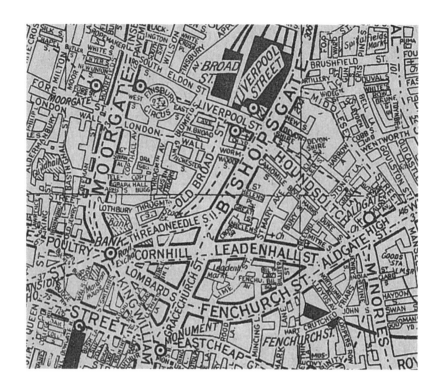

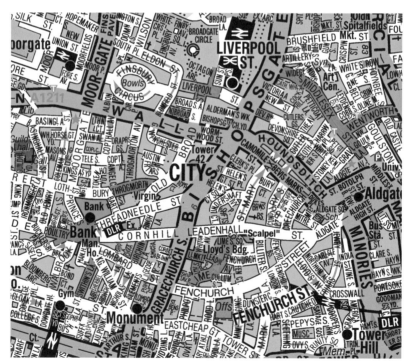

Salvation of a sort came in the emergence of the Eurobond market in the 1960s – the trading in bonds denominated in a currency other than that of their issue – which London came to dominate. But it was not until 1986, when the Conservative government of Margaret Thatcher legislated the 'Big Bang' – a wholesale deregulation of the London markets, abolishing restrictions on trading that had held it back – that the City began to thrive again. It prospered in spite of scandals such as the collapse of Barings in 1986, after the activities of a single trader, Nick Leeson, cost the bank £827 million, and the implosion in 1991 of the Bank of Credit and Commerce International (BCCI), under suspicion of money laundering, which cost its investors up to $20 billion.

Foreign banks, particularly American giants such as Morgan Stanley and Merrill Lynch, set up or expanded headquarters in the City, or in the new financial district to the east that opened after the development of Canary Wharf from 1991. Even the global financial crisis of 2007–8 barely caused the City to break step. By April 2018 it was the centre for over 2.7 trillion dollars of foreign exchange trading each day, contributing around 7 per cent of Britain's GDP and providing employment for over half a million workers.

Such heady growth could not be contained within the existing infrastructure. The old Victorian offices of the City, designed for Dickensian clerks scratching away with quill pens, were woefully inadequate. The transformation was already underway before the Big Bang, with the new Lloyds building designed by Richard Rogers going up between 1978 and 1986. The pace of development then quickened: One Canada Square, the tallest tower in Canary Wharf, opened in 1991, and in the City proper a series of buildings with irreverent nicknames sprouted: the Gherkin (more properly 30 St Mary Axe) completed in 2003 on the site of the former Baltic Exchange; the Cheesegrater (122 Leadenhall Street), opened in 2014; and, soaring over them all, the striking silhouette of the Shard, at 310 metres the tallest building in the United Kingdom (whose first tenants moved in in 2013).

Storm clouds gathered over the City because of the effect of Britain's vote in 2016 to exit the European Union, which threatened to cause jobs and revenue to move to other European countries. But where there is money to be made, there will be banks, and London's centuries-old experience of financial excellence will ensure that the descendants of the medieval goldsmiths will continue to operate in London for a while yet.

◁

The City, London's financial district, had evolved comparatively slowly until the 1970s, its shape in 1938 much that of a century earlier. However, the 1970s saw the construction of the Lloyds Building, the first of a series of new financial buildings that brought a more modern architectural feel to the City.

industry

Like any large town, London has always had its share of industrial manufacturing, from the Roman pottery industry along the Walbrook in the heart of the City to Tudor leather-workers in Bermondsey and Southwark. But it was during the Victorian age that London's industry really came into its own.

Although not so characterized by the textile mills as the heavy industrial centres of the Midlands and the North, London was a major centre of shipbuilding, pharmaceutical and food production and for the manufacture of electronic, communication and maritime products. Traditional industries such as the silk weaving centre in Bethnal Green and Spitalfields were steadily driven out by rising prices, but an arc of small workshops providing specialized services clustered in the inner suburbs (with some particularly niche markets, such as the piano manufacturers concentrated around St Pancras). Outside the centre, heavier industry took a hold, like the chemical factory in Greenford in Ealing, where William Perkins discovered the world's first artificial aniline dye in 1856.

The Great Slump of the 1930s did not affect London as badly as other areas of the country, and around 500 new factories opened in the capital in the period 1932 to 1938, some four-fifths of the national total. The ready supply of young female labour and access to waterways and rail links fuelled this growth, and new industrial estates were established, such as Park Royal in Ealing, which expanded to house 250 factories by 1939. It was an era when London acquired factories whose architecture had a pretence of grandeur about it, such as the Hoover Factory in Perivale (opened in 1932) and the Nestlé chocolate factory in Hayes (which the company took over in 1929). Some trades did contract, however, such as London piano-making (the total number of instrument makers in the capital collapsed from 23,000 in 1929 to 8,000 in 1938), while clockmakers virtually disappeared from Clerkenwell.

666,000

the number of jobs lost in manufacturing between 1974 and the 1990s

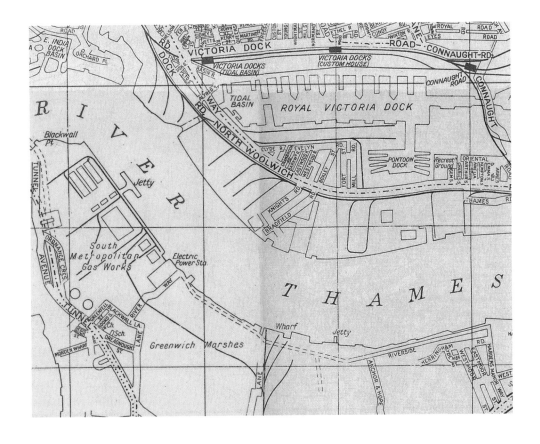

△

Tate and Lyle's Plaistow Wharf factory on Knight's Road was at one edge of
Silvertown's 'Sugar Mile'. Opened by Abraham Lyle in 1880, it is the home of the
company's famous golden syrup, and was originally the rival to Henry Tate's Thames
Refinery, a mile downstream. In 1921 the two merged, creating the sugar giant of today.

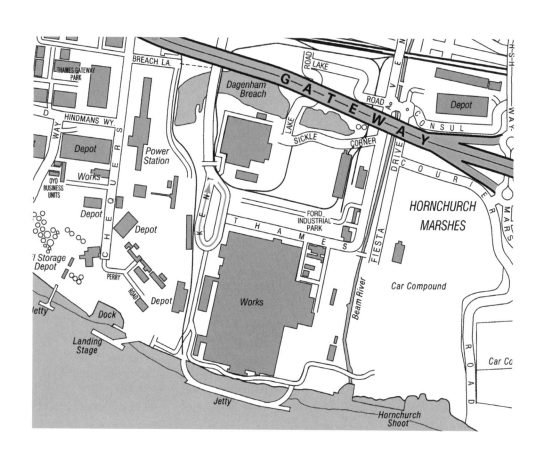

The war dealt London's industry a near-fatal blow. The conversion to war work and the destruction of factories by German bombing, particularly in the East End, meant that many never re-opened, and between 1938 and 1947 London lost a fifth of its manufacturing jobs. Although there was a slight rebound in the 1950s, when 66,000 jobs were gained, more competitive global trading conditions left Britain's companies struggling to keep up. The opening and expansion of Heathrow Airport also pulled London's centre of gravity westward, further disadvantaging established industrial areas to the east. Park Royal virtually ceased to be a significant manufacturing zone and one-by-one London's traditional manufacturers moved out. Tate & Lyle closed down its factories at Plaistow, Fulham and Hammersmith, leaving only the Silvertown refinery. The Beckton Gasworks shut in 1969, while losses in the 1980s included Battersea Power Station, the Royal Small Arms Factory in Enfield, British Leyland's West London plants and the Whitefriars glass factory in Wealdstone. By the 1990s, the number of London manufacturing jobs had declined to 274,000, a fraction of the 940,000 Londoners who had worked in industry as recently as 1974.

There are still survivors, such as Ford's Dagenham Plant, which pulled large numbers of workers into the East End in the 1930s, and which still remains as one of the world's largest producers of diesel engines, and the Tate & Lyle sugar factory, which was sold to American Sugar in 2010. Yet even now, some of the oldest established industries in London are still packing their bags. The very oldest of all, the Whitechapel Bell foundry, which dates back to 1570 and cast Big Ben (the bell that tolls the hour in what is more properly called the Elizabeth Tower) was forced to close down in May 2017. These days a Londoner is more likely to manufacture software than soap, and the hubbub of inner-city factories has been muffled, to be replaced by the click of keyboards.

◁

On its site beside the Hornchurch Marshes, the Ford Dagenham plant produced nearly eleven million vehicles from its inception in 1929 to its conversion in 2002 to manufacturing only diesel engines (of which still over a million a year roll off the production line).

london retailers

The French emperor Napoleon is alleged to have once remarked that Britain was 'a nation of shopkeepers'. Although the expression was probably erroneously attributed to him, it is true that Britain's high streets, and those of London in particular, have always been centres of thriving commercial activity, from the hawking of pungent fish sauce by Roman vendors to the retail of hi-tech gadgets in the twenty-first century.

London's original shops were traditional street stalls or small affairs with narrow frontages, clustered into concentrations of vendors of a particular good. A very early form of shopping centre appeared in the late sixteenth century, when Thomas Gresham opened the Royal Exchange in 1567 in the City. There were over 100 shops within the red-brick emporium selling a range of goods, although haberdashers made up over a quarter of the businesses. As wider streets began to be built through the central parts of London from the seventeenth century, and as the capital's middle classes grew more numerous, larger shops with wider frontages began to appear. By the Victorian era the demand for more innovative retailing was clear; iconic British shops such as Harrods owe their origins to these years. Beginning life as a small grocery store opened by Charles Henry Harrod in 1849, the store really came into its own during the Edwardian era. By 1910 it had around 6,000 staff, selling from its flagship Knightsbridge store under the proud motto *Omnia, Omnibus, Ubique* ('Everything to Everybody, Everywhere').

Chain stores began to appear in London, too. Marks and Spencer started its life in Leeds in 1884, and by 1903 had a store in South London (with its flagship Marble Arch branch opening in 1930); the first John Lewis branch began business on Oxford Street in 1864. American retailers also entered the market, with the opening by Woolworths of its first London branch in Brixton in 1910. The most famous American retail import, however,

1920
the year selfridges gave london its first taste of a sale

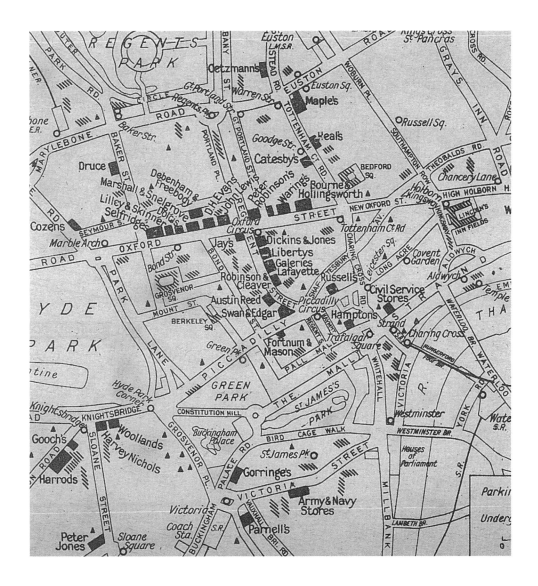

This 1938 map of London's central shopping district contains many stores that were household names at the time, but which have since disappeared (such as Marshall & Snelgrove, which was taken over by Debenhams in 1973; the Army & Navy, which was rebranded House of Fraser in 2005; and Gamages on Holborn, which closed in 1972).

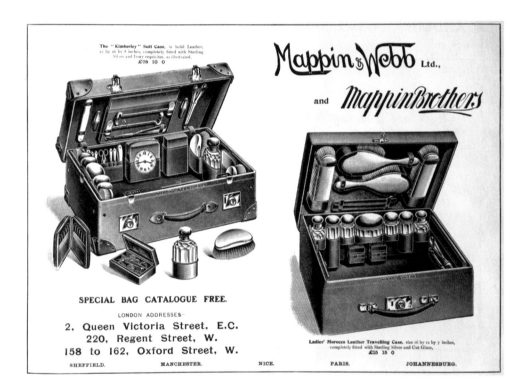

△
Mappin and Webb, the jewellers, was established in 1870 and opened a branch on Oxford Street in 1906. The Kimberley travelling suitcase in this advertisement was named for the area of South Africa from where the company obtained many of its diamonds.

was Harry Gordon Selfridge, who arrived in London in 1906 and found the shopping scene there distinctly pedestrian. He established his own store on Oxford Street, injecting it with a theatrical flair that drew thousands to its opening day in March 1909. He rarely missed a trick, later that year drawing 150,000 shoppers to the main retail hall to see the plane in which Louis Blériot had made the first crossing of the Channel. Selfridge also gave London its first taste of a sale, when in 1920 he cut the price of all goods by 10 per cent. A rather more unorthodox marketing ploy was the national knitting competition that Selfridge sponsored in 1923.

Gradually the retail scene in London diversified, remaining fundamentally conservative while answering the needs of a society in which prosperity was growing, albeit slowly. The Second World War imposed a setback (Selfridges was bombed several times, with the Palm Court set ablaze by incendiaries during a raid on 17 April 1941). The late-1950s saw the opening of new fashion boutiques aimed at a youth market, starting with Mary Quant's Bazaar in Chelsea in 1955 which gave birth to a wholly new fashion district on the Kings Road.

The rising popularity of the motor car began to pose a threat to inner-city retail areas, as shoppers were put off by crowds and congestion, and store chains hankered after even larger spaces in which to show off their wares. Planners looked to out-of-town shopping centres as the solution, and the first such complex in London opened at Brent Cross in 1976, offering an alternative to the traditional shopping areas in Oxford Street and Knightsbridge. The trend continued and the opening of the Bluewater Centre in Thurrock in 1999 on land owned by the Blue Circle cement company proved its pinnacle. By then, concerns were mounting that the life was being sucked out of city centres, as retailers and shoppers decamped to the suburbs.

142 ▷

This shopping map of Oxford Street captures a moment in London's retail history from the 1970s, with businesses such as Lasky's hi-fi radio store and the Athena poster shop which have long-since disappeared.

OXFORD CIRCUS

REGENT STREET
OXFORD CIRCUS TUBE ⊖
SWEARS & WELLS ◐
JOHN PRINCES ST
BALLY □
RAVEL □
H.SAMUEL ❖
BRITISH HOME STORES ■
LORD PETER □
LADYBIRD SHOP ♣
ETAM ●
DAVIS ❖
JOHN STEPHEN ○
WALLIS ●
HOLLES ST

JOHN LEWIS ■

OLD CAVENDISH ST

D.H.EVANS ■

CHAPEL PL
K SHOES □
REGENT FUR ●
NEATAWEAR ●
VERE ST

MARSHALL & SNELGROVE ■

MARYLEBONE LA
STRATFORD COURT HOTEL
DOLCIS □
MARYLEBONE LA.
N.W.KIOSKS ✳
MATES ◐
NATIONAL WESTMINSTER
STRATFORD PL
LILLEY & SKINNER □
TAKE SIX ○
BARRIE ○
GEES CT
LORD JOHN ○
BALLY □
SWEARS & WELLS ●
JAMES ST
C & A MODES ■
BIRD ST
GILDA ●
GUYS N' DOLLS ◐
BARRATT □
DUKE ST

SELFRIDGES ■

ORCHARD ST
NATIONAL WESTMINSTER
FAIMAN ●
CHARCO ▨
WOLF HERBERT ❖
RATNERS ❖
RICHARD SHOPS ●
ETAM ●
STONE-DRI ◐
WALLIS ●
JUST LOOKING ●
RAVEL □
ERNEST JONES ❖
SAXONE □
PORTMAN ST
LITTLEWOODS ■
LORD JOHN ◐
DOROTHY PERKINS ●
JAX ●
SALISBURY HANDBAGS
PAIGE ●
DOLCIS □
EVANS OUTSIZE ●
OLD QUEBEC ST
MAISON LYONS ▨
Leisure wear Camping MILLETTS SUPERSTORE
ORIENT JEWEL CO. ❖
MARBLE ARCH TUBE ⊖
CUMBERLAND HOTEL

STREET

OXFORD CIRCUS

REGENT STREET
⊖ OXFORD CIRCUS TUBE
S.A.AIRWAYS
SWALLOW PASS
◐ STONE—DRI
○ GET KNOTTED
❖ DAVIS
● RICHARD SHOPS
◐ UPWEST ARCADE
❖ ERNEST JONES
● GIRL BOUTIQUE
● GARB GIRL
□ BATA SHOE
▨ OLD KENTUCKY
◐ JEAN JUNCTION
NATIONAL WESTMINSTER
HAREWOOD PL
□ SAXONE
□ BABERS
□ FREEMAN HARDY WILLIS
□ DOLCIS
● BERKERTEX & BRIDAL WEAR
○ ALYCE
■ WOOLWORTH
◐ MATES
DERING ST
❖ SANFORD BROS.
○ LORD JOHN
□ MANFIELD
NEW BOND ST
□ DOLCIS
✳ N.W.SHOPS
◐ JEAN JUNCTION
□ SACHA
▨ INDIA TEA CENTRE
WOODSTOCK ST
□ SACHA
● BEIGE
❖ R.BOWMAN
○ SQUIRE SHOP
SEDLEY PL
● DENISE Furs
● DOWNTOWN
▨ H.M.V. RECORDSHOP
❖ DAVIS
S. MOLTON ST
DAVIES ST
⊖ BOND STREET TUBE
BOOTS .Chemist
○ COLES
● EVERON
GILBERT ST
▨ GARNERS STEAK HO.
BINNEY ST
PFAFF SEWING CENTRE
◐ JEAN MACHINE
DUKE ST
○ HORNE BROS.
○ BURTON
LUMLEY ST
○ QUEENSTREET
▨ WIMPY
BALDERTON ST
◐ SHEEPSKIN SHOP
○ THACKERAY'S
MILLETTS
◐ JOHN STEPHEN
ATHENA REPRODUCTIONS
N. AUDLEY ST
▨ ANGUS STEAK HO.
♣ MOTHERCARE
◐ WESTERNER
○ GUY'S & DOLLS
○ HEPWORTHS
○ TAKE 6
▨ GOLDEN EGG
▥ LASKYS Hi-Fi Radio
● I SPY
○ VILLAGE GATE
● REVONE
○ LORD JOHN
PARK ST.
CHINACRAFT
■ C & A MODES
◐ MARBLES MARKET
✳ INDIACRAFT
◐ SUEDE . LEATHER SHOP
⊖ MARBLE ARCH TUBE
PARK LANE

MARBLE ARCH

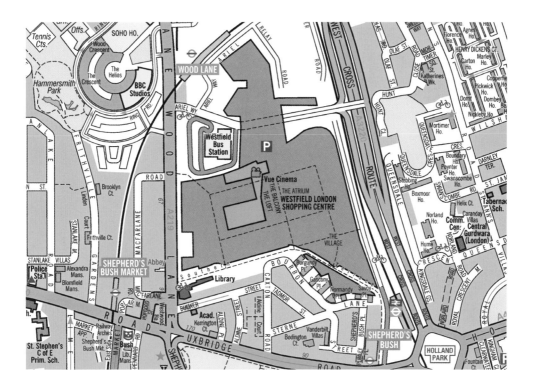

London's retailers began experiencing new pressures in the late twentieth century, as the rising proportion of internet sales bit into their margins. In January 2019, a report revealed that Britain's high streets had experienced their fourteenth successive month of decline in footfall. The sense of gloom was reinforced by a number of high-profile retail failures that left many wondering if the shop had a future any more.

Yet London's retailers have hit back. The trend for shopping mega-complexes has been brought into the inner city, with the opening of two massive new shopping centres at Westfield White City (opened in 2008) and Westfield Stratford (2011); the former is the largest covered shopping centre in Europe. Retailers, too, have been forced to rediscover the sense of theatrical retail flair that Gordon Selfridge pioneered over a century ago. London is truly a city of shopkeepers, and those shopkeepers will not go down without a fight.

△

The Westfield London shopping centre which opened in White City in 2008 was built on the site of the Franco-British exhibition precisely a century earlier. With an extension, completed in 2018 to enlarge it to 2.6 million square feet, it became the largest shopping centre in Europe.

MOVING LONDON

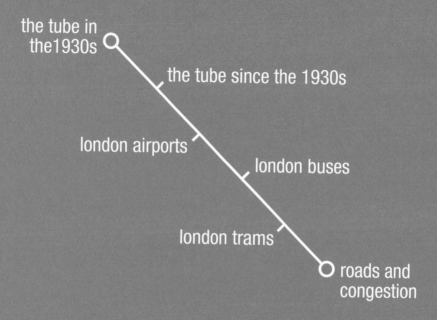

the tube in the1930s

the tube since the 1930s

london airports

london buses

london trams

roads and congestion

THE tube IN THE 1930s

By 1930, the London Underground system was almost seventy years old. Dubbed 'the Tube' since 1900, the system had spread out like a spider's web from the very first stretch of line, which opened between Baker Street and Farringdon in January 1863 (a day on which the prime minister, Lord Palmerston, had declined to join the other 40,000 travellers, on the grounds that he had little time left and wanted to spend as much of it as possible above ground). A confusion of competing companies had pushed the Tube to the north, west, east and, to a much more limited extent, to the south, opening up whole new suburbs for easy commutes.

In 1923–4 the Hampstead Line (part of the future Northern Line) was extended to Edgware, while the City Line was pushed down to Morden in 1926. More ambitiously, the Metropolitan Line added track to Wembley Park and then beyond, cannily establishing estates of cheap semi-detached houses alongside it, whose virtues the company promoted tirelessly in annual *Metro-land* guides.

The Piccadilly Line was further extended to Cockfosters in 1930–3, as part of a plan to rationalize the line (which included the closing down of several Central London stations that became 'ghosts', such as Down Road along Park Lane). Charles Holden, the architect of many of the new stations, designed some of the underground system's most glorious stations, including the cylindrical Arnos Grove building and the flying-saucer-like silhouette of Southgate.

Further expansion was hampered by a lack of funding, made worse by the fractured nature of the system and the tendency of companies to build competing tracks along the same routes rather than servicing new areas. Finally, the Government imposed a solution and on 1 July 1933 the London Passenger Transport Board was born, uniting all the

250,000 and 10,000
the number of umbrellas handed in to lost property annually in the 1930s and today

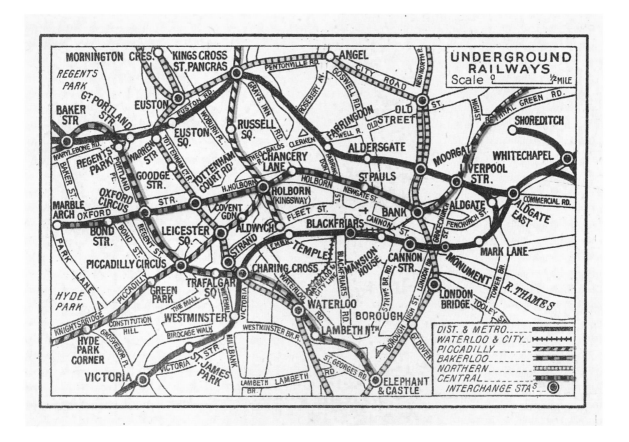

△

By the 1930s, the underground network in the centre of London was nearly complete (save for the addition in the late 1970s of the Jubilee Line). The spur on the Piccadilly Line from Holborn to Aldwych is clearly visible; this underused section, despite hopes that it would be extended at one stage, was finally closed in 1994.

underground operators, as well as the trams and buses, into one company, so creating the lineal ancestor of today's Transport for London.

No sooner was it up and running than the Transport Board began planning new additions to its realm, with a New Works Programme announced in 1935–40. The programme foresaw the extension of the Central Line into Essex, with stations at Epping and Ongar (which did happen) and an ambitious programme of electrification to push the Northern Line to Alexandra Palace and Bushey (which did not).

One thing the newly enlarged Tube lacked was an adequate map. Until 1933, all attempts at mapping the system superimposed it on the street grid above ground, making it easy to find the stations, but vexingly difficult to navigate a journey once underground. In the centre, maps looked like spaghetti, further out, extended skeins of string that seemed to lead nowhere. Salvation for confused travellers came from an unlikely source: a junior draughtsman in the Signal Engineer's office named Harry Beck. In 1933, he submitted an elegantly schematic design for a new map that prioritized simple horizontal and vertical lines to show the routes between stops, without any regard for the distance the journey took above ground. Underground maps ever since have been based on the Beck map, and if the Tube is in need of a patron saint, generations of passengers might opt for Harry Beck.

Another icon of the Underground opened in the year that Beck's map was first published. The London Underground Lost Property Office began operations in 1933 from premises on Baker Street. In its early years it received around 250,000 umbrellas a year (a number that, curiously, has since diminished to today's more modest figure of 10,000). Since then the flotsam and jetsam of London travel has washed up there, from the mundane, such as bags and mobile phones, to the outlandish, like the life-sized gorilla toy that one passenger must have mislaid and the urn, containing a loved-one's ashes, that arrived at the Lost Property Office after being stolen.

By 1939 the system was running smoothly, with over a thousand new carriages delivered in 1938 to transport passengers in the latest style. Plans for further extensions and improvements, however, were abruptly curtailed by geopolitics, when the Second World War broke out in September 1939.

THE tube SINCE THE 1930s

The last eighty years have seen huge changes on London's Underground system as it experienced enormous expansion, periodic upgrades, corporate reorganisations and terrible tragedy. Despite occasional suggestions that the system was becoming overloaded and outmoded, it now transports Londoners and visitors on over a billion journeys a year and has become firmly embedded in the capital's economic life and its folklore.

The period did not begin auspiciously. The outbreak of the Second World War in September 1939 abruptly put the New Works plan for extending several lines on hold. The extension of the Northern Line crawled along with the commencement of services to Mill Hill East in May 1941, but after that the shutters came down. Trains between Strand (later renamed Charing Cross) and Kennington were halted to allow the tunnels under the Thames to be blocked as a safeguard against flooding.

The onset of the Blitz in September 1940 almost threw the system into chaos, as thousands of people flocked nightly onto station platforms to take refuge from the relentless above-ground aerial bombardment. At first London Transport was discouraging of this, putting up posters telling passengers that stations 'must not be used as air raid shelters', but the 'tubites' who slept underground were not deterred, and one estimate put their numbers at 177,000. Some formed committees and issued newsletters such as the *Swiss Cottager*, which lobbied for better conditions – a campaign that bore fruit when the Government allowed metal bunks to be installed at more than seventy stations and arranged for special trains to distribute seven tons of food each night to the subterranean refugees.

The sense of safety provided by the tube shelters sometimes proved illusory and nearly 200 people lost their lives when they were hit during Luftwaffe raids. In the worst incident,

2013, embankment station
the original 'mind the gap' announcement was reinstated to allow the actor's widow to hear her husband's voice while she travelled on the line

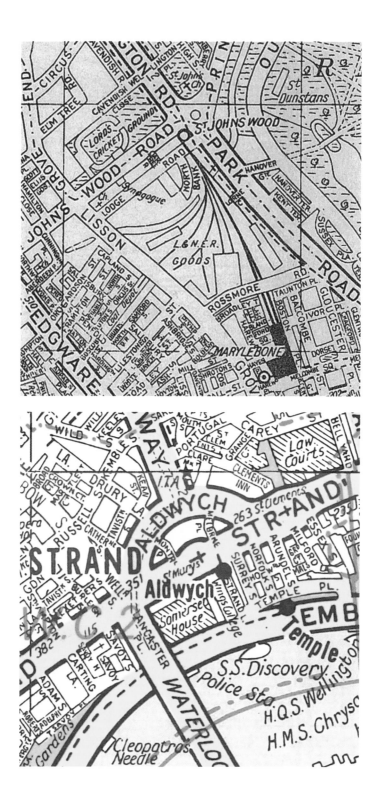

on 14 October 1940 at Balham tube station, sixty-four people died when a German bomb seared down through the road surface above and smashed into the platform, filling the tunnel with sewage from fractured mains and the carcass of a red London bus that toppled into the bomb crater. The single highest death toll was not caused by enemy action, however. On 3 March 1943, a panic on a stairwell at Bethnal Green Station led to the deaths of 173 people, most of them crushed to death, a tragedy contributed to by poor lighting and a lack of supervision by officials.

As the war dragged on, people returned to their homes and the number of tube-shelterers dipped to around 5,000 in 1942, before spiking up to 150,000 during the German V-1 and V-2 rocket offensives against London in 1944/45. When finally they left in May 1945, the clearing out of the beds, first-aid posts and other evidence of their stay took only a short while. The reconstruction of the Underground would take a lot longer as physical damage, shortage of materials and a chronic lack of funds for investment left war-weary commuters struggling in overcrowded and antiquated rolling-stock, and suffering the indignity of steep fare rises as London Transport desperately tried to cover its operating costs.

The management of the Underground tried valiantly to revive pre-war expansion plans, and by late 1947 tubes were running as far as Newbury Park and Woodford at the eastern end of the Central Line. But there was little prospect of more, and in January 1948 the Government took the ailing system in hand and nationalized it. Responsibility for London's transport infrastructure was transferred to the British Transport Commission (BTC), which operated the Underground through the London Transport Executive. Although the LTE oversaw the further extension of the Central Line west to West Ruislip in 1948 and east to Epping in 1949, it could do little more. As a result, the 1950s were a lost decade for the Underground, as it trod water and tried to stem the falls in passenger numbers resulting from disenchantment with the Tube's crumbling infrastructure and Londoners' growing love affair with the car.

The introduction of the first aluminium train carriages in 1952 at least meant that tube-goers had a shinier ride, and the phasing out of the last steam trains from the Central Line in 1961 gave them a considerably less smoky one. LTE's management was conscious, though, that this stasis could not last, and in 1949 it commissioned a report that

◁ top
A number of tube stations have closed down over the years as the needs of the system changed. The original St John's Wood tube station, shown on the 1938 atlas, was opened in 1868 near Lord's cricket ground. It finally closed in November 1939 and was replaced by the current St John's Wood station further to the north.

◁ bottom
Aldwych underground station was opened in 1907, when it was called Strand. At the end of a short spur line from Holborn, it was always of doubtful viability, despite occasional plans to extend that section of the Piccadilly Line further. The station was closed in 1994.

recommended the construction of a new line to relieve congestion across Central London. Concerns about the high cost involved and parliamentary opposition meant that it was fourteen years before construction began on what would – appropriately enough in the Underground's centenary year – become the Victoria Line.

It took six years to excavate the tunnels and test the trains, which were supposed to be one-man operated (though union opposition prevented this for more than fifteen years) and which were designed to carry a total of 25,000 passengers an hour. The line, from Walthamstow to Victoria, was opened with great fanfare by Queen Elizabeth II on 7 March 1969, who reminded onlookers that this was only her second-ever tube journey, before she inserted her ticket in the new magnetic-strip-reading platform barriers that had been erected.

In the same year, tube passengers began to hear one of the system's most iconic announcements, enjoining them to 'Mind the Gap' as they stepped out from trains into the void caused by the disjuncture between the Tube's straight trains and its notoriously serpentine platforms. Initially using the voice of an Underground sound engineer (to avoid paying royalties), LTE gradually switched to a series of actors, whose mellifluous tones encouraged passengers to exercise suitable caution. In the twenty-first century, however, the management gradually transitioned to digital recordings and phased the old voices out, though in 2013 an unusual bout of sentimentality led them to restore that of actor Oswald Laurence to the Northern Line at Embankment station, where his widow, who travelled the route, had loved to hear his voice since he passed away in 2007.

The Tube's mini-renaissance suffered a terrible setback in 1975, when the system's worst ever crash occurred on the Northern City Line at Moorgate. Forty-three people died when a train failed to stop at the terminus and smashed into the wall at the end of the tunnel. The inquest that followed led to the installation of fail-safe systems that automatically cut the train's engine if the driver failed to hit the brakes at critical moments. More positively, the Underground's reach extended, as the Piccadilly Line acquired a branch to Heathrow Airport in 1977 (to which a loop passing through Terminal 4 was added in 1986, and services to Terminal 5 in 2008). The long-mooted Fleet Line, intended to take over Bakerloo Line services to Stanmore in the north, and to break new ground to Lewisham in the south, finally received approval. By the time tunnelling got underway in 1976, the proximity of Queen Elizabeth's Silver Jubilee in 1977 led the Underground's management to change the name, and when it opened in April 1979, it had been rechristened the Jubilee Line.

▷

This poster from the 1930s proclaims the 'Lure of the Underground' as commuters are sucked from buses into the tube system, not a marketing angle today's fully-integrated system would adopt.

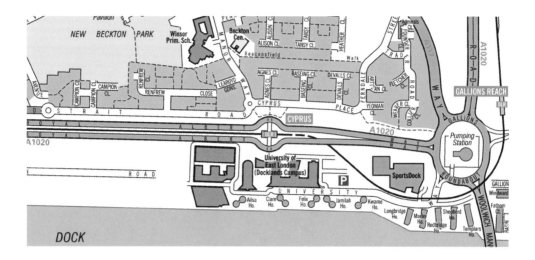

Despite this, passenger numbers on the Tube had been declining from 720 million a year in the 1960s to 498 million in 1982, leading to a revenue crisis and a further lack of money for badly needed investment. A political battle erupted between the Greater London Council, which had responsibility for the tube system, and the Government. In 1981 the GLC introduced a new zonal fare structure, which cut average fares by a third under the slogan 'Fares Fair'. It led to a dramatic high court ruling, which reduced the subsidies the GLC had received from the borough councils, and forced London Transport to almost double fares to make up the shortfall.

The whole battle bequeathed London the Travelcard, vastly simplifying life for the capital's commuters, but the demise of the GLC and the transfer of control of the Underground to the Secretary of State for Transport seemed to herald a new era of stagnation. A further blow was suffered on 18 November 1987 when a lit match dropped onto a wooden escalator at King's Cross caused a fireball to erupt that engulfed part of the station, killing thirty-one people and injuring dozens of others through burns and smoke inhalation. Smoking – which had still been permitted on platforms – was banned in the aftermath and the management turned to a new more customer-centred approach, focusing particularly on safety. It was the worst tragedy on the Tube until a series of Islamist suicide bombings on 7 July 2005 killed thirty-nine people in three separate explosions at Aldgate, Edgware Road and on the Piccadilly Line near King's Cross (thirteen people died in a related attack on a bus on Tavistock Square).

△

The extension of the Docklands Light Railway to Beckton in 1994 brought new areas such as Gallions Reach into the network for the first time, aiding the regeneration of areas where transport links had been historically poor.

A new management culture was needed to steer the next phases of the Underground's evolution as developments above ground led to the regeneration of London's Docklands following the establishment of the London Docklands Development Corporation in 1981. The capital's latest financial district around Canary Wharf needed transport infrastructure to make it viable, and in 1992 the Government approved the extension of the Jubilee Line down to Canary Wharf and then in a loop back round to Stratford. The new section opened in stages in 1999, just in time for the national celebrations to mark the turning of the millennium.

By then the Underground had acquired a sister, in the shape of the Docklands Light Railway, an above-ground system designed as a cheap way of relieving congestion in and around Canary Wharf. It opened in 1987 running driverless trains to fifteen stations on two routes from Tower Gateway and Stratford to Island Gardens. Since then there have been further extensions, adding routes to Beckton (1994), Lewisham (1999), London City Airport (2005) and Stratford International (2011), and the initial miniature single-car trains have been upgraded to three-car as passenger numbers have swollen, reaching 110 million in 2014. A further branch to what was already the world's most extensive urban passenger transport network was added in 2007 when Transport for London (TfL) – which had taken over control of the Underground in 1999, following the demise of the GLC – began to operate a series of lines in North London that had previously belonged to Network Rail. Rebranded as the Overground, this new system took over the Underground's former East London Line in 2010 and added a southern arm from Surrey Quays to Clapham two years later. While adding the new sections and stations, its tendrils snake out with the ultimate intention of creating a massive outer orbital circle line around London.

To simplify the logistics of travel within its increasingly complex empire, in 2003 Transport for London introduced the Oyster card, a plastic card pre-loaded with travelcards or cash for individual journeys that did away with the need for paper tickets. Smart new ticket barriers guarded entry to the stations after 1987. Even busking became more controlled as in the same year TfL introduced a licensing system for buskers, granting 100 licences a year to carefully auditioned hopefuls who had to play on designated pitches, doing away with the old anarchic game of cat-and-mouse in which musicians would set up illicitly, play a set, and then be chased away by Underground staff to begin all over again at a different station.

With 1.35 billion passenger journeys made each year by 2018 (100 million of them alone at Waterloo, making it not a place for the fainthearted at rush hour), the Underground now has 270 stations along its 402-kilometre network. Each year, trains travel 83.6 million kilometres, equivalent to the distance to Mars and half-way back again. It is almost impossible to be a Londoner or to visit London without making use of its network, which knots together the capital and unites its denizens in a shared experience of freedom and frustration. Much as Buckingham Palace, Hampstead Heath or Big Ben, London would simply not be London without the Tube.

london airports

London was not a city designed for the airport age. Its urban sprawl had reached far out by the time commercial aviation became a pressing need for any capital city ambitious for a position at the head of the international rankings. As a result, the siting of its airports was determined by piecemeal development, availability of green space, and a long series of political rows and protracted planning disputes. The five London airports that resulted are Heathrow, Gatwick, City and, further out beyond the metropolitan area, Stansted and Luton.

The capital's senior airport, Heathrow, began its life in 1930 when Richard Fairey paid the vicar of Harmondsworth in southwest London £15,000 for a 1,150-acre patch of land on which he created a grass runway. From the 63,000 passengers his Fairey Airways transported in its first year of operation, the airport would eventually grow to host sixty-seven million passengers in five terminals, the development of which had progressively obliterated surrounding villages.

Initially called Harmondsworth Airport, Heathrow's heady expansion was stemmed by the outbreak of war and its conversion for use by a squadron of Hurricanes. After the war was over it was not transferred back to its original owners (who sued for losses in a marathon legal case that dragged on until 1964) and operations were instead taken over by the Civil Aviation Ministry. The airport opened again for commercial flights in May 1946, its terminals housed in army marquees and huts. Passengers had to navigate a series of wooden walkways to avoid floundering in the airfield's all-engulfing mud. By 1953, a million of them a year were having to cope with these makeshift arrangements, but the first permanent passenger terminal was opened in 1955, to be followed in 1961 by the Oceanic Building (which was ultimately rebranded as Terminal 3).

£15,000
the fee paid to the vicar of harmondsworth for 1,150 acres to create a grass runway at what is now heathrow airport

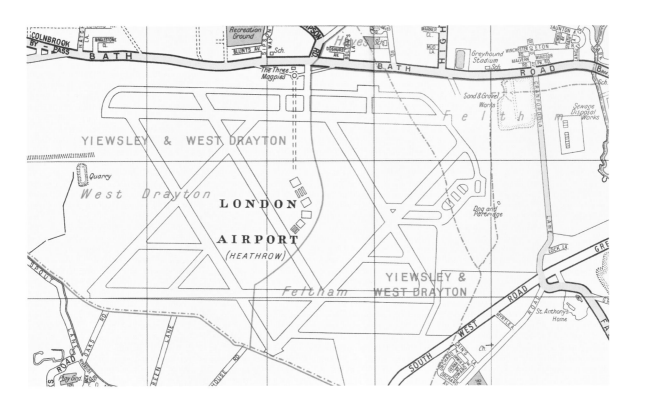

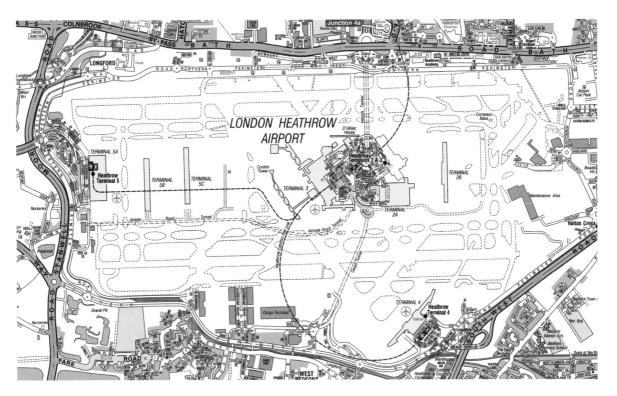

In 1966 the airport, now under the management of the new British Airports Authority, was renamed London (Heathrow), finally definitively receiving the current name. Its expansion continued apace, with the opening of Terminal 1 in November 1968, and the arrival of an extension to the Piccadilly Line, which opened in 1977. Amongst its more noteworthy passengers was James Earl Ray, the assassin of Martin Luther King, who was apprehended at a check-in desk for a flight to Rhodesia on 8 June 1968, when a security official noticed his passport (which was forged) was under the name of a criminal wanted by the Royal Canadian Mounted Police.

The growing passenger numbers – which reached thirty million by the early 1980s – could not be contained even within the four terminals that had by then been built (the last of these to be opened was Terminal 4 in 1986). A long battle broke out to win Heathrow an additional terminal, beginning with a public inquiry, which began its hearings in 1997. After finally receiving approval, Terminal 5 eventually opened to passengers in 2008. The building of a third runway to ease flight congestion was even more bitterly contested, being sanctioned in 2009, only to be cancelled the following year. In 2015, an Airports Commission established to resolve the growing problem of capacity in the London area again gave the green light for a third runway, despite the opposition of a prominent local MP who threatened to lie down in front of the bulldozers (a threat which, in the event, he did not carry out).

Heathrow's main rival for a share of London's airspace had long been Gatwick Airport, which developed out of a modest aerodrome built at Tinsley Green in West Sussex in the late 1920s (a measure of quite how far out of the urban centre 'London' was deemed to extend for the purpose of its airports). Just as Heathrow, it began as a private airfield, until Allied British Airways (the ancestor of British Airways) began operating there in 1935. The first scheduled flight – to Paris – took off in May 1936. During the war it, too, was requisitioned by the Air Ministry and used as a base, mainly for transport and communication aircraft, before returning to civilian use in 1946 when it was officially selected as London's second airport.

◁157
The footprint of the airport in 1936 and that of its vastly enlarged successor today, show how Heathrow has expanded to engorge surrounding villages and dominate its immediate area. Further large-scale expansion in an urban area will, however, be challenging.

For a long time it was principally a base for charter flights, and for less high-profile airlines such as Dan Air, which moved there in 1960. Gatwick was nonetheless the site of several significant passenger aviation innovations, such as Freddy Laker's Skytrain – the model for the future no-frills airlines – which began services to North America in 1977, and Concorde, whose first commercial flights took off from the airport in 1985. Extensions to its runway in 1970, 1973 and 1998 and the addition of a second terminal to the north significantly increased the airport's capacity and allowed the new generation of low-cost airlines such as EasyJet to begin flights in 1999, bringing Gatwick's passenger numbers up to forty-five million by the early twenty-first century.

Even this was not enough to sate the seemingly inexhaustible supply of people wishing to fly to and from the capital. Journey times between the airports and Central London were considerable, and there was limited capacity for air travel to and from the north of the city. As a partial solution to these problems, in 1981 an airport was proposed for London's Docklands, to tie in with the general scheme for regeneration of the area. The approval process was accelerated and in 1986 construction began at a site on the Royal Docks in Newham, with the first aircraft landing just a year later in May 1987. Despite its proximity to Central London, however, the airport's short runway was only suitable for a limited number of aircraft, and City Airport, as it became known, only handled 133,000 passengers in its first year. Technical improvement to allow larger planes to land, and the opening of a Docklands Light Railway station there in 2005, immeasurably improved the appeal of the airport. It reached 4.5 million passengers in 2017, while its use as a centre for arrivals during the 2012 London Olympic Games raised its profile significantly.

City Airport simply does not have the potential to react to large increases in passenger numbers. The strain of this has been taken up by London's two other airports, far out of the capital's traditional bounds, at Stansted and Luton. Both are long-standing transport hubs – Stansted first opening as an airbase in 1943 and Luton beginning operations in 1938 – and have attracted significant business as low-cost alternatives to Heathrow and Gatwick. Stansted's passenger numbers reached twenty-seven million in 2018, just over half the level of Gatwick, and a third that of Heathrow (putting in it on a par with Stockholm or Vienna). That London's third airport could be such a comparative titan shows how vital air transport has become for the city's well-being and how far it has developed since the days of turbo-prop aircraft disgorging handfuls of passengers into muddy fields fringed by makeshift immigration and customs posts.

london buses

London's buses are its oldest form of mass public transport. They originated in a service started in 1829 by the enterprising George Shillibeer, whose horse-drawn buses carried twenty-two passengers at a shilling apiece from Paddington into the City. Since then the system has spread to all parts of the capital, and now around 2.3 billion passenger journeys are made on Transport for London's bus network annually, a far cry from those modest beginnings.

By the 1930s, London's buses had already experienced great changes. Horses had been phased out in 1911, to the great relief of the capital's street cleaners, to be replaced by fleets of motorized buses, whose exhaust fumes have tormented Londoners' lungs ever since. The chaos of competing Victorian bus operators – who would routinely tear down side streets to get ahead of the competition on popular routes – had been partially resolved by amalgamations, but by 1924 there were still over 200 independent bus companies. The largest of them, the London General Omnibus Company (LGOC), was forced to paint its vehicles red to stand out from its rivals, a colour that has stuck ever since.

In 1933 the bus system was unified under the control of the London Passenger Transport Board, which operated the buses until 1948. This was succeeded by a variety of quasi-governmental bodies, which oversaw the buses through difficult times after the war, when Londoners' growing affection for the car, and frustration with a decaying bus fleet, led passenger numbers to drop (and a seven-week strike in 1958 caused them to fall further, and never to fully recover). In 1985 the system was split into twelve business units, which were privatized in 1995 under the umbrella supervision of London Transport. Its successor, Transport for London, which took over the network in 2000, had to shepherd it through the

200
the number of independent bus companies in 1924

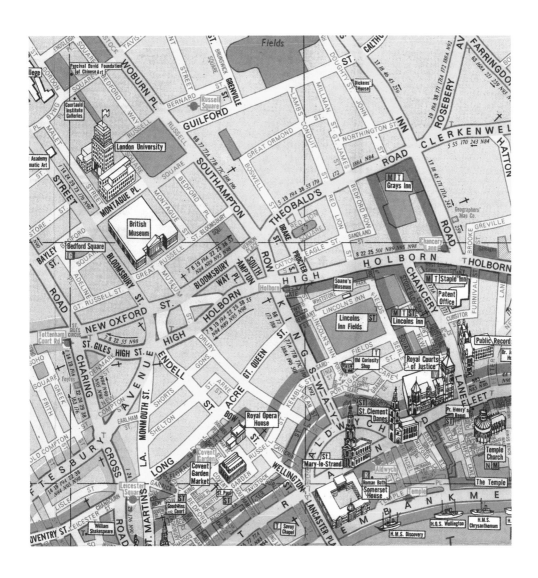

Bus route maps, such as this A-Z Sightseeing map of Central London, were once an essential aid for travellers in the capital. Now, with phone apps and digital timetables at bus stops, they are a relic of the past.

IT'S DANGEROUS TO FLAG
A BUS WITH YOUR TORCH

difficult days after London's worst tragedy on the buses, when an Islamist suicide bomber killed thirteen people travelling on a number 30 bus near Tavistock Square.

Bus passengers have enjoyed a variety of vehicles over time (or endured them, as fully covered buses were only introduced in 1925, and exposure to London's notoriously fickle weather and the fumes of other buses hardly made for a comfortable ride). The system's most iconic vehicle was the ATE Routemaster, much-beloved of Londoners due to its sleek lines and open platform at the back, which made it possible to jump acrobatically on and off the bus even while it was moving. Introduced in 1958, the Routemaster's production run was surprisingly short and the last of the 2,876 built came off the assembly line in 1968 (the same year that the introduction of bus lanes started to speed the buses through London's sclerotic traffic arteries). Even so, red Routemasters plied London's bus routes until they were phased out in favour of articulated 'bendy buses' from 2001. Nostalgia, or constant newspaper stories that the bendy-buses caused traffic jams or were prone to catching fire, prompted a piece of political opportunism when Boris Johnson, during his campaign to be elected London Mayor in 2008, promised the return of the Routemaster. A modified version duly returned to London's streets in 2012 (with an adapted door shield to enclose the back platform and prevent the accidents that had plagued its predecessor, and a lack of openable windows that made it unbearably hot), only for Johnson's own successor, Sadiq Khan to announce in 2017 that they would be discontinued.

The demise of the Routemaster also saw the end of the bus conductors who had taken passengers' fares right from the birth of the system. They were replaced at first with racks of bright pre-printed tickets that were then validated with a special punching machine and then, from 1953, with new-fangled Gibson machines that issued their own tickets from an internal roll. The new Routemasters had Oyster reader machines, just like regular buses, further reducing the romance of travel along London's streets. Yet with digital departure boards at bus stops and transport apps making navigation through the tangle of the network easier than it ever has been, today's bus passengers can probably summon little nostalgia for the good old days of Shillibeer's horse-buses plodding their weary way down the Marylebone Road.

◁

Although London buses continued to run during the Blitz in the Second World War, passengers faced particular challenges. This poster reminds them not to flag down buses with their torches, as these could dazzle the driver. Instead, they were invited to wave a white object, such as a handkerchief.

london trams

In the pantheon of London's transportation systems, the tram has always been a poor relation, overshadowed by its easier-to-understand and seemingly more flexible brethren, the buses, tubes and trains. Yet it has a venerable pedigree, with London's first horse-drawn tram beginning operations in 1860 on a route along Victoria Street. Its architect, unfortunately, was a hyperactive American eccentric named – appropriately enough – George Francis Train. His attention was rapidly diverted by financing the Union Pacific Railroad in the United States, a run for president, and a quixotic round-the-world trip in eighty days that inspired Jules Vernes' later novel.

The trams, when they did finally achieve more orthodox backing, always struggled with a perceived lack of adaptability and with finance. The onerous conditions of the 1870 Act that authorized them allowed local authorities to siphon off too much of their revenue for improvements. Even so by 1932 there were 329 miles of tramway carrying a billion passengers a year. But the warning signs were there, as that number was barely up on what it had been twelve years earlier, and in the intervening time the tram system as a whole had made a profit in just three of those years. Ticket revenues were falling as passengers were travelling less far, in fewer numbers and demanding lower fares. What profit there was to be made had come from the surplus electricity that tram companies sold off as a sideline from their generating business.

In 1933 disaster struck, as the newly installed London Passenger Transport Board made a strategic decision to wind up the system and replace the trams with trolleybuses which, as they did not require tracks – only overhead cables – could be installed and operated much more cheaply. The 1935 New Works Programme that envisaged large-scale expansion for the Tube sounded the death knell for the trams. Line-by-line the tram system was adapted

'tramatorium'
the name given to the yard at charlton where all the redundant trams were incinerated

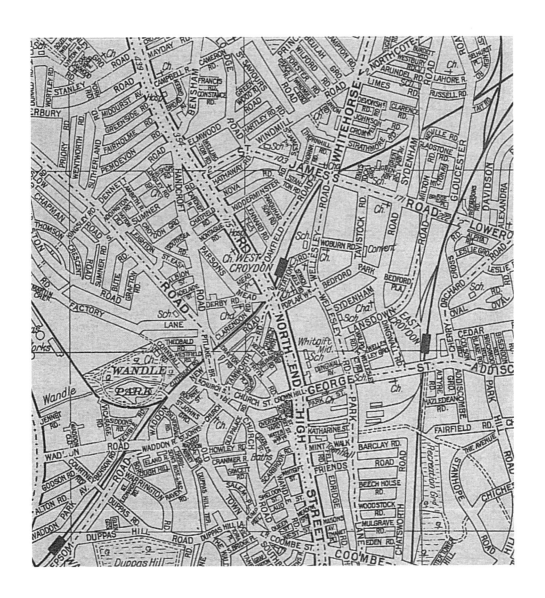

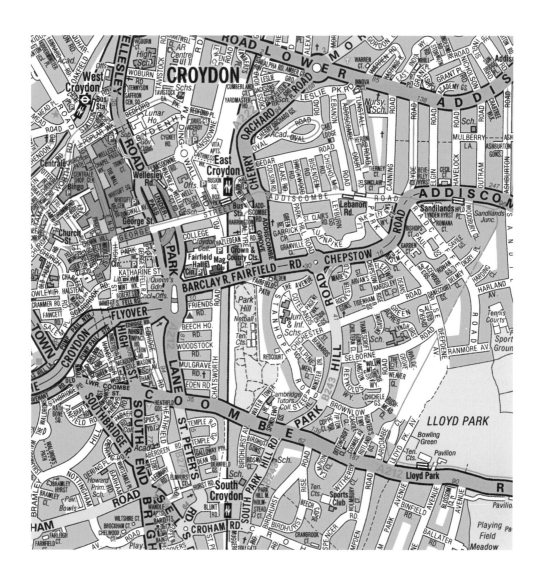

to take trolleybuses, accelerated by an Act in 1938 that provided new funding for the conversion. By the time the war broke out in 1939 and local authorities found better things to do with their resources than rip up tram lines, all that remained was the network around Croydon and a few lines running through Kingsway into North London.

After the war, the trolleybuses themselves fell out of favour – only 127 were ever purchased and they were all phased out by 1961 – and diesel buses replaced the remaining tram lines. A final push was announced in July 1950 with 'Operation Tramaway', to extinguish the last vestiges of the network. When all that remained was a few lines running through East London, a grimly celebratory 'Last Tram Week' was laid on in July 1952. The very last one ran on the night of 5/6 July through New Cross, Woolwich and Abbey Wood, serenaded by huge crowds, who placed coins on the track to be crushed by the tram as a kind of memento. The redundant trams were then gathered in a special yard at Charlton where they were incinerated – in what was, with macabre humour, dubbed the 'tramatorium' – until the very last one had gone up in flames on 29 January 1953.

This was not the end of the line for the trams, however. As London's transport system began to creak under the sheer weight of commuters, especially as the capital's economy began to revive in general after the 1980s, planners cast around for cost-effective solutions. There were those who had never forgotten the tram and there had been schemes in circulation for its revival which rapidly crystallized into a proposal to install a service around Croydon (which had been one of the pre-war tram's last bastions). The scheme was authorized by Parliament in 1994 and it opened as Tramlink in 2000, with the first of the new-style Bombardier trams bearing the service number 2530, in homage to the very last 1952 London tram, which had been number 2529. Since then it has extended to three routes and branch lines around Croydon, amounting to a total of eighteen miles, with periodic further proposals to extend it further, in particular by joining Sutton and Wimbledon with a tram line.

The renaissance of the tram has been so thorough that there were even suggestions that the proposed pedestrianization of Oxford Street could be accompanied by a tram line that would run along its centre from Oxford Circus to Marble Arch. It is a scheme whose grand flourish would be more than worthy of George Train, the tram's flamboyant Victorian progenitor.

◁ 165–6
Croydon was one of the last bastions of the pre-war tram system, and it was only appropriate that the revival of the network, in the form of Tramlink, took place there.

roads AND congestion

London acquired its first roads around AD 50 in the shape of the north–south and east–west axial streets that characterized any planned Roman town, and the matter of weaving land transport through the capital's road network, in the form of carts, carriages, buses, and latterly cars, has been a pressing one ever since.

Although London has long since deviated from the neat Roman grid pattern into a bewildering labyrinth of twists and narrowing alleys, where even straight streets change their name with confusing regularity, its roads proved in general just about adequate to carry the traffic seeking to navigate the maze. Adequate that is, until the age of the car. The 23,000 cars registered in the whole of Britain in 1904 barely made a dent against the horse-drawn trams and motorized buses that plied London's streets, but by the outbreak of the Second World War there were 1.6 million cars in private ownership, many of them trying to fight their way into the crowded centre of the city.

The Government's solution was to build – or at least to plan – more roads. Already by the 1930s the North and South Circular Roads had opened up in a bid to divert traffic around, rather than through, Central London. The mania for ring roads or ringways caught on and Abercrombie's 1943 County of London Plan envisaged a series of sweeping circular routes around London that would render much of the outer suburbs into a grand urban motorway. Needless to say, the plan was not popular with local residents and stalled, with only relatively short sections – the East and West Cross Routes – ever being built. A version of the scheme, though, was revived in the early 1960s, including the proposal for a 'motorway box' that would enclose Central London in the concrete embrace of four urban motorways, that would have obliterated much of Camden Town, Hackney, Battersea and Earls Court. When the final version of the plan was released in 1967, there was outrage,

263,000
the number of vehicles per day on the ten-lane M25 near heathrow

and a concerted campaign by lobby groups such as Homes before Roads caused its cancellation in 1973.

Fragments of the envisaged network did survive, in the form of the Westway, an elevated urban highway running from Paddington to Shepherds Bush, intended to feed traffic into the western arm of the motorway box, which opened in 1970. A more important legacy was the M25, which began life as the outermost ringway of the scheme, and which finally completely opened in 1986. This created a 117-mile orbital route around the whole of London. As the backdrop for some quite epic traffic congestion, it was widened in places, in particular around Heathrow, where ten lanes carrying 263,000 vehicles a day make it Britain's busiest section of road.

The M25, however, does not bear the title of Britain's most expensive section of road, an accolade won by the Limehouse Link. This scarcely one-mile section of carriageway was intended to relieve the congestion between Limehouse and Canary Wharf created by the regeneration of the Docklands. Its £293 million price tag caused a furore but it, and the immense cost of constructing additional river crossings at Dartford and Blackwall in the 1960s, presented the only reasonable solution to London's growing numbers of cars.

It seemed that more vehicles meant more roads, which attracted more vehicles. Attempts to break free from this spiral and actively discourage, or at least curb, cars from entering Central London began late. Parking meters were introduced in Westminster in 1958 exacting a price (small at first, just sixpence) for motorists wanting the luxury of leaving their cars close to shopping or entertainment districts, and traffic wardens inevitably followed soon after. Speed cameras, to moderate cars' speed in those areas where they were not reduced to a crawl by traffic jams, were first trialled in Twickenham in 1992, and caught 22,939 drivers exceeding the limit in the first three weeks alone. These soon spread throughout London's boroughs, to the chagrin of motorists in too much of a hurry.

A more comprehensive effort to stem the tide of London's traffic began in 1993, when the Congestion Charge, a £5 daily fee for entering the central zone of London during

170 ▷
The authorities in London have tried a number of means to reduce the level of traffic clogging the city's streets. The introduction of parking meters in 1958 led to a demand by motorists for products that would tell them where they could park (such as this Motorists Map).

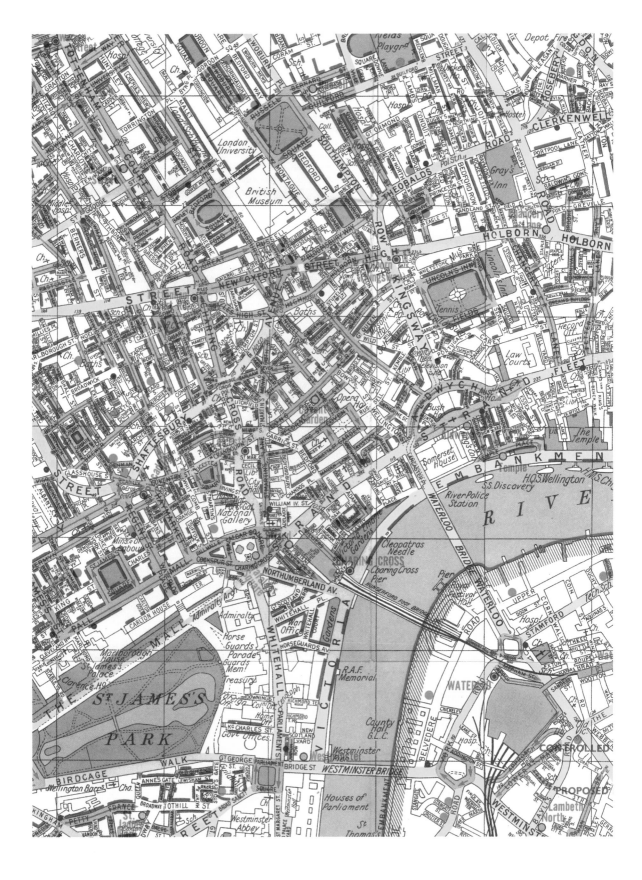

working hours, was introduced. Its initial success in diminishing journey times by about 14 per cent and reducing the numbers of vehicles entering the zone by around 60,000 a day led to its extension westward to include Chelsea, Kensington and Notting Hill in 2007. This addition, however, was particularly unpopular and was cancelled in 2011, though the charge itself continues to creep up, reaching £11.50 in 2014. The Low Emission Zone, introduced in 2008, added an additional fee for the most polluting vehicles. This measure was strengthened in 2017 by the T-Charge, which levied £10 daily on polluting cars and £100 on lorries and coaches, and the imposition in April 2019 of an Ultra Low Emission Zone with even stricter criteria and heavier charges.

The 2.6 million cars owned by Londoners now face tighter controls than ever before to keep them from clogging up the capital's roads and its citizens' lungs. Despite this their numbers show few signs of declining and in twenty-first-century London the car is still king of the road, even if a slightly frustrated one.

△
The congestion charge, introduced in 1993, proved so successful that it was extended westwards from the initial central zone in 2007. There were limits to motorists' (and voters') tolerance, however, and the extension was rescinded in 2011.

ENTERTAINING LONDON

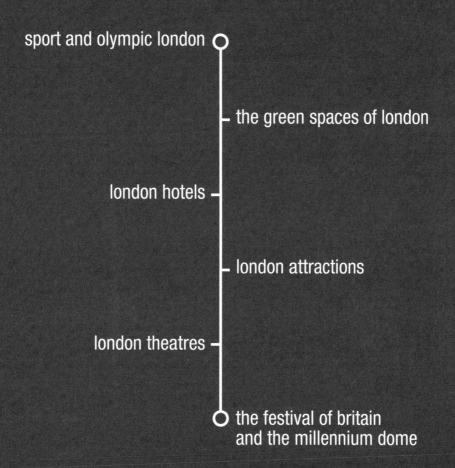

sport and olympic london

the green spaces of london

london hotels

london attractions

london theatres

the festival of britain
and the millennium dome

sport AND olympic london

The Victorians invented modern sport. As the amount of leisure time available to workers increased (particularly when a two-day weekend became the norm from the 1870s), mass participation in sport led to the codification of the rules of a number of sports including football, rugby, tennis and cricket. Many of those sports had their origins in London, from where they spread out across Britain, the Empire and the wider world.

The rules of the modern game of football were drafted by the Football Association, which first met at the Freemason's Tavern on Great Queen Street in October 1863, and which has presided over the game ever since. The first English football league kicked off in 1888, although it was not until the 1893–4 season that a London club (Woolwich Arsenal, now Arsenal) participated, and not until 1930–1 that one (also Arsenal) topped the table. London had more luck in the Football Association's own competition, the FA Cup, won in its inaugural 1871–2 season by Wanderers, whose peripatetic existence took them to home grounds from Epping Forest to Battersea. (Despite winning the cup three times in a row in the 1870s, Wanderers had descended into obscurity by the next decade.)

Since then, London has taken football to its heart. A range of top-rank teams such as Chelsea (who have played at Stamford Bridge since 1905), Arsenal and Tottenham Hotspur (founded in 1882 as a non-league side) regularly vie for domestic and international honours. The home of the game is Wembley Stadium, as it has been since the venue was opened in April 1923 and which, after its redevelopment in 2007, has a crowd capacity of 90,000 (almost twice that of the Colosseum in Rome). It did, though, have to share its space with greyhound racing, another perennial London favourite, as the stadium housed a track from 1928 until as recently as 1998.

25 lb
the amount of food foreign visitors were allowed to bring with them to the 1948 olympics because of rationing

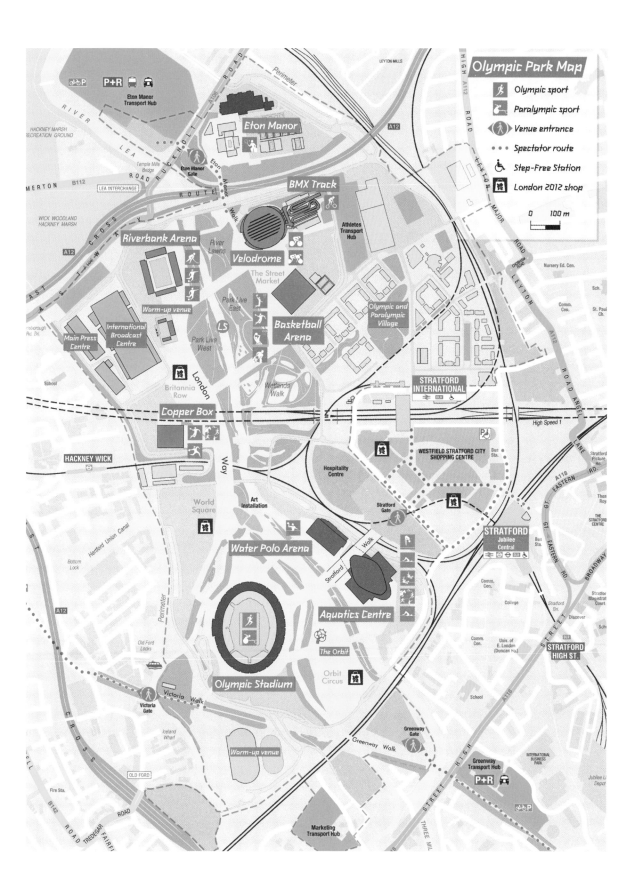

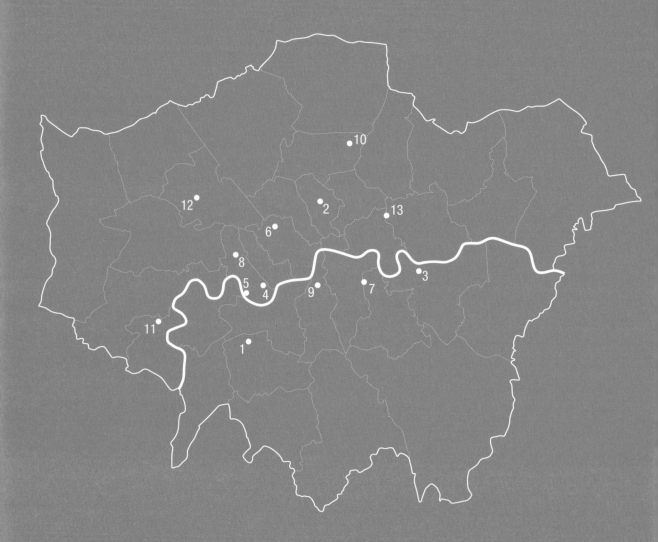

◁ 175

The 2012 London Olympics brought much-needed regeneration to part of East London. This map shows the extensive series of venues that were constructed in the area, much of which was redeveloped later to provide new housing.

1. All England Tennis Club (Wimbledon)
2. Arsenal Football Club
3. Charlton Athletic Football Club
4. Chelsea Football Club
5. Fulham Football Club
6. Lord's Cricket Ground
7. Millwall Football Club
8. Queens Park Rangers Football Club
9. The Oval Cricket Ground
10. Tottenham Hotspur Football Club
11. Twickenham Stadium
12. Wembley Stadium
13. West Ham United Football Club/ Queen Elizabeth Olympic Park

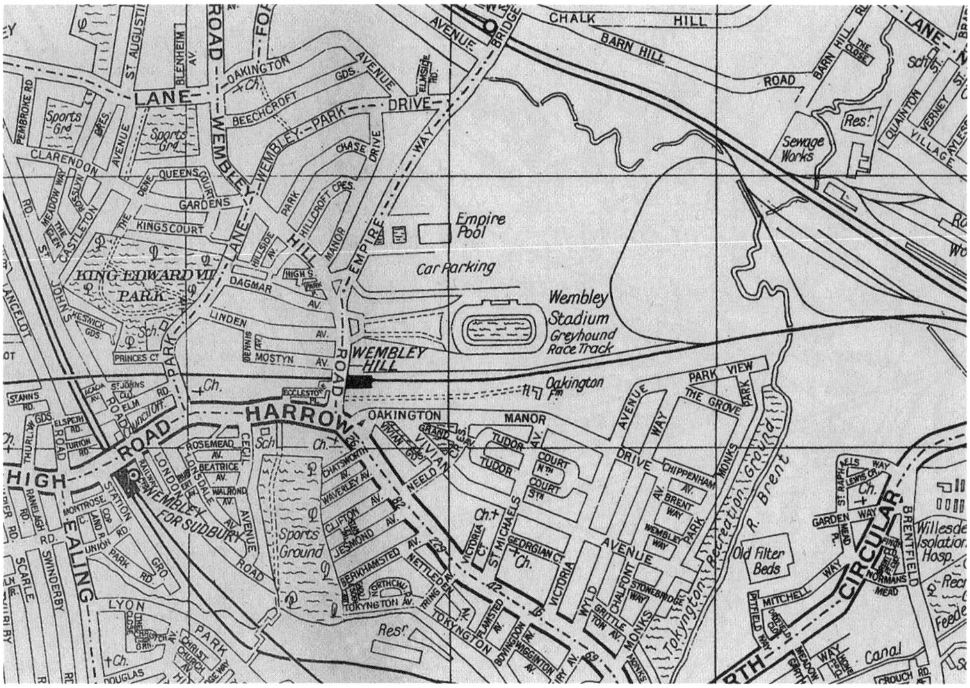

△

In 1936, Wembley Stadium was still better known as a greyhound track than a football stadium, a relative balance-of-power that soon began to shift at a venue which now prides itself as being 'the home of football'.

Cricket has an even more venerable history in the capital, having been played there since the eighteenth century. The oldest club, the Marylebone Cricket Club, first held matches in 1787 and moved to its current location at Lord's in 1814, where it has become the international headquarters of cricket. There, regularly every other year since 1882, one of the international Test matches in the Ashes series against Australia has been played. It was after a match at The Oval cricket ground in Kennington that the Ashes were named, in mock reference to English cricket after the first defeat by Australia on home soil.

London plays host to a huge number of other sports, including rugby, whose stadium at Twickenham was built in 1907 on the site of a former cabbage patch, and from where the BBC broadcast its first ever coverage of a rugby match in 1938. The All England Lawn Tennis Championship has been played at Wimbledon since 1877 (with the addition of Ladies' Singles for the first time in 1884), while newer sports have been added over time, with the first London Marathon in 1981.

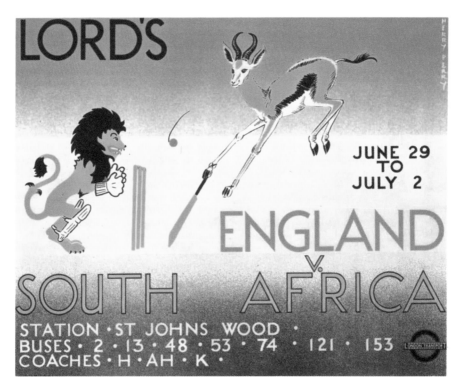

London has also hosted the greatest sporting gathering of them all, the Olympics, no fewer than three times. The first, in 1908, was held at the White City Stadium, where the Americans caused controversy by refusing to dip their flag to Kind Edward VII during the opening ceremony. The 1948 Games were held in the same venue, but in straitened circumstances as the ravages of the war had left London as almost the only European city capable of holding the event. As defeated nations, Germany and Japan were not invited (although the Japanese caused a scare by almost insisting at the last minute that they would participate). Because of rationing, foreign visitors were allowed special dispensation to bring in 25 lb of food with them (to avoid their not having sufficient to tide them over the two weeks of the games), while athletes were forced to sit on the rubble of uncleared bomb sites while they waited to enter the stadium for the opening ceremony. The crowds who did brave the inconveniences were treated to some astonishing performances, as 30-year-old Fanny Blankers-Coen from the Netherlands – dubbed the 'Flying Housewife' by the British press – made off with four gold medals, and the Czech Emil Zátopek won his first Olympic gold in the 10,000 metres.

It was all a far cry from the 2012 Games, which London won in a tough round of bidding against four competitor cities and for which a lavish new stadium was built in a redeveloped 500-acre Olympic Park in Stratford in East London. The final cost was around £9.3 billion, but the boost to London's morale and its international image meant it was deemed worthwhile. When it ended, Londoners knew they had hosted a spectacle unlikely to be repeated in most of their lifetimes.

◁ top
This 1933 poster invites spectators to alight at Southfields before going by bus to the Wimbledon champion-ships. The men's singles competition was won that year by the Australian Jack Crawford, while the American Helen Wills won the ladies' championship (one of her eight Wimbledon titles).

◁ bottom
The second test match against South Africa at Lord's in July 1935 was unusually short, at a scheduled three days. Those home cricket fans enticed to attend by this London Transport poster were disappointed as South Africa won by 157 runs.

THE **green spaces** OF **london**

London's parks and green spaces seem to have an immemorial and immutable air about them, timeless barriers against the encroachment of the tide of buildings that jostle around them. In one sense this cannot be true, for until the eighteenth century even areas now commonly regarded as being in the centre of London, such as Marylebone or Islington, were mere villages surrounded by green fields.

Yet as the city grew, somehow areas of greenery survived, often in the guise of former royal hunting lodges (in turn commonly the relic of land confiscated from monasteries by Henry VIII). These Royal Parks were private domains, and the common Londoner was not initially welcomed. In the case of Regent's Park, it wasn't until a change in sensibility and the emergence of a larger, vocal middle class that it was forced to open in stages from 1835.

The Royal Parks now number eight, from Greenwich in the southeast to Richmond Park in the southwest and a string in the centre from Hyde Park to Regent's Park. They cover an area of around 2,000 hectares and give the centre of the city a set of green lungs of which many other cities are envious. The inner parks experienced their fair share of history before reaching today's sedate state, for instance St James's Park was the site of a former leper hospital which Henry VIII coveted and confiscated to build a palace on. It was the scene of Charles I's last walk in 1649, swathed in a black cloak, before he went to his execution on a scaffold erected in the courtyard of nearby Whitehall Palace.

London has more than 3,000 parks and open spaces, though not all are of such venerable pedigree. The twentieth century gifted the capital's residents a small number of new green areas in which to take their leisure. Burgess Park in Southwark had its origins in a bomb-damaged industrial and residential area which was cleared from 1951 and converted into a park, while Cutty Sark Gardens in Greenwich was built in 1954–7 to act as the backdrop of the preserved tea-clipper *Cutty Sark*. Some new parks have stemmed from modern urban regeneration projects, such as Thames Barrier Park, built in the shadow of the river's huge flood barrier in 1995, with a sunken green garden providing much-needed natural respite in the area. New forms of park opened too – the London Wetland Centre, established in 2000 on the site of several disused Victorian reservoirs near Barn Elms, acts as a haven for wildfowl in an unlikely urban setting.

3,000
the number of parks in london

Existing parks and gardens have been modified, too, receiving new features and monuments. In Regent's Park, Queen Mary's Gardens – named for the wife of George V – were laid out in 1932, and two years later had the much-loved rose garden planted there, which today showcases more than eighty-five varieties. Amongst the later additions were the Kyoto Garden, installed in Holland Park in 1991 as part of a Japanese festival, which encourages visitors to walk along a gravel path to view beautifully manicured and curated areas as an aid to contemplation. There are also the similarly oriental Peace Pagoda erected in Battersea Park in 1985, and the Princess of Wales Memorial Playground opened in Kensington Gardens in 2000, which features a life-size pirate ship as part of the playground's theming around the Peter Pan stories.

In some cases the parks have been put to new uses. In 1932 the Open Air Theatre in Regent's Park opened for the first time and has laid on performances every season since, even during the Second World War when it continued to operate matinees (making it one of only two London theatres to remain open). Hyde Park became the venue of regular summer rock concerts from 1968; at the very first on 29 June some 15,000 fans attended to watch a bill topped by Pink Floyd, while the Rolling Stones made an appearance in July 1969. In 1996, the organisers of the London Prom concerts began to organise Proms in the Park (beginning with Hyde Park) to cater for classical fans who preferred their Beethoven or Handel outdoors. The art world was not to be outdone: in 2003 the Frieze Art Fair was put on in Regents' Park for the first time, and it has since become one of the largest contemporary art fairs in the world, attracting over 60,000 visitors in its 2018 season.

There were some who grumbled at the 'privatization' of the parks, with large sections roped off for long periods of the summer to allow concert stages to be built or exhibition marquees to be erected. Yet the twenty-first-century Londoner's access to green spaces is a boon of which their ancestors, gaping through the fences of the large parks owned by royalty, nobility and great corporations, could only have dreamed.

182-3 ▷

The large area of Central London occupied by parks and other green spaces is clear from this 1949 A-Z map. In many cases their history as royal hunting lodges (in turn often areas confiscated from former monasteries in the sixteenth century) explains why, despite their location on prime land in London's heart, they had not been built upon.

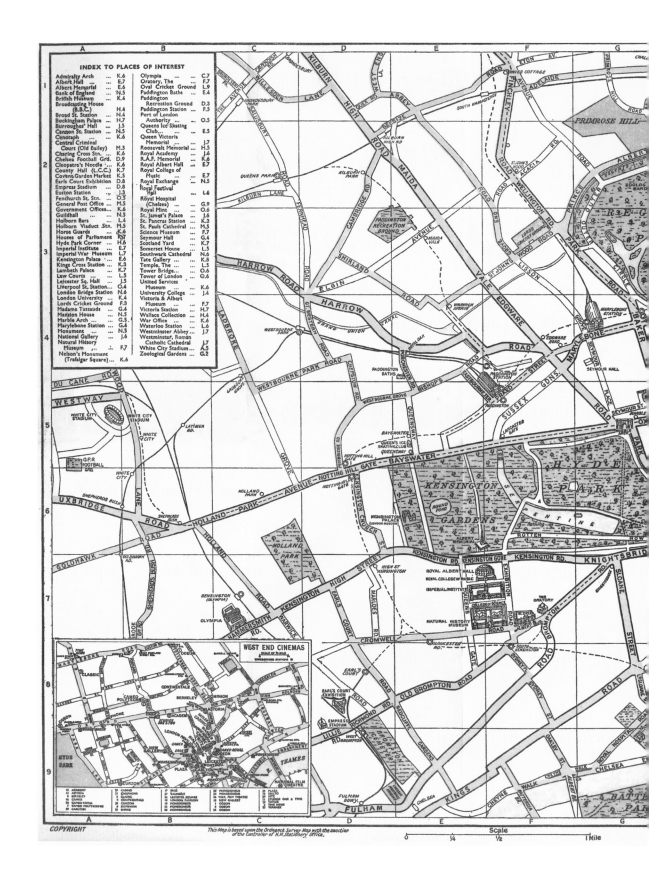

SHOPPING
CENTRES

HYDE
PARK

KENSINGTON
GARDENS

Serpentine

GREEN
PARK

Underground Stations
Scale

WEST END THEATRES
SCALE OF ⅛ MILE
Underground stations

WIGMORE HALL
(CONCERT)

THAMES

london hotels

L ondon has had hotels right from the very beginning. There would have been inns in Roman London, and in the Middle Ages, and travellers had little choice but to make use of their rather unsalubrious services. Geoffrey Chaucer's pilgrims in *The Canterbury Tales* gathered at the Tabard in Southwark, which dated from 1307 and was only demolished over 500 years later, in 1873. Such lodging houses were largely of very dubious quality, however almost none have survived (with the sole exception of the George Inn, London's last galleried hotel, which dates from the sixteenth century, but is now a pub).

It was only in the late Victorian era and with the advent of the railways that hotels inspired by some notion of service and dedication to the comfort of their new middle-class patrons began to emerge. Each railway terminus had its sumptuous hotel, including the Midland Grand at St Pancras, whose extravagant red-brick Gothic pile was designed by George Gilbert Scott. It opened in 1873 and survived for seven decades before shutting up shop in 1935 and eking out a half-life as offices, constantly under the threat of demolition, before its rebirth as the Renaissance St Pancras in 2011.

These pioneers were soon joined by a second generation of even more luxurious hotels, such as the Savoy, opened in 1889, which was the first to have private en-suite bathrooms for all guests, the Ritz whose opening dinner on 24 May 1906 established its reputation as a centre for haute cuisine, and the Dorchester, which first welcomed guests in April 1931 and became a haunt for literary giants such as Cecil Day Lewis and Somerset Maugham.

The Second World War hit the London hotel trade badly, as the flow of visitors to the capital dried up, although the Dorchester's robust construction gave it the reputation as one of the safest buildings in air raids, allowing patrons to dine and party in the knowledge that they could take refuge in its cellar shelters should the Luftwaffe strike. The hotel

60,000
the number of air bnbs listed in london

△
The Charing Cross Hotel, depicted in this 1902 painting, opened in 1865, just a year after the nearby station. It was designed by E. M. Barry, the son of the architect of the new Houses of Parliament, and an early description lauded it as a 'noble edifice'.

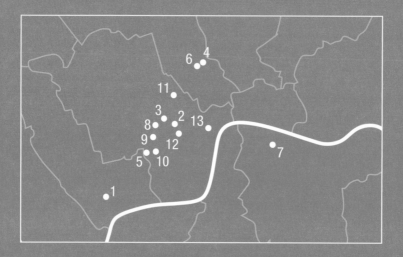

1. Blakes
2. Brown's
3. Claridge's
4. Great Northern
5. Mandarin Oriental
6. Renaissance St Pancras
7. Shangri-La at the Shard

8. The Connaught
9. The Dorchester
10. The Lanesborough
11. The Langham
12. The Ritz
13. The Savoy

even became Eisenhower's headquarters for the planning of the Normandy landings in 1944, providing a new stream of uniformed guests. The end of hostilities in 1945 and the difficulties in financing reconstruction led to a downturn in the hotel trade, and in the 1960s what new openings there were tended to be modernist towers such as the London Hilton in Park Lane. This began operating in 1963 and, with over 450 guest rooms, it was the largest hotel built in post-war Europe.

The Sixties and Seventies saw the growth of hotel chains, a global phenomenon which reduced the diversity of London's hotel scene, while at the same time ensuring a general improvement in quality. The growth of cheaper air travel from the 1970s then led to an increase in the number of tourists visiting London, which reached six million in 1974, and an accompanying shortage in rooms to accommodate them. Hotels of all kinds mushroomed, including the arrival in London of boutique hotels – small establishments with individual designs, appealing to a niche market – beginning with Blakes in South Kensington in 1978. At the luxury end of the spectrum, five-star hotels continued to open apace, until by 2019

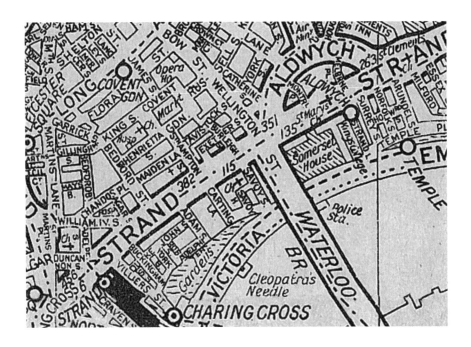

London had around a hundred, including the Shangri-La, incorporated into the Shard building, where guests can enjoy a spectacular view of virtually every part of London.

Even the 123,000 rooms in traditional hotels, hostels, guesthouses and bed and breakfasts struggled to keep up with the tide of London tourism, despite a spike in hotel building around the 2012 London Olympics. To help house the nineteen million visitors who came to the capital in 2017, the market devised new solutions and many Londoners began to offer rooms in their flats and houses through internet services such as Air BnB. By 2017, over 60,000 London properties were listed on its site, and it accounted for around 7.5 per cent of all stays in London. Unlike their medieval forebears, travellers (and the odd pilgrim) to London now have an embarrassment of choice about where to lay their weary heads.

△

Savoy Court, just to the east of Carting Lane, which acts as the entrance to the Savoy Hotel, is the only road in London where cars are required to drive on the right.

london attractions

The capital's citizens have always had an appetite for the curious, the macabre and the titillating. Alongside the theatres that appeared in Elizabethan times and the public galleries and museums established by the Victorians, a parallel world of attractions developed, from bear-baiting to freak shows, which catered to a less highbrow taste.

Some of these survive today, welcoming millions of visitors to a version of what Victorian thrill-seekers experienced nearly two centuries ago. Prime among them is Madame Tussauds, established in 1835 by Marie Tussaud, a Frenchwoman who had begun to learn the trade of wax sculpture from her uncle at the tender age of six. The waxworks moved to their present site on the Marylebone Road in 1884, by which time it housed hundreds of figures of the great, the good and the villainous. A catalogue from 1892 began with a worthy procession of kings and queens of England, and included a large section on Napoleon (prominently featuring his 'apotheosis'), reflecting Madame Tussaud's French heritage. Then came the section most visitors had probably been most eagerly anticipating, the 'Chamber of Horrors' which contained wax likenesses of famous murderers and the Victorian graverobbers Burke and Hare (as well as an incongruous recreation of an opium den).

Madame Tussauds survived all the vicissitudes of taste in the twentieth century (including the German air raid that destroyed hundreds of head moulds in 1940), adding famous sportsmen, film stars and politicians to its repertoire (Winston Churchill has had ten likenesses, beginning with one made in 1908, near the start of his career). Super celebrities such as Michael Jackson are now star attractions and the museum keeps up with the latest political trends, unveiling a statue of Donald Trump in January 2017. To sculpt them requires care – more than 350 hours of work, including the insertion of each strand of hair by hand – and patience on the part of the subjects, who are required to sit for three hours and have 250 measurements taken. All this attention to detail is rewarded with 2.5 million visitors a year, who line up in great snaking queues on Marylebone Road, much like their Victorian predecessors.

350 hours
the time to create each waxworks at madame tussauds

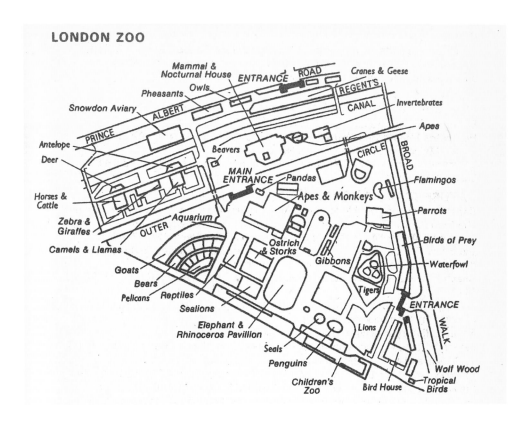

LONDON ZOO

London Zoo is another Victorian survival. It was founded on the northern edge of Regent's Park in 1828, in part to bring a sense of scientific rigour to a field that had previously been monopolized by those with little care for the animals' wellbeing or for studying their habits, and in part to take refugees from the menageries at the Tower of London. Early visitors to the zoo could see exotica such as Obaysh, the first hippopotamus to be seen in Britain since Roman times, who arrived in 1850, and a selection of monkeys that were chained to poles so that visitors could get close to them, but who had the unfortunate habit of purloining mountains of hats, gloves and ladies' bags.

The twentieth century brought new animals and architectural splendour to the zoo, with the building of enclosures such as the Mappin Terraces (originally for mountain goats, but now used for kangaroos) in 1913, the Penguin Pool in 1934, and the splendid tent-like mesh of the Snowdon aviary in 1964. The zoo's first panda arrived in 1958, and the charismatic animals became a symbol of 'panda diplomacy', used by the Chinese government to reward improved ties with Western nations (Prime Minister Ted Heath came back from Beijing in 1974 with a pair named Chia-Chia and Ching-Ching). By 1990, the zoo had almost 7,000 animals, but was facing severe financial difficulties. The following year, the Zoological Society of London announced that the Regent's Park site would close so that resources could be concentrated on its open-air zoo at Whipsnade in Bedfordshire, which had been established in 1932. An outpouring of public support, donations and a surge in visitors wanting to catch the zoo one last time resulted in its unexpected reprieve. By 2017 the zoo was again receiving over a million visitors a year, conducting world-ranking breeding programmes for species such as the Amur tiger, and unveiling new attractions, such as a troupe of western lowland gorillas and a female baby okapi born in 2018, named Meghan after the Duchess of Sussex.

London has of course welcomed new attractions in more recent decades. The London Dungeon opened on Tooley Street in 1976 as a horror museum offering macabre competition to Madame Tussauds, and the London Aquarium commenced operations in 1997, giving tourists and Londoners the chance to see sharks at close quarters, a delight that London Zoo could not match. Perhaps the most famous of these new crowd-pullers is the London Eye, a giant observational Ferris wheel erected to celebrate the turn of the new millennium. Not quite the first such structure in London – a huge wheel had been constructed at Earls Court in 1895 for the Empire of India Exhibition – it was without doubt the largest, with its 120-metre diameter increased to a height of 135 metres by its base.

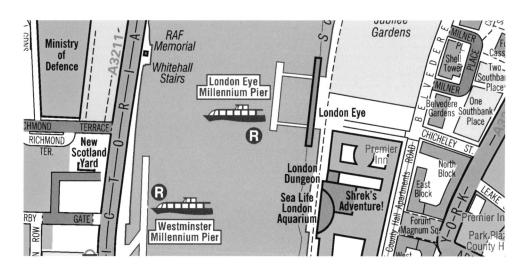

△
The London Eye and the London Aquarium are just two of the more recent additions to London's attractions scene, and have established themselves firmly on the itineraries of hundreds of thousands of tourists.

◁ 189
Although the layout has changed somewhat – wolves no longer prowl in their wood, and a whole enclosure has been built for the western lowland gorillas – much of the plan of London Zoo in 1986 would be familiar to today's visitors.

The enormous wheel was floated up the Thames in sections on barges before being assembled and then raised into place in October 1999. On clear days – not a given in London – visitors could see a breathtaking panorama of the entire city from its thirty-two glass passenger capsules. Originally only intended as a temporary structure which would be dismantled after five years, it proved so popular that in 2002 permission was granted to make it permanent.

From there the observant visitor can see how much London has changed since 1895, when the Eye's predecessor wheel was in operation – the transformation in the Docklands, the appearance of skyscrapers such as the Gherkin and the Shard – and how much has remained the same, including, for the keen-eyed, the padding around of a hippopotamus at London Zoo, just as its ancestor did 170 years ago.

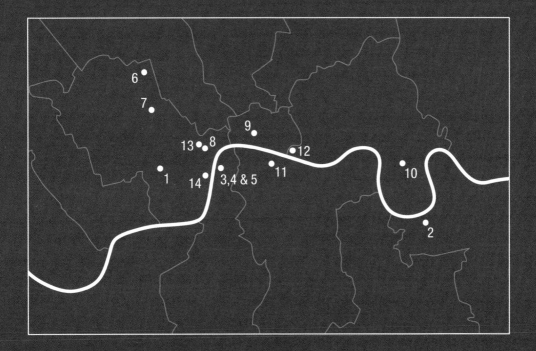

1. Buckingham Palace
2. Greenwich
3. London Aquarium
4. London Dungeon
5. London Eye
6. London Zoo
7. Madame Tussauds
8. Trafalgar Square

9. St Paul's Cathedral
10. The Docklands
11. The Shard
12. Tower of London
13. Piccadilly Circus
14. Westminster Abbey/
    Palace of Westminster/Big Ben

london theatres

Unless one counts the Roman amphitheatre of the second century AD – where the spectacles were of a distinctly bloodier nature – London's first theatre was established in 1567 at the Red Lion in Whitechapel, a short-lived venture at the very threshold of London's golden age of drama (which featured such greats as Shakespeare and Marlowe). Four-and-a-half centuries later, the capital boasts over 240 theatres with a capacity for over 110,000 people (just over twice that of the Colosseum in Rome), and has been in the intervening 450 years the centre of a thriving dramatic culture, from the highbrow and innovative to crowd-pleasing music-hall variety (with the genius of Shakespeare somehow managing to balance its appeal at all levels).

London theatre underwent a renaissance during the late Victorian and Edwardian era, as a result of which many of the capital's dramatic venues sport gorgeous neoclassical architecture and beautiful interior flourishes, but are hopelessly expensive to run, have cramped seating and limited facilities for the audience. Serious maintenance issues meant that some were forced to close, including the Windmill Theatre whose proud boast 'We Never Closed' during the whole of the Second World War (unlike every other West End theatre, which all shut their doors) was rendered hollow when it was forced to shut down in 1964. Others had to make severe cutbacks or hope for a long-running show.

A few were lucky, such as St Martin's Theatre, where Agatha Christie's *The Mousetrap* opened in 1952 and has run continually ever since, rendering the job of scheduling planner somewhat redundant as the play approaches its eighth decade. Musicals, a mainstay of the London theatrical scene, drawing on the rich tradition of Victorian music halls, have also provided a succession of blockbusters. Most notable is *Les Misérables*, which by 2019 had run for thirty-four continuous seasons at the Queen's Theatre on Shaftesbury Avenue.

8th november 2012
the date *the mousetrap* reached its 25,000th performance

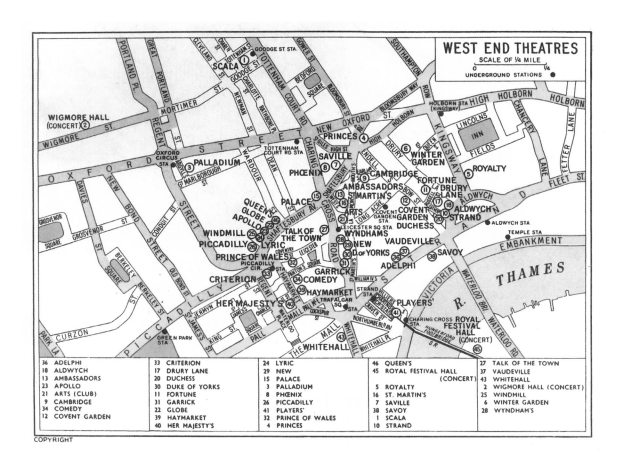

London's concentration of theatres in the district along the Strand and Shaftesbury Avenue led to its being dubbed 'Theatreland'. Although some have closed down since the heyday of the 1930s, there are still around forty theatres in the area.

THEATRE ROYAL
DRURY LANE

CHAIRMAN—PRINCE LITTLER   GEN. MANAGER—FRANK C. MARSHALL

Prince Littler
presents

Carousel

As originally produced by **THE THEATRE GUILD** in the U.S.A

Based on Ferenc Molnar's " LILIOM "
As Adapted by Benjamin F. Glazer
Music by RICHARD RODGERS
Book and Lyrics by OSCAR HAMMERSTEIN 2nd
Original Production Directed by **ROUBEN MAMOULIAN**

Dances by **AGNES de MILLE**
Costumes Designed by **MILES WHITE**
Orchestra Directed by **REGINALD BURSTON**
Orchestrations by **DON WALKER**

| EVENINGS at 7·15 | Matinees : WED. & SAT. at 2·30 |

Reproduced by **JEROME WHYTE**—Production Manager, Theatre Guild, N.Y.
Original Production supervised by } **LAWRENCE LANGNER & THERESA HELBURN**

Post-war London did acquire new theatre venues, as the drama scene became both more diverse and professional. The Royal National Theatre opened in 1963 amid the concrete utopia of the South Bank, its opening night featuring Peter O'Toole playing Hamlet, while the Barbican Theatre opened in 1982, nestled among the brutalist architecture of the surrounding estate. Less traditional venues began to appear in the 1970s, with the opening of the Young Vic Theatre on the South Bank – its 420-seat auditorium partly carved out of a former butcher's shop – and the Donmar Warehouse, which put on its first performances in Covent Garden in 1977 and acquired a reputation for innovation under directors Sam Mendes (1992–2002) and Michael Granage (2002–2011).

The most unexpected addition to the London theatre scene came in 1997, when actor and director Sam Wanamaker achieved a long-held dream by opening Shakespeare's New Globe in Southwark. A close replica of the Elizabethan original – which had stood close by and burnt down in June 1613 when a cannon let off during a performance of *Henry VIII* caused the roof to catch fire – it includes an open area at the front of the stage apron in which standing 'groundlings' can savour the experience of seeing the performance through the eyes of a Shakespearean audience.

Despite mounting costs, the London theatre scene has proved itself resilient to setbacks such as the Gulf War of 1993, when audience numbers fell by nearly 5 per cent as tourists curtailed their travels. Gross sales rose in 2016 to over £644 million, with total audiences amounting to 14,328,000. The centuries-old story of London theatre is not about to end.

◁

Rogers and Hammerstein's much-loved musical Carousel opened at the Drury Lane theatre on 7 June 1950 and enjoyed a four-month run. It had two West End revivals, in 1993 at the Shaftesbury Theatre and in 2008 at the Savoy.

THE festival OF britain
AND THE millennium dome

Londoners have always loved pageants and festivals, from the religious processions and mystery plays of the Middle Ages to the outpouring of royalist devotion surrounding modern coronations. By the mid-nineteenth century, it seemed only right that Britain's burgeoning industrial might should have its very own celebration and so it was – in part at the prompting of Prince Albert – that the Great Exhibition opened in 1851, housed in a sumptuous glass crystal palace in Hyde Park. Six million people attended the showcase of the vast range of products produced in the empire (with a smaller section allowed for foreign powers), with devices from weaving frames to an automatic voting machine, as well as more exotic exhibits, such as the Koh-i-Noor diamond and a range of unpickable locks brought over by the Americans.

The Great Exhibition set a high bar and though there were imitators, in the form of World's Fairs in other countries (notably the United States), nothing was contemplated on a similar scale in Britain until the 1940s. Then, conscious of the need to reconstruct Britain's self-confidence, as well as its physical infrastructure, when the war finally ended, the Royal Society of Arts in 1943 proposed a festival to mark the centenary of the Great Exhibition. This Festival of Britain would, as its director Kenneth Morgan declared, lift 'a people curbed by years of total war and half crushed by austerity and gloom'.

The Government was much taken by the idea of a celebration of Britain and what it meant to be British (ignoring the diminution in global ambition that this implied compared

£400,000,000
the overspend on the millennium dome

to the Great Exhibition). Bids were invited and dozens were received, ranging from the absurd – the demolition of Wormwood Scrubs prison to construct a series of pavilions and marquees; to the practical – the redevelopment of a series of derelict and post-industrial sites. Finally, the bomb-damaged area along the south bank of the Thames by Embankment was selected and bulldozers moved in rapidly to clear and level it for the grand celebration to come.

The exhibition planners co-opted a series of high-profile figures from the arts, including the architect Hugh Casson, to design buildings and exhibits intended to show Britain as a forward-looking nation, conscious of its past, but well prepared and enthusiastic for its role in shaping the future. The heavily themed areas included sections on the 'Land' (which encompassed minerals, ships and nature from the Poles to the Deserts, as well as Outer Space); and 'the people' (which featured sections on the seaside, schools and sport). There was, though, a certain self-regarding complacency about the whole thing: the 'Lion and the Unicorn Pavilion' was designed to show the 'realism and strength' of the British character (the Lion), as well as its 'fantasy, independence and imagination' (the Unicorn), and the exclusion of other nations' products gave the Festival an unbalanced feel.

Even so, 8.5 million people visited the South Bank site, each paying five shillings to enter, meaning the Festival actually made a small profit of £2.5 million. They were treated to the Dome of Discovery, the largest dome in the world at the time (at 365 feet in diameter), which contained many of the exhibits; the telekinema, a 400-seat state-of-the-art cinema that could show 3-D films; and – possibly most famously of all – the Skylon, a curious cigar-shaped metal needle suspended fifteen metres off the ground by cables that resembled an alien ship hovering over the site. Further fun was to be had at the Festival Pleasure Gardens in Battersea, where an amusement park (which later became the Battersea Fun Fair) and a miniature railway were among the diversions on offer. Less immediately popular was the 'Live Exhibition' of architecture at the Lansbury Estate in Poplar, and also an exhibition of books in South Kensington that attracted only 63,000 visitors.

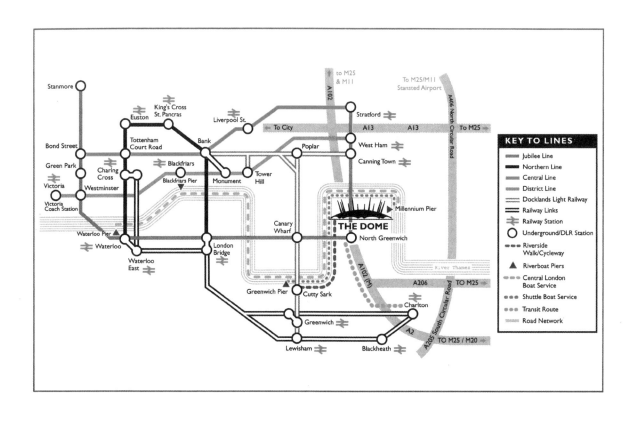

The Festival was always intended only to be temporary and it closed on 30 September 1951, just short of five months after King George VI had presided over its opening ceremony. The exhibition buildings were dismantled, the Skylon was sold for scrap metal, and all that survived were the new concert venue in the Royal Festival Hall and a regeneration programme that later populated the South Bank with a rash of identikit concrete arts venues.

The notion that a national festival could overcome national self-doubt and inspire a renaissance in Britain's image was a seed that did not go away. It germinated once more in the late 1990s, when politicians awoke to the advantage to be gained from commemorating the forthcoming millennium. This crystallized around the idea of reviving the spirit of celebration by putting on an exhibition venue to revisit the triumphs of the Great Exhibition and the Festival of Britain. After receiving sixty-one bids, the government of John Major rejected the more outlandish (including one to convert the Isle of Wight into a huge festival venue) and chose the site of the former Greenwich Gasworks to build a giant dome – another homage to the Festival – in which to put on a similarly themed exposition of modern British life.

The Millennium Dome opened for business on 1 January 2000 and immediately attracted a stream of negative press for its cost overruns (the final price tag was around £800 million, over double that originally envisaged) and for being a pale imitation of the Festival of Britain, with a similar arrangement (into 'Who we are', 'What we do' and 'Where we live' zones). Instead of a celebration of national self-confidence, it seemed simply another entertainment mega-venue, a symbol of a society that was becoming more fractured and self-centred.

After its closure, the Millennium Dome was indeed turned into a concert venue, sponsored by the telecommunications company O2 (after original plans to convert it into a football stadium were scrapped). Britain, it seemed, was now more interested in exhibitionism than exhibitions.

◁

The 6.5 million people who visited the Millennium Dome during the year that the exhibition ran there were able to take advantage of a series of newly constructed transport links in the area, including the Jubilee Line extension, which ran directly to North Greenwich, and the Docklands Light Railway, which had stations at nearby Cutty Sark, Canary Wharf and Canning Town.

COMMUNICATING LONDON

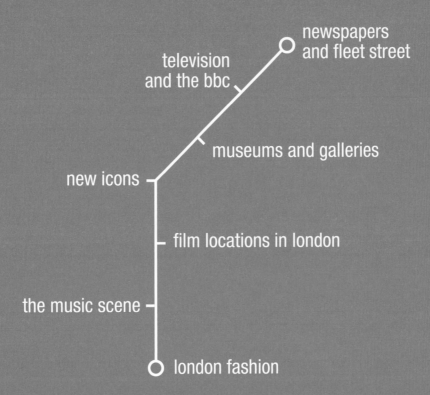

newspapers
and fleet street

television
and the bbc

museums and galleries

new icons

film locations in london

the music scene

london fashion

newspapers AND fleet street

Londoners' appetite for gossip and tidings from overseas has always been insatiable and for centuries Fleet Street was at the heart of the industry that grew up to satisfy them. Newspapers began to appear in England in the 1620s, and right from the start the gossipmongers, scribes and printers gathered around the alleyways and coffee houses bordering the long street which led from St Paul's westwards to the Strand at Aldwych.

London's first daily newspaper, the *Daily Courant* first appeared in March 1702 and before long was being published 'at the sign of the Dolphin, Little Britain', a little way north of St Paul's. By the early twentieth century Fleet Street was firmly established, with a clutch of watering holes such as Ye Old Cheshire Cheese and the Punch Tavern servicing the journalists and printers on the dozens of newspapers and magazines that made the area their home.

The *Daily Telegraph*, the *Daily Express* and *The Guardian* had their offices on the street while the *Evening Standard* occupied premises up Shoe Lane to the north and the *Daily Mail* on the corner of Whitefriars Street and Tudor Street to the south. Only *The Times* stood relatively aloof – as befitted the country's oldest continuously published daily and the nation's newspaper of record – presiding in a now-demolished building at Printing House Square, north of Queen Victoria Street.

A powerful duopoly of lords, Rothermere and Beaverbrook, dominated the last golden age of the newspapers. This was interrupted rudely by the Second World War, when censorship and paper shortages muted their style and German bombs wrought havoc in their offices (such as the Luftwaffe air raid on 20 September 1940 which scored a direct hit on the *Daily Telegraph*, deluging the press room in a metre of oily water). Those publications that dared criticise the Government were punished: the left-wing *Daily Worker* was closed down for nineteen months from 1941 and the *Daily Mirror* narrowly avoided a similar fate.

Yet the newspapers published on, and after the war their circulations soared – by 1949 the *Daily Mirror* was selling four million copies daily and a coronation special edition in 1953 reached the unprecedented level of seven million on the newsstands. It could not last: inefficient working practices, defended by exceptionally strong printing unions, meant that

4,000,000
daily sales of the *daily mirror* in 1949

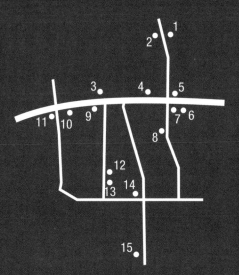

Former newspaper offices
in and around Fleet Street

1. Evening Standard
2. The Daily Sketch
3. Sunday Post
4. Daily Telegraph
5. Daily Express
6. Press Association
7. Reuters News Agency
8. Press Gazette
9. Glasgow Herald
10. London News Agency
11. The Guardian
12. News of the World
13. The Sun
14. Daily Mail
15. Evening News

technology passed the world of Fleet Street by. As antiquated linotype presses bashing out hot metal continued to produce London's grand broadsheet papers, sleeker phototypesetting composition became irresistible to frustrated proprietors in search of an end to their losses, if not an actual profit.

Gradually the newspapers drifted a little further from Fleet Street, where some minor gains in efficiency might be had in new offices. *The Times* transferred to Gray's Inn Road in 1974, and *The Guardian* to a new headquarters in Farringdon in 1976. It was not enough. In 1978 the owners of *The Times* proposed the installation of new printing machinery, unleashing a strike that closed the newspaper and its sister title the *Sunday Times* for eleven months. At the end, almost bankrupt, it was bought by Rupert Murdoch's News International, to sit alongside his rather racier titles *The Sun* and the *News of the World*¸ which had by then become the nation's best-selling tabloids.

In 1986 the storm broke. Murdoch announced the transfer of production to new purpose-built premises in Wapping, sparking a strike by 5,000 print workers, most of whom had been told they were no longer required. Mass picketing of the Wapping plant failed to stop the production and distribution of the newspapers and the strike collapsed after thirteen months in February 1987. Murdoch's success paved the way for an exodus from Fleet Street as other proprietors, seeing that the unions could not hold them back, moved

204 ▷

Right from the eighteenth century, London's newspapers (and its journalists and printers) clustered in a small area around Fleet Street, a tradition that was still strong in the 1930s and only finally died out in the early twenty-first century.

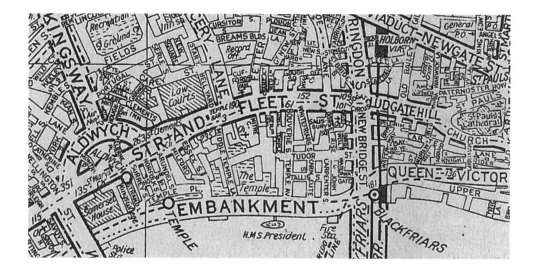

out to new offices and adopted the latest technology (which they had to do to compete with the News International titles). *The Guardian* opened a new print centre soon after on the Isle of Dogs, and Associated Newspapers, publisher of the *Daily Mail*, moved their offices to Kensington High Street, while their bitter rivals the *Daily Express* stayed close to their old haunts at Ludgate House on Blackfriars.

As the newspaper scene transformed – with a brief infusion of life caused by the cost efficiencies gained by the new production techniques followed by a long slow decline as audience and advertising revenue was lost to television and then the internet – new titles rose and fell. *The Independent* launched in 1985 and surpassed *The Times* with a circulation of 402,000 in 1992, but it ceased to produce a print edition in 2016, becoming an internet-only title as blogs, social media and internet news agencies complicated the terrain of news dissemination and swallowed up audience attention.

Fleet Street's last journalists left in 2016, when two reporters from the London outpost of Dundee's *Sunday Post* handed back the keys to their office. As four hundred years of tradition died out in a final toast, London's journalists found themselves dispersed, from the *Daily Telegraph* in Victoria, to *The Guardian* at King's Cross. Some, liberated by technology from the tyranny of the fixed news room, even produced the news from laptops in London's cafés. In one sense, therefore, journalism had come home.

television ^{AND}_{THE} bbc

As national institutions go, the BBC is a Johnny-come-lately – founded only in 1922 – but its rapid establishment as a national icon is a sign of how deeply television has embedded itself in Britain's popular culture and sense of itself. The British Broadcasting Corporation was set up as a quasi-governmental body, funded by the state, but operated at arm's length by an independent management as a way of bringing a sense of order and decorum into the field and avoiding the free-for-all that had broken out in the United States, the pioneer of radio and television.

The BBC's first home was in a studio operated by Marconi's 2LO company on the Strand, but it rapidly established its own identity, still as a radio broadcaster, in nearby Savoy Hill. It was not until 1932 that the corporation moved into its own purpose-built headquarters at Broadcasting House on Portland Place. There it has remained ever since, where its imposing building of Portland stone – faintly resembling a ship – was twice bombed in the Second World War and now boasts a modern extension accessible by a glass corridor.

The first television programmes were actually broadcast from Alexandra Palace in North London, leased by the BBC in 1935, and where trials took place in 1936 in a head-to-head between a Marconi-EMI system and one installed by television's pioneer John Logie Baird. The inventor lost out and so it was using Marconi's 405-line machinery that the first BBC programmes went out before wartime exigencies caused the BBC to halt television broadcasts in September 1939. They were only resumed seven years later with a re-broadcast of the same Mickey Mouse cartoon with which they had ended.

By then, the BBC had added Bush House on Aldwych to its portfolio of London studios. The building was acquired in 1940 when the corporation's European radio services were

1936
the year that trials took place between the marconi-emi system and the one installed by television's pioneer john logie baird

bombed out, and it hosted many of General de Gaulle's morale-raising speeches to the Resistance against the Nazi occupation of France. George Orwell briefly worked there, though he found it a thoroughly dispiriting experience. By 1972, Bush House had become a veritable tower of Babel, with 750 hours of programming a week going out in forty languages. The fall of the Berlin Wall in 1990 and the removal of the need to support dissident opinion behind the Iron Curtain, together with budget cuts, caused the linguistic hubbub to recede, and in 2012 operations at Bush House ceased.

Programmes were made at Elstree in Borehamwood (which ultimately became the home of EastEnders after its first broadcast in 1985), and Lime Grove in Shepherd's Bush (which the BBC occupied from 1949 to 1992 as a temporary measure that became semi-permanent, and which hosted seminal dramas such as *Doctor Who* and *Steptoe & Son*). To these studios was added Television Centre at Wood Lane in White City, which from 1960 was the main headquarters of BBC Television. In a move to consolidate its London property portfolio in the early twenty-first century, BBC Television transferred its headquarters to a newly extended Broadcasting House. Although Television Centre is still in use by the BBC's commercial arm, the BBC ceased to broadcast from there in 2013, causing many politicians to breathe a sigh of relief as it removed the need for a taxi ride away from the Westminster bubble for interviews.

Political dramas and crises were meat and drink to the BBC's news service, but the occasions that really stuck in the collective memory were the London Olympic Games in 1948 (the first ever to be televised), and their reprise in 2012 on the new Stratford site; the coronation of Queen Elizabeth II in 1953, which was seen by over twenty million people throughout Europe and which led to a surge in the purchase of television sets; and the wedding of Prince Charles and Lady Diana Spencer in 1981, which attracted a total of over twenty-eight million viewers. Nearly a third of those watched the ceremony on ITV, an independent service that had begun broadcasting in 1955 after parliamentary lobbying to ensure that the BBC faced some competition, and which was based initially at Television House on Kingsway.

▷

In the 1930s, the BBC was firmly associated with its flagship headquarters at Portland Place. By the 1960s, its portfolio of buildings had diversified to include the BBC Television Centre at White City.

In 1982, Britain gained yet another television channel, when Channel 4 opened up in Charlotte Street, and from then the diversification of the field became vertiginous. The explosion of digital television services after the turning-off of the analogue TV signal in 2007 has meant that the single channel that could pioneer the first children's broadcast (Muffin the Mule in October 1946) or the first television weather forecast (in 1949) now faces dozens of competitors and in areas such as news, has lost significant market share to news websites and social media services.

Yet, despite it all, the BBC, and its monolithic headquarters, remain one of the most recognizable symbols of Britain and of London.

 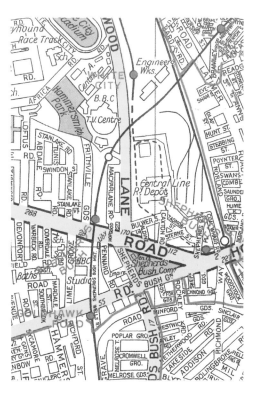

museums AND galleries

London, it seems, has a museum on almost every corner. They range from the huge national collections of the British Museum and National Gallery, to esoterica such as the Grant Zoology Museum in Bloomsbury and Greenwich's Fan Museum. Their origins are in the cabinets of curiosities assembled by seventeenth- and eighteenth-century noblemen, mostly gathered from their excursions on the Grand Tour round Europe's sites of historical interest (though the very oldest museum, the Royal Armouries, is based around the collection of weapons held in the Tower of London, to which paying visitors are recorded from as early as the sixteenth century).

In 1753, London's most famous museum, the British Museum, was founded after an Act of Parliament sanctioned a lottery to purchase the treasures assembled by Sir Hans Sloane. It grew steadily, its collection enhanced in 1802 by the acquisition of the Rosetta Stone, the key to the decipherment of Egyptian hieroglyphs. The visitor experience was improved by the construction of its main building, with its grand neo-Classical façade, from 1825. Establishing itself as a must-see for visitors to London (5.9 million of whom entered its gates in 2017), the 'BM' also pioneered the blockbuster exhibition, with *The Treasures of Tutankhamun*, which nearly 1.7 million people paid to see in 1974. Since 2000, it has also boasted the splendid glass-covered Great Court, in a central area of the museum, which was formerly largely occupied by temporary offices, but which also housed the famous circular Old Reading Room of the British Library (in which Karl Marx wrote *Das Kapital*).

The nearest the British Museum has to a direct competitor is the National Gallery, sporting a similarly grand frontage overlooking Trafalgar Square. Established in 1824, its world-class collection of paintings was deemed so vulnerable to destruction in German air attacks during the Blitz in 1940 that it was moved in its entirety to the safety of a slate

1802

the year the british museum acquired the rosetta stone, the key to the decipherment of egyptian hieroglyphs

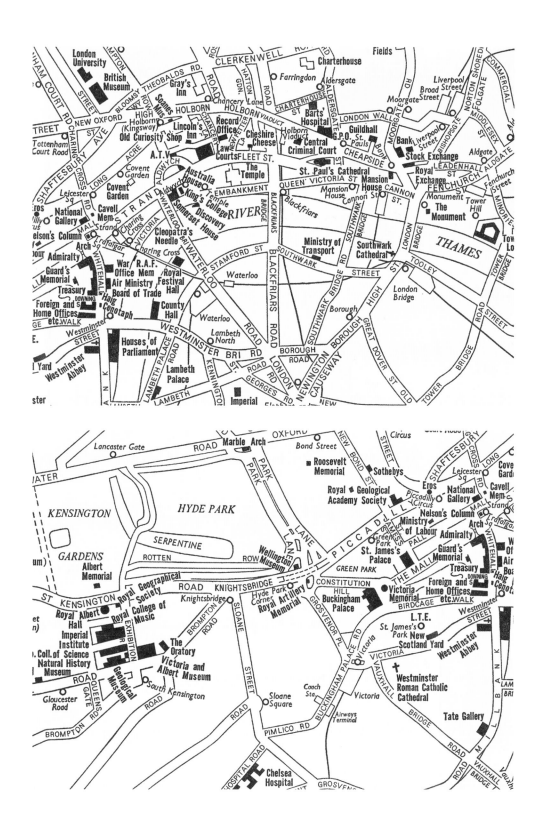

quarry at Blaenau Ffestiniog in North Wales, and the empty galleries were used to put on morale-raising lunchtime concerts. The Victoria and Albert Museum (V&A), funded in 1852 with part of the profits from the Great Exhibition, similarly had its treasures dispersed (part to a Wiltshire quarry and part close by, to a tunnel at Aldwych tube station), while its interior was made over into a makeshift camp for child evacuees from Gibraltar.

The late twentieth century saw a renaissance in London's museums, with new museums opening up and extensions to several others that had long suffered from cramped accommodation. Most notably the National Gallery acquired its Sainsbury Wing in 1991, which blended more gently with the gallery's original sections after a more modernist plan, complete with tower, was branded a 'monstrous carbuncle'. The Museum of London opened in 1976 to gather together the collections previously held at the Guildhall Museum and London Museum, and became a compelling destination for those interested specifically in the history of the capital (enhanced by a £20 million redevelopment completed in May 2010). It also acquired an outpost in East London when the Museum of London Docklands opened in 2003, in a nineteenth-century warehouse, as a specialist gallery charting the development of London's ports.

The list of other museum openings seems endless. The Tate Modern became a showcase for Britain's contemporary art collection in 2000, housed in the great hulk of the former Bankside Power Station, whose enormous turbine hall allows the display of installations of astonishing size. The Garden History Museum was established in 1977 by Rosemary and John Nicholson in the abandoned church of St Mary's at Lambeth, as a homage to John Tradescant (d. 1638), Britain's first great plant hunter. And the Cartoon Museum was established in Holborn in 2006 to bring together a collection of the nation's humorous graphic art.

There are scores of others, but to balance so much additional diversity in the museum scene, a few old friends have had to close. The London Gas Museum at Bromley-by-Bow shut in 1998; the Theatre Museum in Covent Garden, with its dazzling array of costumes and other theatrical paraphernalia, ceased business in 2007, its collections absorbed into the V&A; and the Bramah Tea and Coffee Museum closed down in 2008 when its founder died. Yet for each museum that closes, another opens, making the museum scene itself a living and vibrant thing. London may be a city of museums, but it is not a fossil.

◁ 209
The wealth of London's museums is clearly indicated in this 1967 A-Z map which shows monuments, churches and other cultural institutions as well as museums and galleries.

new icons

London's cultural scene has an imposing permanence about it, its theatres and galleries seeming to date from time immemorial and – despite the shock of occasional closures – having the air of institutions that will grace the capital forever. Yet some of the capital's best-loved cultural venues are not so old, and have either been extensively reconstructed since the Second World War, or are in fact entirely new.

The Royal Opera House in Covent Garden was one such venerable fixture receiving a major facelift. Its origins lie in 1732, when its first manager John Rich used the not inconsiderable profits from putting on *The Beggar's Opera* to build a dedicated theatre. The structure itself proved vexingly flammable, burning down twice (in 1808 and 1856) before the present building was designed by E. M. Barry, the son of the architect of the new House of Commons. Over time, the facilities began to decay and by the 1980s the Floral Hall was virtually derelict. A major redevelopment announced in 1984 was given a huge boost by the awarding of a £55 million grant from the National Lottery. After a farewell concert in July 1997, the Opera House then closed for three years, and a refurbishment by architects Dixon and Jones was followed by a grand reopening in 2000. With improved technical and rehearsal spaces and new bars and restaurants in the Floral Hall, the Opera House now provides London with a facility ready to face the twenty-first century.

London's main classical concert venue in the years before the Second World War had been the Queen's Hall on Langham Place. Its destruction by an incendiary bomb on the last day of the Blitz in May 1941 left the capital without a world-class auditorium, and the Labour government of Clement Attlee lost little time in announcing in 1948 that, as part of the plans for the Festival of Britain, a new concert hall would be built on the South Bank. Attlee laid the foundation stone in October 1949 and eighteen months and £2 million later, the Royal Festival Hall opened with a concert attended by King George VI. Outside, its modernist architecture, a conscious attempt to escape the shackles of neo-classicism,

5,900,000
the number of visitors to the tate modern in 2019, making it the most popular tourist attraction in the uk

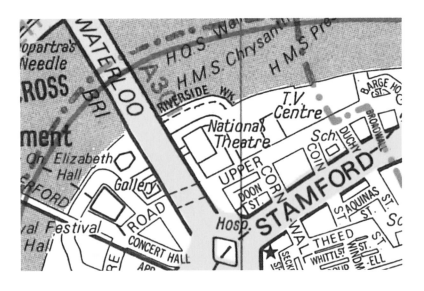

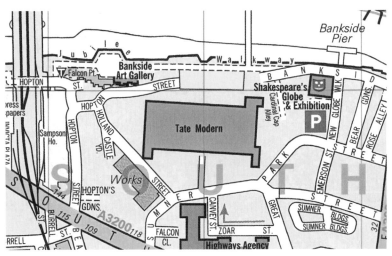

△
Two of Britain's new post-war cultural icons were located along the south bank of the River Thames: the National Theatre which finally opened in 1976 just by Waterloo Bridge, and the Tate Modern (formerly the Bankside Power Station) further east, between Blackfriars and Southwark Bridges.

would become progressively less loved as its concrete declined into middle-aged brutalism. Inside, however, the flowing spaces, designed to give audiences the freedom to roam foyers and floors where traditionally they were confined to cramped bars and the auditorium, gained more friends. The acoustics too won plaudits and a Harrison and Harrison organ, installed in 1954, with 7,700 pipes, added grandeur to its orchestra, the Royal Philharmonic – which took up residence there in 1992. The opening of the Queen Elizabeth Hall and the Purcell Room in 1967 then enriched London's most splendid classical music complex with two smaller venues.

The road to the construction of a National Theatre was a far more tortuous one. A movement to build a national theatrical auditorium began as early as 1902, and two sites were actually purchased: one behind the British Museum in 1913 and another opposite the V&A in 1937. The Second World War, however, prevented its construction and in 1942 the plot was swapped for land on the South Bank beside the future Royal Festival Hall. A foundation stone was actually laid there in July 1952, but the next year it was agreed that the site would move further eastwards. Following this, nothing was done, and in 1955 the critics Kenneth Tynan and Richard Finlater staged a mock funeral beside the foundation stone, in a gesture of frustration that the national theatre might never come to fruition.

The saga had a few twists yet, and in 1963 the National Theatre Company had its opening night (a staging of *Hamlet* with Peter O'Toole in the lead role), but it had been forced to take up residence at the Old Vic pending the building of its longed-for permanent home. The exile lasted thirteen years. In 1973 a new bill funding the National was passed by Parliament and on 16 March 1976, the Lyttleton, the first of the National Theatre's three auditoriums, finally opened, again with a performance of *Hamlet* (this time played by Albert Finney). The Olivier auditorium followed in October, and the inauguration of the Cottesloe completed the trio in March 1977. Since then the National, in a modernist, but rather more subdued building than the Royal Festival Hall, has showcased a wide theatrical repertoire and under directors such as Peter Hall and Trevor Nunn, has ensured London's reputation as an innovative centrepiece of English-language drama.

London, it seems, has no shortage of gallery exhibition space, but the Tate, with a remit that covered the more modern end of the artistic spectrum, chafed at the lack of space that it had in its Millbank gallery (now Tate Britain) to show more contemporary and European pieces. Its need coincided with the campaign to save the Bankside Power Station, a hulking

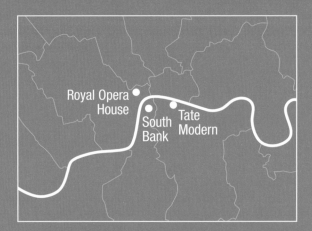

red-brick giant on the South Bank opposite St Paul's. Designed by Giles Gilbert Scott, its operational life had been comparatively short, with the first section opening in 1953 and the station being finally decommissioned in 1981. The Trustees of the Tate announced their intention to open a new gallery in December 1992, and sixteen months later the Bankside site was designated as the venue for the New Tate Modern. The architects Jacques Herzog and Pierre de Meuron began work on a complex conversion in 1995, and finally, just too late for the millennium celebrations, the new gallery opened in May 2000.

The space had been challenging. The massive turbine hall of the power station was retained as a venue for enormous installations, and a two-storey glass extension was added to the roof to house exhibition spaces. The Tate Modern, however, surpassed its founders' expectations and the crowds who came to see the latest in contemporary art and a series of imaginative installations made it clear that further expansion was needed. Part of the building that had been retained by the electricity company EDF was released to the Tate, and in 2016 a major new extension was constructed around the power station's old switch house (which was renamed the Blavatnik Building in 2017). By 2019, the Tate Modern had leapfrogged the British Museum to become London's most visited tourist site (with 5.9 million visitors, just ahead of the museum's 5.8 million). As the twenty-first century enters its third decade, London's newest cultural icons are proving that they have just as much allure as its old favourites.

film locations in london

London is a photogenic city, its vast spectrum of urban landscapes encompassing iconic historical landmarks, classic architecture, gritty down-at-heel districts and a fair sprinkling of greenery. It is therefore no surprise that it has provided the locations for a wealth of films, from the first ever colour film, shot by the Edwardian pioneer Edward Turner in 1902, which included street scenes in the capital and shots of his family's pet macaw, to ultra-futuristic epics such as *Thor: The Dark World* (2013) in which the convergence of the realms takes place at the Prime Meridian in Greenwich.

Plenty of movie action has been set against the backdrop of London landmarks. Doctor Who's great adversaries the Daleks were caught trundling across Westminster Bridge in 1964 in an early foray at galactic domination, while James Bond took part in an epic speed boat chase along the Thames in *The World Is Not Enough* (1999). Tower Bridge, meanwhile, has been the backdrop in a large number of London-set films, including *Tomb Raider*, *Mission: Impossible*, *The Mummy Returns* and *The Edge of Reason*.

A gentler, more humorous side to the English cinematic genre was showcased in *Passport to Pimlico* (1949), a whimsical example of the classic Ealing comedies, in which the residents of the Thameside district decide to defy Whitehall bureaucrats by declaring independence. Not in fact filmed in Pimlico at all, most of its scenes were shot in sets constructed on a bomb-damaged site in Lambeth on the other side of the river.

Several neighbourhoods genuinely have appeared in the films for which they were named. *Notting Hill* (1999) takes a loving look at a district that was just then emerging from struggling suburb to chic quarter, with a wealth of scenes including some showcasing Portobello Road and its market. *84 Charing Cross Road* (1987), which charts the interactions between an author and the chief buyer of a second-hand book shop, is a loving tribute to

at least 12
the number of times london has been destroyed in the movies

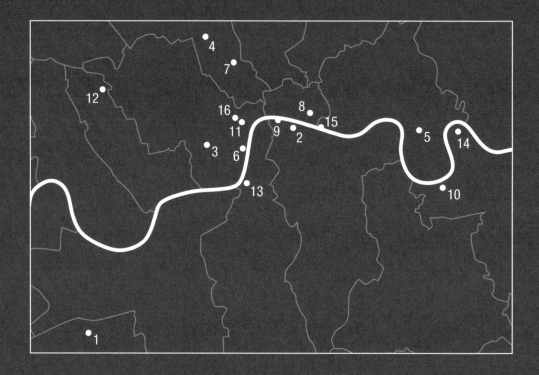

A selection of films set or filmed in Central London

1. All England Tennis Club
   Wimbledon

2. Borough Market
   Bridget Jones's Diary
   Harry Potter:
   The Prisoner of Azkaban

3. Buckingham Palace
   The BFG

4. Camden
   Eyes Wide Shut
   Four Weddings
   and a Funeral

5. Canary Wharf
   Star Wars: Rogue One

6. Houses of Parliament
   28 Days Later
   Suffragette

7. King's Cross
   Harry Potter

8. Leadenhall Market
   Harry Potter:
   The Philosopher's Stone

9. Millennium Bridge
   Harry Potter:
   The Half-Blood Prince

10. Old Royal Naval College,
    Greenwich
    Thor: The Dark World
    Les Misérables

11. Trafalgar Square
    Captain America
    V For Vendetta
    St Trinian's
    Edge of Tomorrow

12. Portobello Road Market
    Notting Hill

13. South Bank/MI6 Building
    Skyfall

14. The O$_2$
    The World is Not Enough

15. Tower Bridge
    Mission: Impossible
    The Mummy Returns
    Tomb Raider
    Bridget Jones:
    The Edge of Reason

16. Piccadilly Circus
    Harry Potter:
    Deathly Hallows I
    An American Werewolf
    in London

a narrow strip of London long dedicated to the bookselling trade (though the eponymous address is now a fast-food restaurant). And, while there is no Platform 9¾ at King's Cross Station (or at least none that we muggles can find), scenes from the Harry Potter series of films were shot at the Central London terminus from which the wizarding children depart for Hogwarts School of Witchcraft and Wizardry (while the external shots of Diagon Alley used Leadenhall Market to create just the right ambience).

Not fixed to a specific suburb, some films have nonetheless encapsulated an era in London's history. Michael Antonioni's seminal Sixties film *Blow Up* (1966) takes a photographer through a wide variety of London locations, including an arch just east of Peckham Rye station, the former El Blason restaurant off the King's Road (just then becoming the epicentre of Swinging London), and Maryon Park in Woolwich. Closer to the present day *Withnail and I* (1987) sets some grimly dark scenes in what purports to be Camden Town (but is actually Notting Hill) and includes high-speed scenes around the M25 near Rickmansworth, even though the motorway had not actually been built at the time the film purported to be set.

Horror and dystopian visions of London's future have provided enticing quarries for film directors drawn to the capital. In *An American Werewolf in London* (1981) a grizzly chase through darkened tunnels as a city broker is hunted down and savaged by a hungry lycanthrope, was filmed in tunnels at Tottenham Court Road tube station, while in *The Day the Earth Caught Fire* (1961), a cautionary tale about a mega-heatwave caused when an atom bomb sends the earth careening out of orbit towards the sun, was largely shot in the *Daily Express* office on Fleet Street. More darkly humorous, *Attack the Block* (2011) charts the adventures of a set of streetwise South London teenagers when aliens make the fatal mistake of invading Brixton, though the city comes off distinctly worse in *Hellraiser* (1987), in which a doorway to hell is inadvertently opened up in a suburban semi in Dollis Hill.

218-9 ▷

Sometimes it seems as though most of Central London has acted as a location in one or more films; from the gentle Ealing Comedy *Passport to Pimlico* in 1949, to the aspirational *Notting Hill* in 1999 and the altogether rougher-edged violence of *London Has Fallen* in 2016.

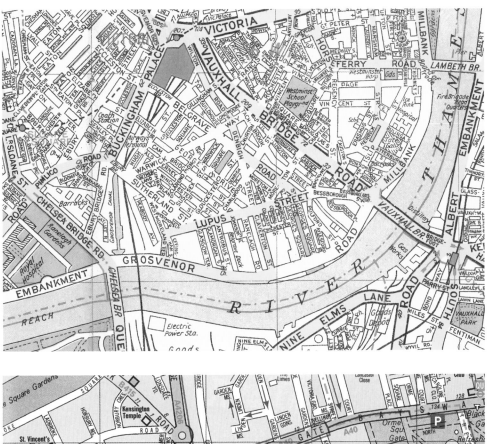

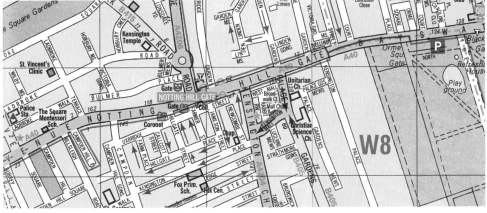

London has been destroyed around a dozen times by Hollywood filmmakers, including *28 Days* (2000), when it is overrun by flesh-eating zombies, *The Reign of Fire* (2002) in which it is reduced to a crisp by dragons, and *Mars Attacks!* (1996), when humanity's old adversaries from the red planet have another go at the capital. Yet if they keep obliterating it, directors keep coming back to set their stories in London. As Dr Johnson might have said, if a film director is tired of London, he is tired of life.

THE music scene

The capital's popular music scene was once confined to the streets, making Victorian (and most likely Shakespearean) London a riotous cacophony of organ grinders, singers and jobbing minstrels. It was only when formal venues began to grow up, with the explosion of organized leisure which characterized the late Victorian era, that we can begin to trace the careers of London's popular musicians.

Artists such as Marie Lloyd graced the stage of Victorian London's music halls, the showcases for acts which enthralled the masses: from her first appearances at the Theatre Royal, Drury Lane in the 1890s she encapsulated a kind of earthy romanticism with songs such as 'The Boy I Love is Up in the Gallery'. Lloyd and her successors continued to woo London audiences well into the twentieth century, leavened with singer-comedians such as George Formby and Flanders and Swann. Little, though, prepared the London music scene for the transformation that it would undergo in the 1950s.

Jazz had already taken a hold from the 1930s and the influx of American music that accompanied the GIs who were stationed in Britain during the Second World War accelerated this trend. In the aftermath of the war, pioneers such as Ronnie Scott began to experiment with jazz venues, culminating in the establishment of his club in a Soho basement in 1959. By then other musical strands had developed, starting with skiffle, which exploded onto the London scene in 1956.

These, though, were just the first wavelets of a great musical tide that engulfed London in the 1960s, with an explosion of youth culture and the rock and pop bands that underpinned it. By the middle of the decade the Beatles could routinely be seen at the Abbey Road Studios in North London, where most of their albums were recorded from 1962.

next-door neighbours
the composer george frideric handel and rock musician jimi hendrix on brook street – albeit two hundred years apart

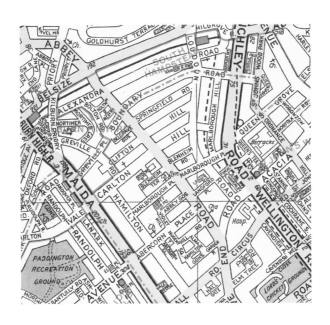

Denmark Street in Soho became known as 'Tin Pan Alley', the epicentre of a thriving music scene, where new music magazines such as *New Musical Express* and *Melody Maker*, appealing to a youth audience, had their offices. Studios sprang up in which Elton John and David Bowie recorded, while downstairs at street level music shops sold instruments, both to the aspiring and the adept (Bob Marley is said to have bought his first guitar in the Alley).

New venues emerged as popular music's appeal widened, such as the Marquee Club, which first opened on Oxford Street in 1958 and hosted the first live performance by The Rolling Stones in July 1962. Music also moved out of niche clubs and into more mainstream settings, such as the Roundhouse in Camden, a former railway shed, which opened for concerts in 1964, while a series of concerts in Hyde Park also featured the Rolling Stones in 1969. As the 1970s progressed, new musical genres appeared in London, including punk, which colonized the 100 Club, a former jazz venue on Oxford Street, while the 1980s brought the New Romantics, such as Culture Club, who could be heard at the Blitz Club on Queen Street.

The 1990s saw the birth of Britpop, with bands such as Blur and Suede playing London gigs, and Prime Minister Tony Blair extolling the virtues of 'Cool Britannia', a very marketable version of London culture aimed at exporting a vision of Britain that would perpetuate its reputation as the beating heart of pop music. Tourists today can explore any number of popular music circuits of the capital, taking in Abbey Road, Tin Pan Alley, perhaps popping into Berwick Street – home to a number of traditional vinyl music shops, and which appears on the cover of Oasis's second album *(What's the Story) Morning Glory?* – and maybe taking in an evening concert at London's new mega-venue, the O$_2$ at Greenwich (which took over the Millennium Dome once the twenty-first century had got into its stride). And those of a more historical bent can take in a wider arc of London musical history by visiting the house on Brook Street where the composer George Frideric Handel lodged between 1723 and 1759, and its next-door neighbour, where the rock musician Jimi Hendrix lived in 1969. It is the kind of serendipitous juxtaposition that makes a London musical odyssey such a joy.

◁ 221

Two London locations that lodged themselves firmly in the heart of London's youthful music fans in the 1960s were Abbey Road, in St John's Wood, where the Beatles recorded some of their best-known albums and Denmark Street in Soho, where one might bump into rock stars, music journalists or simply a music-lover in search of an electric guitar.

223 ▷

Melody Maker, one of Britain's oldest music magazines, was founded in the 1920s, but really came into its own in the 1960s, when it covered the new musical genres that swept the London scene. Early July 1969 was a busy time for music news, with Jimi Hendrix splitting with his bass guitarist Noel Redding and the Rolling Stones headlining at a gig at Hyde Park.

Melody Maker

JULY 5, 1969   1s weekly

HENDRIX AND REDDING, parting company

Exclusive!

STONES AT HYDE PARK

WHAT YOU'LL SEE
WHAT YOU'LL HEAR

'and if you can, bring a drum or a tambourine even a tin to bang on or something,' urges Mick Jagger

TURN TO PAGE 4 AND CENTRE PAGES

Hendrix split: Redding goes, group grows

MITCHELL: may return

PLANS by Jimi Hendrix to enlarge his Experience have led to British bass guitarist Noel Redding quitting the group.

Noel decided to end his association with Hendrix, begun in September 1967, last weekend. The crux of the split, it appears, is that he was not consulted by Jimi over his plans to expand the group from a trio into a "creative commune" which would include writers as well as more musicians.

Chas Chandler, ex-manager and record producer of the Experience, said at

MITCH MITCHELL'S PLANS UNKNOWN

presstime that Noel was expected to return to London from the States at the end of this week to discuss his future.

Said Chandler: "Obviously it is too early to make any statement until we have had a chance to sit down and work things out, but there are a lot of exciting possibilities for Noel."

When he was last in London, Noel said he expected to stay with the Experience until September, at least.

It is not yet known whether drummer Mitch Mitchell will remain with Hendrix or also return to Britain.

Noel Redding's own group, Fat Mattress, have been set for the 9th National Jazz And Blues Festival — renamed the London Jazz Blues And Pop Festival — at West Drayton, Middlesex, on Saturday, August 9 (see Page 2).

Hendrix is currently reported to be grossing over 100,000 dollars a night on his appearances in the States.

The Hendrix Experience last played in Britain in February when they gave a sell-out concert at the Royal Albert Hall.

What the disc price war means to you

Record prices took a dive following the ending last weekend of Resale Price Maintenance. One chain of London retailers immediately marked down singles to 30s for four (instead of 34s) as previously. And ten shillings was knocked off LPs. The recent Beatles double album was being sold fifteen shillings cheaper — £3 instead of for £3 15s. For the full story

see page 3

london fashion

With its vast array of boutiques, mainstream fashion retailers, independents, designers and a less constrictive atmosphere than most other major capitals, London is an undoubted global leader in international fashion. It was not always so – the British capital long chafed in the shadow of its French rival, with 'Paris fashion' being considered the epitome of clothing.

Nonetheless, tailors and craftsmen established themselves in Savile Row and Jermyn Street from the 1750s as a particular sense of British style began to develop which, despite bouts of flamboyance, became progressively more staid and controlled as the Victorian era progressed. The latest fashions began to be more accessible to middle-class Edwardians with the opening of large department stores such as Selfridges in 1909, where ready-made garments could be purchased without the need for bespoke tailoring.

The Second World War brought a more utilitarian style to fashion, shortages of material militating against the more expansive femininity of the pre-war period. There was in turn a further reaction once the conflict was over, with Christian Dior's New Look, launched in 1947 with large swirling skirts and sweeping necklines. Yet the London fashion scene could not yet be said to be dynamic, dominated as it was by a smaller number of established names such as Norman Hartnell and Hardy Amies.

It was the birth of youth culture in the late 1950s that gave the London fashion scene a much-needed shot in the arm. First, young men adopted a neo-Edwardian style with velvet-trimmed draped jackets and drainpipe trousers, with extravagant coiffed hairstyles. These Teddy Boys clashed on Bank Holiday weekends at the beach with their Mod rivals, who instead affected a European-influenced style with smart, slim tailored suits or parka jackets and polo shirts.

London now found its fashion heart for the first time as Carnaby Street emerged from the early 1960s as a centre for cheap youth fashion, and where rock icons such as Jimi Hendrix and the Beatles could be seen shopping for clothes. The Kings Road offered a more considered, chic style, with the springing up of a series of boutiques, beginning with

£28,000,000,000
the fashion industry's contriburion to the uk economy in 2017

Mary Quant's Bazaar in 1955. The area reached the height of its fashion influence after Barbara Hulanicki opened Biba on nearby Abingdon Road in 1964, and now young women, in particular, had unparalleled access to innovative styles at an affordable price.

London was now 'Swinging London' (the title of an edition on the city that *Time* published in April 1966) and it retained its edge through all the subsequent changes in style: with the move in 1976 to punk, an edgier, darker musical and fashion strand, which was self-consciously iconoclastic, with leather, safety pins, spikes and extraordinary hair styles all featuring in its repertoire. London boutiques and fashion houses followed the rest of the world in the 1980s with big hair and shoulder pads, and renewed itself with a new wave of designers, such as Katharine Hamnett (who picked up the Designer of the Year award at the first London Fashion week in 1984) and Jasper Conran, to be followed in turn by a fresh generation, such as Stella McCartney.

By 2017, the fashion industry was directly contributing £28 billion pounds to the British economy, much of it flowing through London. As well as dressing Londoners in whatever style they desired, fashion made it rich.

△
By the mid-1960s London's fashion boutique scene was diversifying from the Kings Road, with the opening by Barbara Hulanicki of Biba on Abingdon Road in 1964 part of a trend that would see boutiques become mainstream.

DIVERSE LONDON

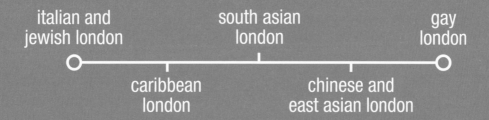

italian and
jewish london

south asian
london

gay
london

caribbean
london

chinese and
east asian london

italian AND jewish london

Although migrant communities have enhanced the demographic and cultural diversity of London for centuries, two in particular – the Italians and Jews – have a claim to be to the capital's most long-standing minority groups. In one sense, indeed, the Italians were the original Londoners in the form of the Roman soldiers who founded it as Londinium around AD 50.

The Romans did not stay, and the Italian merchants and craftsmen who drifted back in the Middle Ages, a group of goldsmith-bankers giving their name to Lombard Street in the City, were a tiny community. It was not until the nineteenth century that increasing numbers of Italians moved to Britain, in part impelled by the political uncertainty and agrarian crises that accompanied the birth of a united Italy in 1871. By 1915 there were nearly 20,000 of them in Britain, the majority in London, centred around a colony in Clerkenwell, where they were employed in trades such as organ grinding, the manufacture of mosaic and terrazzo surfaces, and food retailing.

The early 1920s marked the nadir of Italian immigration, but a golden age for the community itself, as it diversified and its members began to open their own businesses (the 1931 census recorded 2,000 Italian waiters, but also 1,183 restaurant owners). The heart of Italian London began to move from its old Clerkenwell haunts – where the annual procession of the Madonna del Carmine had been a central focus since 1883 – northwards

131,000
the number of italian-born residents in the capital in 2011

and into Soho, where some of London's oldest Italian restaurants opened (notably Quo Vadis in 1926).

The advent of Fascism was a disaster for Italian Londoners. At first it seemed to offer a sense of belonging, as Mussolini promoted the idea of a worldwide family of Italians, and the *Fascii*, the Fascist clubs, offered a secular focus for cultural life (with the Italian fascio in London opening in 1921). In the 1930s in particular, when British Fascism was on the march in urban areas, the fact that large numbers of Italians joined the fascio (even though they were in no way politically committed Fascists) did not seem out of step with the times.

It proved a catastrophic misjudgement. The British press, its nationalistic and patriotic instincts accentuated by the outbreak of the Second World War, rounded on the Italians – as the *Daily Mirror* put it in April 1940, 'We are nicely honeycombed with little cells of potential betrayal'. Worse was to come: when the Italian dictator Mussolini gave a thunderous speech declaring war on 10 June 1940, the London mob reacted furiously with a round of xenophobic riots in large part directed at the Italian community. At a stroke the Italians became enemy aliens and all men and boys between 16 and 60 were arrested – thousands of them in London – and interned on the Isle of Man. Around 750, who were deemed especially undesirable, were sent to Canada on the *Arandora Star*, only to be sunk by a German U-Boat on 2 July 1940. About 450 Italians died, and many of the survivors were shipped far out of sight to Australia.

The Italian community recovered slowly after the war – many businesses had been lost and some changed their name as their owners still felt uncomfortable being identified with a recent enemy power. Cheaper Italian restaurants and trattorias, however, began to proliferate in Soho, as well as the first coffee bar, the Moka, which opened in 1953 and began London's long-standing love affair with espressos and cappuccinos. Those Italians who migrated to London often came through 'chain migration', invited or encouraged by relatives who had made the move earlier.

By the early 1980s, Greater London had 30,000 Italian-born residents, and an overall population of Italian origin of around 100,000. The accession of the United Kingdom to the European Community and the opportunities it offered for freedom of movement to find work led to a rise in the number of Italians in London – in common with many other nationalities from Europe – and the 2011 census recorded 131,000 Italian-born residents

◁

Soho became a focus for the Italian community in the 1860s, and many cheap Italian restaurants were established there, a trend which accelerated in the 1930s. In the 1950s, the first Italian style coffee bars opened up, including Bar Italia, which has been in business for over 60 years.

in the capital. Resident in a wide sweep of London boroughs, and working in occupations as diverse as finance and the restaurant trade, they are the true heirs of their long-distant ancestors who founded London in the first place.

The Jewish community in London might well be as venerable as the Italian. It is more than likely that some Jews came to Britain during the 368-year Roman occupation, but they have left no trace, and so it is only after the Norman Conquest of 1066 that there are certain indications of a small Jewish settlement (though it was expelled by Edward I in 1290, only to be allowed back under the regime of Oliver Cromwell in 1656). Just as for the Italians, it was political crises in the late nineteenth century that brought a surge of Jewish migration to London, although the motive was more pressing. The anti-Semitic persecution and pogroms that swept across Eastern Europe and Russia from 1882 led the Jewish population in Britain to swell from 46,000 in 1882 to 250,000 in 1919, most of them in London.

The newcomers clustered in the East End, London's traditional gateway for the downtrodden arrivals. Many of them set up in the garment industry, cabinet-making or other retailing businesses, establishing a reputation for entrepreneurial flair, and their increasing numbers supported a thriving culture flowing from their native Yiddish. Storm clouds began to gather, however, in the early 1930s, as the rise of the British Union of Fascists (BUF) led to a spike in anti-Semitism, first with sporadic attacks on the burgeoning number of synagogues in the East End, and then with anti-Jewish meetings and marches through Jewish districts. These culminated in the Battle of Cable Street, in which an alliance of Jewish and Socialist activists kept a Fascist column from marching though their district *(see page 36)*.

Although the Public Order Act of 1936 banned marches through areas of the East End with a large Jewish population, Fascism flourished regardless – with the BUF candidates gaining 23 per cent of the poll in London County Council elections in Bethnal Green.

The rise of Adolf Hitler's Nazi regime turned British opinion away from Fascism, but this domestic respite was marred by external tragedy, as the German government's anti-Semitic stance targeted Jews in German-controlled territories with increasingly oppressive legal measures and finally with incarceration in labour and death camps. Although the British government was reluctant to take large numbers of Jewish refugees, some 50,000 from Germany and Austria were permitted to enter, alongside 40,000 Jews fleeing from Italy, Poland and Eastern Europe, and 10,000 unaccompanied children who were brought in on the *Kindertransport* scheme, and whose numbers included the future Nobel laureate in chemistry Walter Kohn and the painter Frank Auerbach.

This new wave of forced migrants tended to settle outside the traditional Jewish East End (many of whose residents had in any case decamped by the 1930s to Hackney and Stoke Newington) and they instead settled further north in Hampstead, Golders Green

and Hendon, which became post-war London's best-known Jewish suburbs. As the Jewish population increased still further, to a peak of around 400,000 in the 1950s, they moved even further afield, including a large Hasidic community, some 30,000 strong, which grew up in Stamford Hill, now the largest such observant Hasidic community in Europe.

From the 1950s, however, the Jewish population of London entered a steady decline. The establishment of the state of Israel in 1948 led some to migrate – sapping around 500 to 1,000 each year from the community's numbers – and intermarriage and the secularization that affected society more generally took its toll. By the 2011 census, only 263,000 people defined themselves as Jewish, but the life of the community in London was still exceptionally vibrant, with over 450 synagogues (including the oldest, Bevis Marks in the City, in continuous use since 1701), successful Jewish secondary schools such as JFS and JCOSS, and a wide range of cultural institutions. Nearly a thousand years on from their first recorded appearance in the capital, Jews are still quintessential Londoners.

△
The East End, and in particular the area around Whitechapel, was long the heart of Jewish London. From the 1930s, Jewish families moved out to suburbs further north, such as Hampstead, Golders Green, Barnet and Stamford Hill, with relatively few remaining in the East End.

caribbean london

Black Londoners have been present in the capital from its earliest years; tests on skeletons unearthed at a Roman cemetery in Southwark dating from AD 50 to 70 showed that some had skeletal features or DNA consistent with an African origin. Their numbers, though, were probably small. Even after contacts with sub-Saharan Africa increased during the age of exploration in the fifteenth and sixteenth centuries, bringing seamen, slaves and servants – such as those who accompanied Catherine of Aragon when she came to marry Henry VIII in 1509 – the community in London remained tiny.

The seventeenth and eighteenth centuries brought disaster to Africa in the form of European involvement in the slave trade, which transported millions of black Africans to a life of servitude in the Americas, but also installed populations of African origin in the Caribbean, from where future black migration to Britain would principally come. Some ended up in London, too, whether in service to European masters, or as sailors who never returned home: in the 1770s Lord Mansfield estimated their population was around 10,000. They lived in a sort of limbo, not quite recognized as citizens, but also in a legal environment where slavery was not recognized. In 1772 the Somerset case ruled that a black fugitive former slave could not be made to leave England against his will, providing a sort of minimum protection under the law.

Living mainly in the traditional migrant quarters of Mile End, Poplar and Stepney, London's black population remained of modest size throughout the eighteenth and nineteenth centuries, though it did produce some high-profile members such as the anti-slavery campaigners Ignatius Sancho and Olaudah Equiano – whose autobiography recounting his experiences as a slave was published in 1789 – and the pioneering nurse Mary Seacole, whose work during the Crimean War is often overshadowed by that of her

42,000
the number of caribbean immigrants in 1957

white counterpart Florence Nightingale. The illustrious career of black Londoners in sport began a little later in Edwardian times, when footballer Walter Tull became the first player of mixed race to play for a club in the capital, after he signed for Tottenham Hotspur in 1909.

The First World War brought a small growth in the number of black residents in London, as more merchant seamen arrived, but in 1950 the community probably numbered fewer than 20,000. All that changed with the labour shortages that followed the Second World War. Suddenly London needed more workers, and it needed them fast. Word spread to the Caribbean of the likelihood of finding employment, and on 22 June 1948, 492 Caribbean migrants arrived at Tilbury Docks aboard the Empire Windrush. The new arrivals were initially housed in a former air-raid shelter at Clapham South, before dispersing to areas such as Notting Hill and Brixton, where landlords of poor quality private housing were prepared to rent them rooms.

More followed throughout the 1950s, swelling the Caribbean-born population of London to 21,000 by 1951, and with 42,000 arriving in 1957 alone. Although the immigrants found jobs on the buses, in the National Health Service and on the railways (London Transport had begun recruitment in Jamaica and Barbados in 1956), they frequently had to accept positions for which they were overqualified: around 22 per cent of West Indian migrants had worked in unskilled or semi-skilled jobs back home, but this rose to 63 per cent after they arrived in Britain. They also met with racism, often overt, as existing residents accused them of taking jobs, houses, or worse.

An unhappy record of London race riots began in Notting Hill in 1958, after attacks by local white youths on the Caribbean community flared up into violence. The starting up of the Notting Hill Carnival that year (initially an indoor affair) was part of an effort to repair relations, which at first bore little fruit. Local authorities installed effective colour bars to social housing by insisting on a qualification of up to fifteen years' residence before receiving a council house; some local politicians campaigned on openly racist platforms;

234 ▷

Brixton, home to a large Afro-Caribbean population, saw serious rioting in 1981 and 1985 after relations between the police and the black community broke down. For a time the area around Railton Road became known as 'the front line'.

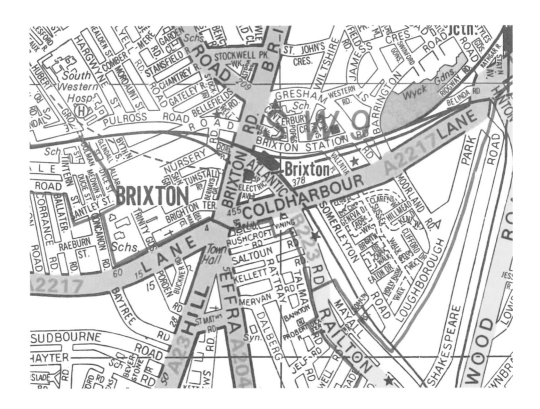

and in 1968 the Conservative MP Enoch Powell made an incendiary speech in which he warned of 'rivers of blood' if migration were allowed to continue unchecked.

The British government had already bowed to this pressure and in 1962 enacted the Commonwealth Immigrants Act, which set in place controls that became gradually more stringent, until by 1972 only those with a work permit, or parents or grandparents born in the United Kingdom, could enter the country. Those already settled faced growing economic problems in the 1970s and 1980s, and unemployment among children of Caribbean families soared until it was three or four times that of white school leavers. Poor quality housing, limited educational opportunities, lack of access to jobs, often harsh police tactics and the rise of racist organisations such as the National Front (which in GLC elections in Newham in 1974 gained a quarter of the votes in several wards) led to an incendiary atmosphere. Riots broke out in Brixton in 1981 and in Brixton and Tottenham in 1985, the spark often provided by a confrontation with police (in 1985 two elderly black women died: one shot by the police in Brixton and the other during a police raid on her house, fuelling community anger).

The aftermath of the raids, which caused millions of pounds of damage in already depressed areas, led to hard questions. A report led by Lord Scarman following the 1981 Brixton riots called for closer police involvement with local communities, while the Macpherson Inquiry, established to investigate policing practices after the racially motivated murder of black teenager Stephen Lawrence in 1993, concluded in its 1999 report that the Metropolitan Police had been 'institutionally racist'. For the first time black political activists came to national prominence and, though Richard Archer had become London's first black mayor as long ago as 1913 when he was elected in Battersea, it was only now that MPs of Afro-Caribbean origin entered Parliament, with Diane Abbott, Bernie Grant and Paul Boateng becoming the first to be elected in 1987.

London's black community today is spread amongst all its boroughs, and the 2011 census found that just over a million people of Black African and Caribbean origin lived in the capital, making up 27 per cent of the population in Lewisham and Southwark and 26 per cent in Lambeth. The community still faces immense challenges in combating racism and in ensuring adequate opportunities for its young people (in 2003 only 23 per cent of Black Caribbean pupils achieved a C grade or above in GCSEs compared to 42 per cent of white British pupils). Yet with a vibrant cultural scene, of which the annual Notting Hill Carnival is only the most high-profile event; with cohesion strong, helped by attendance at black churches (which draw on a strong evangelical tradition with Caribbean roots); and with its members achieving a profile in sport, business, the media and professions of which their grandparents could only dream, black Londoners can rightly celebrate a two millennium-long presence in the capital.

south asian london

The ties between London and the Indian subcontinent are long-standing, with the East India Company, which from 1600 pioneered the British economic – and then its political – domination of India, having its headquarters on Leadenhall Street in the heart of the City of London.

The numbers of Indians who came to London, however, were small, and those who stayed even fewer still. Most were seamen, in large part *lascars* from the Sylhet region of Bangladesh, together with a sprinkling of sailors from Mirpur in Kashmir. Their conditions were poor, often with no fixed contract of employment – in 1857 the Strangers' Home for Asiatics, African and South Sea Islanders was opened by Joseph Salter in Limehouse to provide aid for sailors who had been abandoned by their employers. There were also tensions with other rival migrant groups as they jostled for what few jobs there were: in 1806 there was a riot between 200 *lascars* and Chinese sailors in Wapping.

Despite the small numbers of Indians resident in London – probably no more than a few hundred by 1900 – many of them achieved positions of prominence. In 1892 Dadabhai Naoroji was returned as Liberal MP for Finsbury, becoming the first ever MP of South Asian origin in the United Kingdom, while in 1922 the trade union activist Shapurji Saklatvala was elected MP for Battersea.

In the First World War, around 1.5 million Indians fought in the Allied forces, and a trickle came to Britain, taking jobs in factories such as the Tate sugar refinery at Silvertown, whose European workers had been sent to the front. Once the war was over many went home, though there were race riots in London in 1919 when some remained. Even so, the 1939 Hunter report estimated there were between two and three thousand Indians in London.

1,500,000
the number of londoners of indian, pakistani, bangladeshi or sri lankan origin

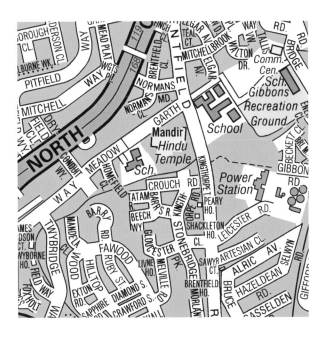

This number expanded enormously after the Second World War, in which even more Indians fought for the British (around 2.5 million). Shortages of labour in industries such as transport (particularly on the buses and at Heathrow Airport), the new NHS and the textile industries led to significant numbers coming to Britain, a movement accentuated by the distress in the chaotic aftermath of Indian partition in 1947. New migrants came in particular from the Punjab, from Mirpur in Pakistan – especially after the building of the Mangla Dam in 1966 inundated part of the district – and from Bangladesh after the civil war and conflict with India that led to its independence in 1971. The first wave, in particular, consisted of young men from modest backgrounds, many of whom had served in the police and armed forces.

The new arrivals faced deep-seated prejudices and tended to cluster in particular areas, finding employment in a small number of industries such as tailoring and catering (as well as over 1,000 South Asian doctors who served in the NHS at its inception in 1948). Many of the Bangladeshis started Indian restaurants and takeaways (although London's oldest, the Veeraswamy off Regent Street, was opened in 1926 by an Anglo-Indian army officer named

△
The Shri Swaminarayan Mandir in Neasden, completed in 1995, was the first example of a traditional stone Hindu temple constructed in Europe. It was built using 5,000 tons of marble and limestone, which was all hand-carved in India before being shipped to London.

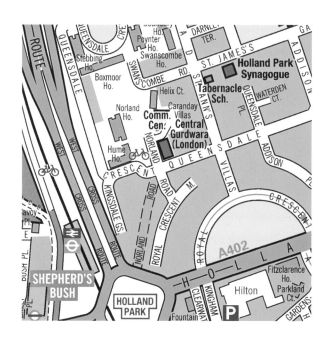

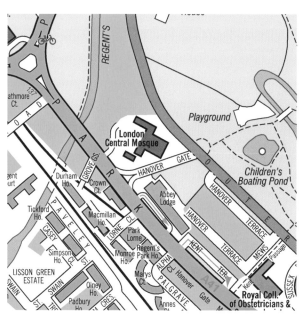

Edward Palmer) and many Sikhs from the Punjab found employment at Heathrow Airport. This Sikh community coalesced around Southall; while Harrow and its neighbouring boroughs became a centre for the Indian Hindu community; Newham, Redbridge and Waltham Forest in East London received large numbers of Pakistanis; and Tower Hamlets and the East End continued its long-standing tradition as a destination for migrant groups with the arrival of substantial groups of Bangladeshis.

These growing communities needed services. These ranged from shops providing a taste of home – Taj Stores, the first Bengali grocery store, opened in the East End in 1936 – to places of worship. The first purpose-built mosque was the Fazi Mosque in Southfields, which opened in 1926. As the Muslim population of London grew, further places of worship were established, most notably the Central London Mosque, with its striking golden dome, on which work was completed in 1977. The Hindu community's first dedicated place of worship was the Shree Ganapathy Temple, opened in Wimbledon in 1981, but further, grander temples were built, culminating in the completion of the Shri Swaminarayan Mandar in Neasden, the first traditional stone-built Hindu temple in the United Kingdom, in 1995. The Sikh community's first place of worship in London was built much earlier than this, as the Khalsa Jatha Gurdwara in Southall opened its gates in 1908, the first of around 300 in the UK.

Today there are around one and a half million Londoners of Indian, Pakistani, Bangladeshi or Sri Lankan origin. They are spread out across all the London boroughs (though still with notable concentrations in the northwest, west and east) and throughout a range of employment and professions. Their presence continues a history of South Asian Londoners that now stretches back almost half a millennium.

◁ top
The Khalsa Jatha Gurdwara is the oldest Sikh place of worship in Europe. Originally in Putney, it moved to the current building in Shepherd's Bush in 1969.

◁ bottom
London's Central Mosque was built on land near Regent's Park donated in 1944 by the British government to the Muslim community. The present building, designed by Frederick Gibberd, was completed in 1977.

chinese AND east asian london

Chinatown in London's Soho is a vibrant place, its heart in Gerrard Street resounding to the colour and hubbub of dragon dances at Chinese New Year and fringed with Chinese restaurants. Yet it was not the capital's original Chinatown, which had its origin in the 1780s when Chinese sailors began to visit the port aboard tea-carrying ships. They settled down by the docks at Limehouse, creating a small community by the 1850s, which then began to spread out towards Deptford and Woolwich.

By 1911, the Limehouse Chinatown had more than thirty Chinese businesses – including restaurants and laundries – but the 1905 Aliens Act, which for the first time imposed immigration controls, together with the gradual decline of the shipping industry, meant that the numbers of new arrivals between the First and Second World Wars were small. The extensive destruction inflicted on the East End by German bombing caused the community to disperse, heading into Central London. There, enterprising Chinese businessmen began to buy restaurants, catering for more adventurous theatregoers, and building on the pioneer Soho Chinese establishments set up around 1908 (various establishments lay claim to being the first, including Maxim's and the Cathay off Piccadilly Circus).

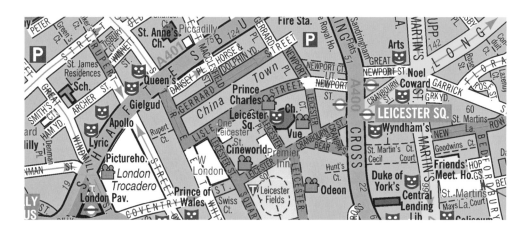

90
the percentage of chinese londoners in employment working in the restaurant trade as recently as 1985

The Chinese community remained focused on the restaurant trade – as late as 1985, some 90 per cent of Chinese Londoners with employment worked in it in some guise. At first the area gained a reputation for crime, rife with vice and gambling dens, but by the 1980s this was cleared up, making Chinatown an attractive tourist destination. Many in the community, however, remained isolated by language, with limited English and trapped within the confines of a Cantonese-speaking environment.

By the 1990s the Chinese community was becoming more diverse. Refugees arriving from Vietnam were often of ethnic Chinese origin and the preponderance of Hong Kong Chinese who had previously made up the bulk of Chinese migrants were replaced by groups coming from mainland China, some of them as students. This led to additional linguistic tension, as many of the newcomers spoke Mandarin, or other mainland languages such as Fujianese, cutting them off from the Cantonese-speaking mainstream. Many, too, were undocumented migrants, with no paperwork to allow them secure residence and, living on the margins of society, they were vulnerable to suffering working conditions every bit as poor as their nineteenth-century predecessors had endured.

London's Chinese community branched out from its traditional Soho haunts, moving into less central boroughs, but still with large concentrations in Barnet, Camden, Westminster, Islington and Southwark. The 2001 census recorded some 80,000 people of Chinese origins in London. Fewer are now employed in the catering trade, with less than half now working in the business; many are in professional jobs, and the children of Chinese families register the best examination results of any ethnic group.

Servicing this growing and successful community is a wide range of institutions, from the ubiquitous restaurants and Chinese grocery businesses to a number of temples, both Confucian (beginning with the very first in Limehouse around 1900) and Buddhist (such as the Fo Guang Shan temple just off Oxford Street, founded in 1992), and facilities such as the London Chinatown Community Centre, established in 1980. Although comparatively small in number, London's Chinese community continues to contribute to the diversity, wealth and culinary delights of the capital.

◁

Gerrard Street forms the heart of London's Chinatown. Its many restaurants serve both the Chinese community, non-Chinese Londoners and tourists, and the street is the scene of enthusiastic celebrations, including dragon dancers, at Chinese New Year.

gay london

Homosexuality in London was long forced to exist in the shadows. The general antipathy of the Christian church meant that, even where a blind eye was turned to homosexuals among the elite, persecution was the lot for those less powerful. There are records in medieval London of actions taken against gay Londoners – such as the arrest in 1394 of John Rykenor, a transvestite prostitute going by the name of Eleanor – but the legal situation was not clarified until the reign of Henry VIII, when the 1533 Buggery Act criminalized sexual relations between men.

Although fashions at court sometimes allowed limited toleration (James I was rumoured to have had a string of relationships with young men) and 'molly houses' proliferated in Georgian London, such as that started by Margaret Clap in Holborn in 1724, the treatment of homosexuals who came to the attention of the law could be brutal. Three men apprehended at Margaret Clap's house were hanged in 1726, and as late as 1835 two men were executed at Newgate for homosexuality. An offence of gross indecency introduced in 1885 caught more gay Londoners in its net, and in 1895 even as high-profile a figure as the playwright Oscar Wilde was sentenced to two years' imprisonment with hard labour in Reading jail.

The twentieth century brought some level of relief, at least in the profile of homosexuality and the options available to gay Londoners, as the first overtly gay pub, The Cave of the Golden Calf, opened on Heddon Street (off Regent Street) and the publication of *The Well of Loneliness* by Radclyffe Hall in 1928 daringly raised awareness of lesbianism among the

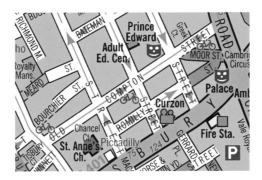

1967

the year sexual relations in private between men over 21 were decriminalized

general public. Yet the authorities continued to pursue homosexuals, actively entrapping men who were seeking same-sex companionship, even those in the upper echelons of society; in 1953, the actor John Gielgud was arrested for soliciting in a public lavatory and the following year the eminent mathematician Alan Turing, who had contributed immeasurably to Britain's Second World War codebreaking efforts, committed suicide after being prosecuted for his homosexuality.

The pressure for reform increased, and in 1957 the Wolfenden Report proposed that homosexuality should be decriminalized. Resistance to the measure amongst tradition-alist politicians and more conservative elements of society was fierce, and the Homosexual Law Reform Society was established in the same year to begin the long struggle of lobbying for the law to be changed. It was not until 1967 that the Sexual Offences Bill was passed, removing the offence of sexual relations between men over 21 in private (which still made it in theory illegal in a hotel, a piece of discrimination only removed in 2000).

The next two decades brought both progress and retrograde measures. The first Gay Pride rally took place in 1972, its 1,000 marchers just the vanguard of the far greater numbers who would attend by the twenty-first century, and *Gay News*, Britain's pioneering newspaper for the homosexual community, was first published the same year. Although homosexuality began to be accepted in public life, with Chris Smith becoming the first openly gay MP in 1984, the introduction in 1988 of Clause 28, which banned local authorities from disseminating information about homosexuality or allowing teaching about it in schools, marked a backward step. The emergence of a strong gay community centred on Soho's Old Compton Street and slightly further afield – with gay pubs such as the Bricklayers Arms and Fitzroy Tavern – did not dispel the anti-homosexual violence that bubbled way beneath the surface. This took a sinister turn with the bombing of the Admiral Duncan, a well-known gay pub, by a far-right militant in April 1999, killing three people.

By then, however, the age of gay consent had been reduced to 18 in 1994 (although it was not lowered to parity with those in heterosexual relationships until 2000). Over the next few years, further legal discrimination against homosexuals was removed, with the repeal of Section 28 in 2003 and the passing of the Civil Partnership Act in 2004 allowing for a legally binding form of partnership between same-sex couples (which was extended to marriage in 2013). As a result, by 2019, although social forms of discrimination persisted, gay Londoners faced as level a legal playing field in living their lives as at any time over the preceding two millennia.

◁

Old Compton Street in Soho became the heart of London's gay and LGBT culture. The street and roads around it house bars, clubs and restaurants catering to the community (including the Admiral Duncan, which was the scene of a far-right bombing in 1999).

LONDON LOCATIONS

covent garden

canary wharf and
the isle of dogs

clerkenwell

the city of london

thames gateway

thamesmead

nine elms

surrey quays

hendon aerodrome
and the raf museum
at colindale

king's cross

paddington basin

covent garden

It takes a keen eye to note the difference between the 1936 map of Covent Garden and its modern equivalent. The market is still there, the road layout is unchanged – perhaps the presence of the London Transport Museum is a clue. In truth, on the ground the difference is both trivial and immense. There is still the bustle of thousands of keen bargain hunters flocking to one of London's key markets, regaled by entertainers from the space in front of St Paul's neo-classical frontage. Yet these twenty-first-century market-goers are not on the hunt for the vegetables and flowers that were Covent Garden's traditional staples. Instead, they are predominantly foreign tourists, here to soak in the atmosphere of an authentically recreated market, one specializing in crafts and souvenirs more aimed at gifts for loved ones than at provisions for the dinner table.

Covent Garden's journey to prime tourist destination – it pulls in about fifteen million visitors a year – has been a long one, but trading has always been at its heart. The area between the modern piazza and the Strand has been home to merchants since Anglo-Saxon times (and their remains have been found at Jubilee Hall and Maiden Lane). Over time it became a garden belonging to the monks of Westminster Abbey (from which its name, a corruption of 'Convent Garden', derives). When Henry VIII dissolved the monasteries in the 1530s, he gave the land to John Russell, the 1st Earl of Bedford, whose family continued to control Covent Garden until 1918.

The Russells built Bedford House on the south side of the square in 1627, and in 1631 the fourth Earl commissioned Inigo Jones to construct an elegant piazza influenced by Italian models, ringed with portico houses in which he hoped aristocratic tenants would congregate. The future turned out very differently. The market that began in 1670, while it brought life to the area, also marked the beginning of a steady downward spiral in the area's social standing. By the mid-seventeenth century, Floral Street was already occupied by tailors, barbers and several licensed victuallers, and the opening of a number of coffee houses around 1700 was followed by gambling dens (in which the writers Henry Fielding and Oliver Goldsmith habitually played), drinking houses and brothels. The immediate hinterland of the market declined too, until by the time of Charles Dickens in the mid-nineteenth century, nearby Seven Dials was one of London's most notorious slums.

1662
the year in which the first punch and judy show was performed – at the piazza

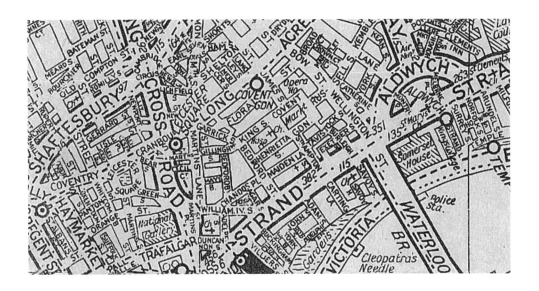

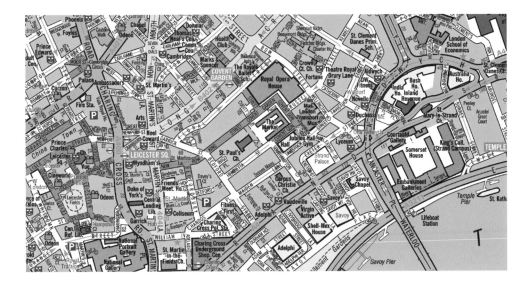

△
Although the street grid around Covent Garden has remained unmodified since the 1930s (despite the ambitions of planners in the 1960s to run several major roads through the district), on the ground the area has been transformed; resounding now to the chatter of tourists and the strumming of buskers in place of the cries of market traders and porters.

The market, at least, prospered, acquiring a formal building built by Charles Fowler on neo-classical lines in 1828-30, which was roofed over in 1872 to provide additional accommodation and shelter from the elements. The building and nearby Floral Hall and Jubilee Hall resounded to the cries of hawkers and market porters for nearly 150 years, but the increase in vehicle traffic after the Second World War and the difficulty of access through narrow lanes to the wider thoroughfares of the Strand and Long Acre gradually choked off its business. By the 1960s, the market was palpably dying, and a plan was announced in 1966 to move all its business to a new site at Nine Elms, south of the Thames near Battersea.

The question then arose of what to do with the market area. It would still have the Opera House, first established in 1732 and by then in its third incarnation after two fires in the nineteenth century. But with a large void at its centre, it risked becoming an urban sinkhole. The plan for its regeneration in 1971 was premised on the supremacy of the car, calling for two side roads to be cut through, parallel to the Strand and Shorts Gardens, and the addition of a large sports centre straddling Long Acre to service the new residents the planners hoped to build houses for. Much of the area bordering the piazza itself was to be demolished. There was an outcry locally; it looked as if the area was to be divided up into islands separated by traffic, ruining the precious unity of Covent Garden. The Government, startled by the outcry, rejected most elements of the plan in January 1973. As a result, the central market buildings were preserved – and the Floral Hall experienced a late reprieve to become the home of the London Transport Museum in 1980. The same year, after a century of internal alterations by store-holders had been swept away and a well excavated into the basement to allow for additional retail space, the market reopened. In its new incarnation it was designed to pull tourists – and their money – into an area that now lay badly in need of regeneration.

The gamble was a success. Covent Garden is now on the 'must-see' list of most visitors to London, a place to watch passers-by, listen to buskers (though perhaps none as innovative as the very first Punch and Judy show, which Samuel Johnson saw on the piazza in 1662) and purchase hand-crafted trinkets for the folks back home. Though the traders' cries are not as raucous as those of their Georgian and Victorian predecessors, and the area has lost its taint of ill repute, Covent Garden today continues a tradition of commerce that dates back well over a thousand years.

canary wharf <small>AND THE</small> isle <small>OF</small> dogs

The Isle of Dogs, a tongue of reclaimed land that juts into the Thames north of Greenwich, has led a triple life. For long a sleepy marshland, offering high-quality grazing and little else, it then became one of the engines of empire, as its massive wharves and docks handled timber, grain, iron, tea and rubber, before a post-war slump threatened to return the isle to its primal state. Finally, in the 1980s, an unexpected redevelopment turned it into a new financial centre for London.

The last two of these phases are reflected in the maps. In 1948 the Isle of Dogs is resolutely a shipping and industrial district, dominated by the West India Docks to the north and the Millwall Docks to the south, with a scattering of residential districts inland very much lying in their shadow. By 2019 the docks remain, but they have been repurposed as watery ornaments to the financial skyscrapers of Canary Wharf, while residential developments have colonized the riverfront on the southern part of the isle and the infilled former locks, docks and basins within it.

The river transformed what had been an ill-omened patch of land – which had only two buildings on it before the seventeenth century and was used as a pirate's gibbet in the eighteenth – into a bustling maritime entrepôt. It began with the West India Docks, constructed between 1799 and 1806 to ease congestion in the main Port of London and transport goods to and from Britain's territories in the Caribbean. Joined by Millwall Docks, constructed in 1868 primarily to handle grain and timber, together the docks provided jobs and a measure of prosperity to Poplar, one of London's most deprived boroughs.

1,500,000
the square metres of office space at canary wharf

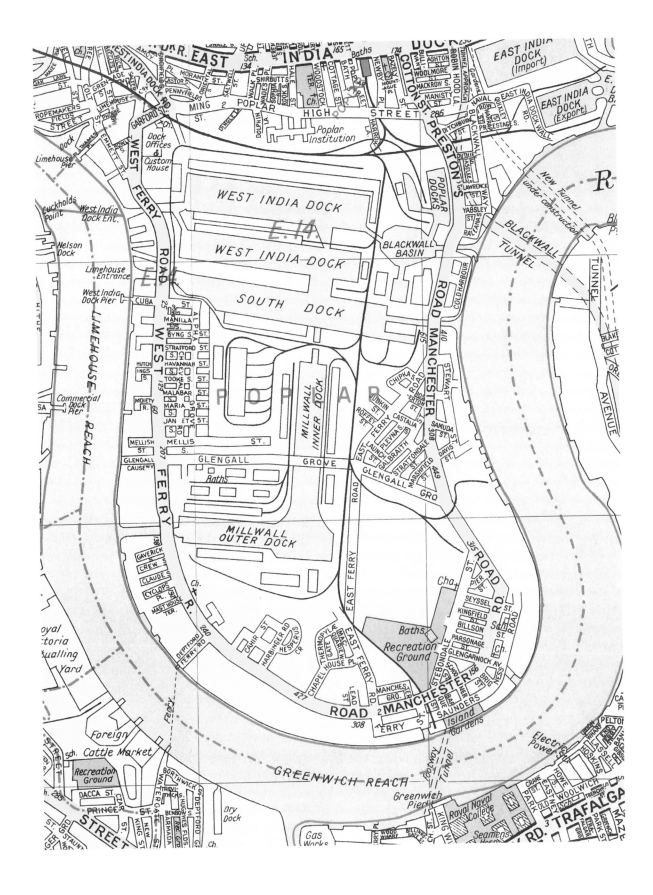

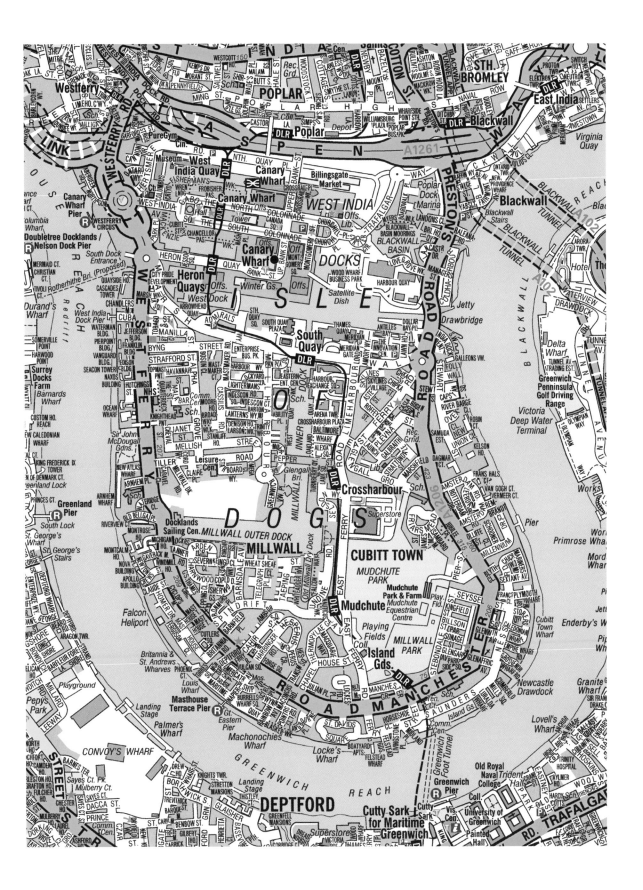

The shift in global trading patterns by the 1930s, as Britain began to lose its unquestioned mercantile supremacy, threatened the docks, and the Second World War inflicted another blow. Serious damage to the West India Docks during a German air raid in September 1940 meant expensive repairs that the Port of London Authority (PLA) struggled to carry out, even when the building of the artificial Mulberry Harbours – used to facilitate the D-Day landings in Normandy – briefly gave it a new purpose. The investment required to convert dock facilities first to palletization and then from 1968 to containerization, together with troubled industrial relations, dealt the death blows. From 1973, the PLA began to transfer operations further west, to the Royal Docks, and finally, in July 1980 the West India Docks closed for the last time.

The Isle of Dogs was now at a low ebb: with the docks gone and transport links to the island clearly inadequate (all rail links had closed down by the 1970s), drastic action was needed. London County Council had already redeveloped much of the residential area. New estates, such as the Manchester and Schooner in Cubitt Town to the southeast, had been constructed in the early 1950s, while pressure from residents led to the preservation of an open space and establishment of an urban farm at Mudchute in 1977. Yet these measures could only mitigate the island's underlying problems and it took the establishment of the London Docklands Development Corporation in 1981 to stem the decline and then reforge the isle in a new image.

In 1982 much of the old docks area was designated as an Enterprise Zone, in which planning was taken out of the hands of the local authority in a bid to attract new investment. In 1985 the Bank of England announced that banking companies would no longer have to retain offices within the traditional square mile of the City of London. The announcement of a huge new office development at Canary Wharf in the north of the Isle of Dogs sparked

◁ 250–1
While the outline of the old docks can still be seen on the Isle of Dogs, seventy years have wrought enormous change. From a predominantly industrial area, the area has been transformed into a banking and financial hub, with large numbers of residential complexes and enhanced transportation links through the Jubilee Line and the Docklands Light Railway.

a rush of financial firms in search of larger (and cheaper) offices. Though the recession of the early 1990s led to the bankruptcy of the initial developer in 1992, the new financial district (dubbed 'Manhattan-on-Thames') weathered the crisis and has continued to grow, until it now consists of around 1.5 million square metres of office space, housing around 100,000 people. Among its new financial palaces was 1 Canada Square, the centrepiece of Canary Wharf, designed by the Argentinian-American architect Cesar Pelli. At 235 metres high it is Britain's second-tallest building, whose flashing beacon can be seen from almost any vantage point in London.

A residential building boom followed as new private residential complexes sprang up, such as the Cascades on Westferry Road (its design a homage to an ocean liner). To service the new offices and to transport their workers, grand new infrastructure projects were needed. Northwest of the isle, the Limehouse Link cost £293 million for just a mile of road tunnel, while the absence of rail links was resolved first by the Docklands Light Railway, an innovative monorail opened in 1987, and the extension of the Jubilee line in 1999 to include a station at Canary Wharf. Just across the river, on the Greenwich Peninsula, London acquired another landmark when the Millennium Dome was built on the former site of the Metropolitan Gasworks as part of the capital's celebration for the arrival of the year 2000.

Three decades have wrought huge changes on the Isle of Dogs, bringing to its traditional community – which by 1961 had dwindled to 22,209 – and its old nineteenth-century terraces, a new world of tens of thousands of commuters, tower blocks and skyscrapers. Although this transformation has brought its own challenges and tensions, nobody could now, as the diarist Samuel Pepys did in July 1665, call it 'the unlucky Isle of Doggs'.

clerkenwell

The district to the north of Farringdon Station and south of the Sadler's Wells Theatre has known many vicissitudes since its beginnings as the home of the priory of the Knights Hospitallers of St John and Jerusalem. The priory was founded in 1140 on a site that stretched from Red Lion Street in the west to St John Street in the east, and from Clerkenwell Green in the north to St John's Gateway in the south. It was from the priory that the area derived its name, Clerkenwell (as medieval clerics were often referred to as 'clerks').

This ecclesiastical origin did not prevent Clerkenwell acquiring a baleful reputation for poor housing, disorderly conduct, beggars and brothels. Situated just outside the walls of London, it escaped the formal jurisdiction of the city authorities and became a byword for forbidden pleasures, so much so that in *Henry IV Part 2*, Shakespeare has Falstaff mock another character for his indiscretions on Turnbull Street (later renamed Turnmill Street in an attempt to wipe clean its dubious past). Clerkenwell also acquired three prisons, including the side-by-side Bridewell and Clerkenwell New Prison, the latter the site of the Clerkenwell Outrage of 1867, when escaping Irish nationalists blew a hole in the jail wall, killing many local residents.

A slightly bohemian atmosphere meant Clerkenwell was ideal terrain for the growing number of theatrical establishments that appeared in London in the seventeenth century, the most long-lasting of which is Sadler's Wells, founded as a spa and theatre, by Richard Sadler in 1683. Other marginal, but more law-abiding, residents gravitated towards the area. It became the centre of London's first major Italian community in the late nineteenth century, and even after the 1950s, when they began to drift away, it remains their spiritual home as the venue of the annual Procession of Our Lady of Mount Carmel. Political radicals, too, took advantage of the low-cost housing to remain both anonymous and solvent. Vladimir Lenin took a house on Clerkenwell Green, from where he published the

1,093
the number of printing and engineering factories in the 1920s

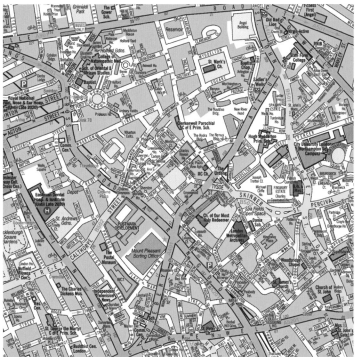

Bolshevik newspaper *Iskra* ('spark') for a year from 1902, before its operations moved to Geneva. The Green retained its radical connections even afterwards with the opening of a Marx Memorial Library there in 1930s, and as the traditional assembly point for protest marches.

During the Victorian era the area became the home for a large number of precision industries, which benefited from the concentration of skilled artisans in one quarter. Workshops for clocks, watches and marine chronometers proliferated, as well as printers to keep them fed with radical literature, and breweries to satisfy their more mundane needs. By the 1920s the area had 12,000 employees in the printing industry in 272 factories, as well as 10,625 engineering workers in 821 factories.

Finsbury, the larger borough that included Clerkenwell, was badly hit during the Blitz, leaving 9,015 of its 9,899 buildings damaged (and 983 totally destroyed). Large parts of the borough found themselves in need of reconstruction, allowing the clearance of bomb-damaged and slum housing to create several new housing estates such as the Finsbury Estate, centred on four high-rise towers north of Skinner Street, which was built in 1965, and the equally modernist Spa Green Estate, whose architect, Berthold Lubetkin, was rewarded with a Grade II listing in 1998.

As rents rose and traditional industries were driven to bankruptcy by successive recessions, Clerkenwell began to transform once more. Warehouses and factories were converted to cater for the loft-living style that became all the rage from the 1990s and, as brewers and printers moved out, designers and architects moved in, preserving the area's reputation for niche concentrations of excellence, even if of a rather different sort. *The Guardian* newspaper, which straddled both worlds and had occupied offices on Farringdon Road since 1976, decamped to new offices in King's Cross in 2008. Clerkenwell may have lost its radical edge, but it remains a haven for innovative ideas, thriving just on the edge of the more constrictive atmosphere of the City.

◁ 255

Between 1936 and 2019, some of the more crowded areas of Clerkenwell were cleared away; the district also lost its concentrations of light industry, although where clockmakers moved out, designers and journalists have moved in to ensure it retains a reputation for creativity.

THE city OF london

At first glance the modern map of the City of London shows little change from its counterpart from the 1930s. Only in the area of the Barbican does a new estate – complete with tower blocks, concert hall and theatre – speak of an altered urban topography. Elsewhere, the comfortingly familiar miscellany of ancient street names, such as Wardrobe Place, Crutched Friars, Hanging Sword Alley and St Mary Axe, act as reminders of continuity with an earlier age.

The last – a reference to a church that was alleged to hold the very axe with which Attila the Hun was said to have beheaded St Ursula and her 11,000 handmaidens when they refused his advances while on the way back to Britain from a pilgrimage to Rome – is a sign of the fundamental conservatism of London's nomenclature. Yet the very fact that the church itself was demolished in the 1560s shows that while street names may change, the streets themselves have undergone huge modifications over time. The very existence of the 'square mile' of the City of London is one side of this phenomenon – it owes its broad shape to the extent of the original Roman settlement of Londinium, while the names of the gates punctuating the defensive wall that was built in the late second century still survive today as Ludgate, Newgate (where the city's most notorious medieval prison was housed), Cripplegate, Bishopsgate and Aldgate.

As with most areas of the capital, the City suffered badly during the Blitz, its collection of cultural and strategic buildings such as the Tower of London and the Bank of England, and its status as the centre of Britain's financial industries, making it an appealing target for the German bombers. At the end, much of the rubble was cleared away, buildings were repaired, or in some cases replaced, but one ward of the City, Cripplegate, was deemed irrecoverable. By 1951, only forty-eight people were listed as living there (as against a population of 14,000

48
the number of people left living in the bomb-damaged ward of Cripplegate in 1951

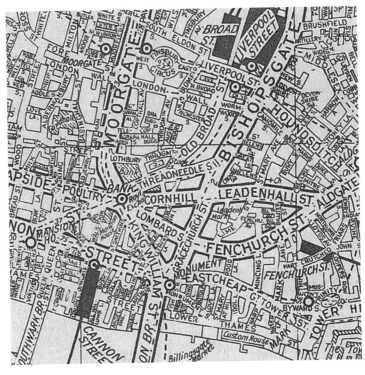

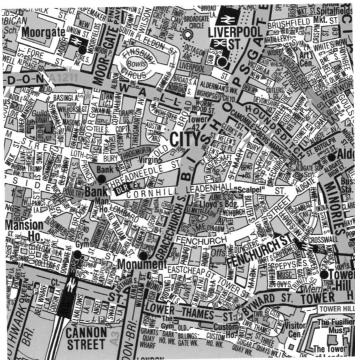

a century earlier). After a lengthy consultation, it was decided not to restore the area to its pre-war condition, but instead to embark on an ambitious programme of regeneration that would create a high-rise estate and a series of new venues for the arts. The estate itself was completed by 1976, and the Barbican Centre by 1982, boasting two theatres, a concert hall and an art gallery, while the addition of a number of other facilities such as the Museum of London and the Guildhall School of Music and Drama created a veritable cultural hub in the heart of the City.

Further developments did take place, including the building of the NatWest Tower (now Tower 42) in 1980 – at 183 metres the tallest building in the City at the time, and its first skyscraper. But it was only the massive expansion in business being done in the City after the 'Big Bang' financial reforms of 1986 that led to an influx of foreign banks, new employees and a demand for modern facilities to house them. The silhouette of the City has radically changed; the transformation to glass-and-chrome towers is a metamorphosis equal to the one from wood to brick that marked London's reconstruction after the Great Fire of 1666. The list of new and innovative buildings grows by the year, many of them possessing both a mundane street address and a quirky nickname. 30 St Mary Axe (more commonly known as the Gherkin), designed by Norman Foster in 2003, towers 180 metres (and forty-one floors) above the ground below, while the tapered glass façade of the Leadenhall Building and its ladder-like frame have earned it the nickname 'the Cheesegrater'. The architects of the new city have let their imaginations run riot; 20 Fenchurch Street, completed in 2014, has a curious top-heavy shape that makes it look like a walkie-talkie; Broadgate, an area on the edges of the City extensively redeveloped since the 1980s, boasts the Broadgate Tower, the fifth-highest in the City, and 5 Broadgate, designed to look like an idealized machine-produced object. Towering over them all is 110 Bishopsgate (the Heron Tower), which at 230 metres is still significantly shorter than its cousins over at Canary Wharf, but a sign that the traditional bounds of the City have a lot of commercial vigour in them yet.

A medieval visitor to London gazing up at these new towers might mistake them for enormous cathedrals (which, in a sense, as temples to money, they are), but keeping their eyes fixed firmly on the ground they would find street signs that would allow them to fix their position in the same lanes and alleys of six centuries earlier: Poultry, Magpie Alley and Old Jewry. The City of London may be one of the world's most technologically advanced places of business, but its ghosts are surprisingly persistent.

◁

After decades of relative stagnation, the City started its late-twentieth-century metamorphosis in the 1970s when the Barbican complex was built, as the rubble of the old Cripplegate ward was swept away. The process has accelerated over the past twenty years with the construction of a series of striking skyscrapers, including the Cheesegrater, the Walkie-Talkie and the Gherkin.

thames gateway

For London to retain its status as a world city, it must grow. There are limits to the number of sites in the centre that can be redeveloped, regenerated or repurposed and so the capital, as it always has done, must expand at its margins, pressing ever further into what are historically the independent counties that surround it.

The decline of London's port and dock area presented a historic opportunity to reshape the industrial land east of the city and to provide new housing and new services to the communities that cluster around the banks of the Thames and the Thames Estuary. A number of development agencies were established in 2004, including the London Thames Gateway Development Corporation and the Thurrock Thames Gateway Development Corporation. Their remit was to devise a masterplan for a funnel of land extending seventy kilometres east of the capital, covering around 80,000 hectares of land and a general area that was home to more than three million people.

The Thames Gateway Delivery Plan, published in 2007, called for 160,000 new zero-carbon homes to be built within this area, and 225,000 jobs to be created, with investment in infrastructure that would include the spending of £1.2 billion on schools. It is planned as the largest single regeneration project in Western Europe, with three main focal nodes in Kent: Kent Thameside (including Ebbsfleet, Dartford and Gravesham); Medway (covering Chatham and Gillingham); and Swale (encompassing Sittingbourne).

The schemes are grand in scope, taking advantage of the transport links made possible by the opening of the Channel Tunnel Rail Link between Ebbsfleet and Stratford in 2007. To the west, the Stratford City development is designed to provide nearly two million

160,000
the number of zero-carbon homes called for in the thames gateway delivery plan from 2007

square feet of office space and 5,000 homes, partly on the site of the 2012 Olympic Village, while 20,000 new houses are planned at Ebbsfleet. Although an ambitious plan to build a Thames Gateway Bridge between Beckton and Thamesmead was cancelled in 2008, a new London Gateway Port opened at Thurrock in 2013, its deep-water port and advanced logistics allowing London to keep up with its competitor ports, such as Rotterdam, well into the twenty-first century.

Additional developments are planned at Basildon, Dartford, Gillingham and Rochester, challenging the logistical capabilities of more than sixteen local authorities to work together. When the Thames Gateway development is complete, it will mark another great leap forward for London and strain our definitions of what exactly constitutes the capital by linking it to new communities far beyond its traditional boundaries.

262-3 ▷

The very definition of what constitutes London is being challenged by the Thames Gateway projects, which coordinate development far to the east of the twentieth-century boundaries of the city. It is all part of a centuries-long trend that began when Roman Londinium began to develop a suburb south of the river.

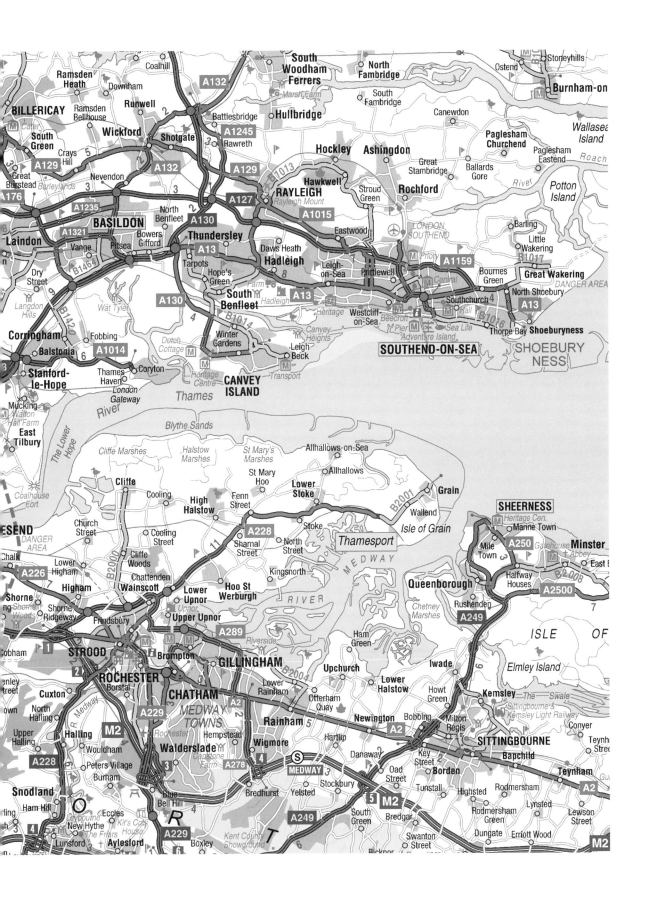

thamesmead

The regeneration of areas of marshland has been a time-honoured way of extending land for cultivation or for settlement, and London has its very own reclaimed district in Thamesmead, situated between Plumstead and Woolwich. The map in 1936 shows a marshy void, not far from the Royal Arsenal at Greenwich, while today a spider's web of roads populates the area, sprinkled with a few parks and criss-crossed by several spinal routes.

Thamesmead began its slow transformation in the Middle Ages, when Augustinian monks from the nearby Abbey of Lesnes began to reclaim land needed for growing crops and grazing. The establishment of the naval dockyard at Woolwich in 1512 brought its workers into neighbouring villages, but Thamesmead itself was reduced to a testing ground for guns and ammunition, its marshy soil providing a satisfying target and insulation from the sound of naval shells thudding into the ground.

The New Towns Act of 1946, mandating the establishment of new urban areas of around 50,000 people in a ring around London, brought to life settlements such as Harlow and Crawley, but planners sought a site close to the heart of London and they found it in the Erith-Plumstead Marshes. In the late 1950s, London County Council obtained 500 acres of old Royal Arsenal land and in 1962 developed plans for a new riverside development 'on stilts' (to keep the houses clear of the waterlogged morass below). However it took the purchase of a further 1,000 acres by the new Greater London Council in 1968 to make the plan viable.

Engineers began the building of two pumping stations and the digging of channels to drain excess water and strengthen the riverbank, and architects laid out a plan for a town, which while not quite utopian, had a certain futuristic vision. Green spaces and parks were to be integrated, traffic was to be kept apart from pedestrians – who would have their own

1971

the year *a clockwork orange* was released, setting the seal on the area's baleful reputation at the time

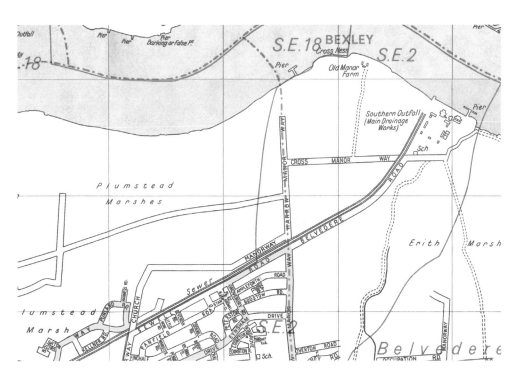

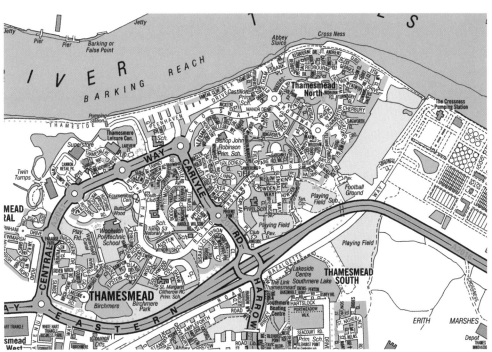

walkways – and the lower levels of blocks of flats and maisonettes were to be occupied by garages, to keep the residential areas well away from possible flooding. Five villages were to be established, each with its own satellite town centre, with the south of the area being primarily residential, the east for commerce and industry and the centre focused on retail and entertainment.

The development opened with a fanfare: a competition was run to name it and the winner, who christened it Thamesmead, won a £20 prize. The very first residents, who moved into Coralline Walk in July 1968, attracted newspaper attention and were whisked to their new home in a chauffeured limousine. Unfortunately, the high hopes were not fulfilled. By the early 1970s plans had been scaled back, and the envisaged tunnel crossing over the Thames was scrapped, making it unfeasible to commute into Central London. Demand for housing dropped and vacant flats were vandalized, while the concrete pedestrian walkways set away from main roads proved a haven for crime and anti-social behaviour. The area's appearance as a violent no-go area in *A Clockwork Orange*, the 1971 film version of Anthony Burgess's dystopian vision of the future, set the seal on the area's baleful reputation.

The success of other parts of London, paradoxically, proved Thamesmead's salvation. As prices for housing rose to unreachable levels in any area within plausible reach of London, it remained one of the few suburbs that people on modest incomes could afford (with many flats having been sold in the 1980s and 1990s under Right to Buy legislation). Since 1986 the town had been operated by a private company in which all residents were shareholders, solidifying some sense of community. Its designation as a Housing Zone in 2015, to kickstart its regeneration, and the investment of £80 million by Peabody to provide 1,500 new homes and reshape the town by reintegrating pedestrian and foot traffic offer hope for the future. A nature reserve at Tump 53, which had fallen into disuse, has revived, and a new reserve opened at Gallions Reach in 2016, featuring wildflower meadows. In danger once of moving from rural marsh to urban swamp, Thamesmead can now hope for a brighter future, after one of London's more troubled transformations.

◁ 265
The transformation in the Thamesmead area between the 1967 and 2019 maps is startling. In the first, the area is almost virgin marsh, with just a few buildings, including Old Manor Farm. In the second, a whole new suburb has colonized the area, with schools, shops, parks and a complex of new residential estates.

nine elms

Nine Elms, a stretch of riverfront between Battersea Park and Vauxhall, is one of London's most transformed areas. The 1948 map shows a predominantly industrial district, dominated by the recently constructed Battersea Power Station and a straggle of railway lines where north–south routes cross those coming westwards from south London. By 2019 a series of newcomers – New Covent Garden and the United States Embassy among them – and the redevelopment of the power station after a series of false starts, had begun to change it into a district to which Londoners might come, rather than one they would by choice pass through or pass by.

Nine Elms derives its name from a farm that stood there in the mid-seventeenth century, but by the Victorian era it had become distinctly less bucolic. Light industry moved in (including the very first incarnation of Vauxhall Motors, which produced marine pumps and cranes at the Vauxhall Iron Works on Wandsworth Road), and the railway arrived with the opening of the first station at Nine Elms in 1838. Its reputation as an industrial suburb was reinforced by the building of Battersea Power Station, whose architect Sir Giles Gilbert Scott was also responsible for London's characteristic red telephone boxes. Constructed in two stages, from 1929–33 and 1944–55, its generators could push out 509 megawatts of power, enough to supply a fifth of London's needs. Gradually, though, it became obsolete and was finally decommissioned in 1983 to begin three decades in which its structure became gradually more derelict, while successive schemes to redevelop it fell through, leaving its decrepit shell and still proud white chimney stacks painfully visible from the train lines.

Finally, in 2010 a new scheme was agreed by which the power station would be redeveloped into one of London's largest luxury residential schemes, together with a sprinkling of prestige offices. By then a series of other projects had already begun to rejuvenate the area. The new MI6 headquarters alongside the river, a gigantic ziggurat-like structure that was completed in 1994, was perhaps not so open to the outside world as New Covent Garden, to where the venerable fruit and vegetable market transferred in 1974,

2018
the year in which the new united states embassy opened

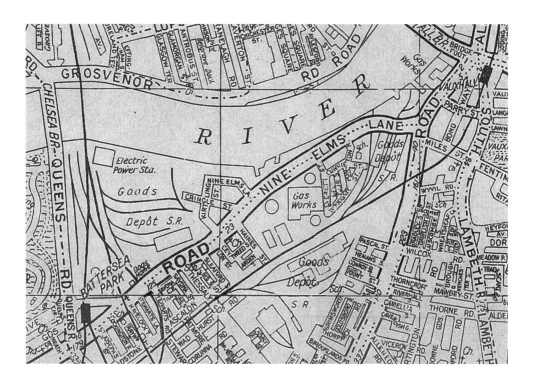

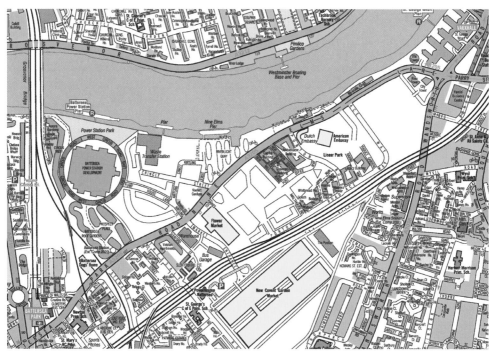

bringing 2,500 jobs to the area and supplying three-quarters of London's florists (as well as 40 per cent of the fruit and veg consumed in its restaurants).

The most high-profile new resident of the area, however, is the United States Embassy, which opened in 2018 at a new address on Nine Elms Lane after an eight-decade tenure at two sites in Mayfair's Grosvenor Square. Despite a certain grumpiness by the Trump administration – the president referred to the site as 'lousy' and accused his predecessors of having got a bad deal on giving up the Grosvenor Square lease – it allowed the building of state-of-the-art diplomatic headquarters, whose bullet-proof glass casing makes it seem like a gigantic crystalline cube. In 2017 the Embassy of the Netherlands also announced it would move to Nine Elms, opening up the prospect of a whole new diplomatic quarter for London.

Some things remain familiar in Nine Elms. Battersea Dogs and Cats Home still has kennels on the site to which its founder Mary Teaby moved it in 1871. Throughout the century-and-a-half since then, it has cared for hundreds of thousands of animals – 145,000 during the Second World War alone, when many people simply could not care for their animals and large numbers were orphaned when their owners were killed during the Blitz. Despite being bombed itself, the home did not close, and now rehouses about 5,000 animals each year. Recognition came in the form of its very own commemorative set of stamps in 2010 and its alumni are keenly sought after – particularly the cats; Battersea has provided Larry, the chief mouser to the Cabinet Office, and his counterparts in the Foreign and Commonwealth Office and the Treasury, who bear the more suitably politically sounding names of Palmerstone and Gladstone.

With a rash of high-rise luxury apartment blocks springing up along the Thames, Nine Elms now needs improved transport links to carry its new generation of workers and residents to the area (rather than simply staring out at it as the trains whisked them by to Waterloo or Victoria). A new bus station opened there in December 2004, which is already London's second busiest terminus after Victoria, and two new underground stations are being built to service an extension to the Northern Line which is due to open in 2021. The one at Nine Elms, ironically, is close to the site of the original 1838 railway station. In forging ahead into the future, some areas do not wholly escape their past.

◁

Although the skyline of Nine Elms is still dominated by the power station, much as it was in 1938, the building has been repurposed as offices and luxury flats. Some old favourites, such as the Dog's Home are still clearly visible on both maps, but the area is being changed by significant newcomers, most notably New Covent Garden Market on the site of an old goods depot and the new United States Embassy on land that formerly housed a gas works.

surrey quays

The Rotherhithe peninsula, a finger of land outlined by the Thames a mile downriver from the Tower of London, has long been a somewhat overlooked corner of London. The map of the area in the 1940s, though, shows a necklace of blue, an interlinked series of docks, ponds, wharves and canals covering most of the land. Some indicate the destinations to which trade from the docks was principally directed: Greenland, Quebec, Russia, Norway. Others are more poetic, such as Lavender Pond, Acorn Pond and Lady Dock. Today, however, they are almost all gone. Only the triangular bulk of Greenland Dock survives, together with a part of Norway Dock and the South Dock (now a marina). Much has become new housing and a retail park, while a sliver of Russia Dock has been wooded over as the southern part of Stave Hill Ecological Park.

Although two possible etymologies of Rotherhithe's name ('sailor's haven' and 'landing place for cattle') suggest a strong trading and maritime connection, the area remained largely marshland – though Canute did cut a channel through it as part of a siege of London in 1016 – and did not even rate an entry in the Domesday Book. Its real maritime heyday dates back to the 1690s and the construction of Howland Great Wet Dock, which in 1763 was renamed Greenland Dock. The early nineteenth century brought the Grand Surrey Canal to the peninsula. Supposed to run from Rotherhithe to Epsom (and some dreamed of extending it even further, to Portsmouth), the waterway would enable goods unloaded at the docks to be carried deep inland. As a consequence, the area thrived, teeming with lumpers and deal porters who carried the timber for which the docks – by now as a group named after the canal as the Surrey Docks – became renowned.

As elsewhere in the Docklands, the Surrey Docks trod water under the new management of the Port of London Authority from 1909. A few improvements were made, with the building in the 1920s of open-sided sheds for storing timbers (which had previously been left exposed to the elements). Yet already there were signs of some retrenchment. Globe Pond was filled in and the blocking of Lavender Lock meant a pumping station had to be

960,000
imports in tons to surrey docks in 1967 – two years earlier, it was 1.6 million

installed to maintain water levels there. The Docks' equilibrium was shattered by the Blitz. Already on the first night in September 1940, more than forty major fires broke out in Surrey Docks as the German bombers sought to destroy the strategically important timber stocks. The area suffered relentless pounding for the next two months. The rubble-choked docks and ruined wharves almost ceased to operate: South Dock was pumped dry and part of it converted for the construction of Mulberry Harbours for D-Day.

At the end of the war, the destruction was too great for Surrey Docks to ever fully recover. The cost of repairs and the difficulties of adapting to containerization meant that the docks became commercially unviable. Imports, which had been 1,617,000 tons in 1965, collapsed to 960,000 tons in 1967 and the Surrey Basin and lock were filled in that year, with Lady Dock being closed in 1968. Over the next two years the other docks all shut down, with the very last ship, a Russian timber vessel, leaving in December 1970. The last remaining short section from Greenland Dock to Deptford was finally closed in 1971.

The abandoned land was sold to the Greater London Council and Southwark Council in 1977, but work on redeveloping the area progressed slowly at first. The Redriff Estate, which had been part of an earlier project for regenerating the peninsula in the 1930s, slowly decayed. The 1980s did see the construction of a new shopping centre and a large printworks on Surrey Quays Road for the *Daily Mail* and *Evening Standard* (which operated until 2012), while Canada Water and Russia Dock were transformed into a nature reserve. However, as elsewhere in the Docklands, it was the establishment of the London Docklands Development Corporation (LDDC) in 1981 that accelerated the pace of change. More than 5,500 new houses and flats were built, and South Dock was converted into London's largest marina. The opening of the Jubilee Line station at Canada Water in 1999 and the transfer of Surrey Quays to become a London Overground station in 2012 brought much-needed improvement to the area's transport links.

The rebranding of the area as Surrey Quays – removing the title 'Docks' and airbrushing out the historic name of Rotherhithe – has displeased many locals. Nevertheless, proposals to develop South Dock Marina with 11,000 new homes, and a Canada Water Masterplan put forward in 2018 with a scheme to add 3,000 housing units, including skyscraper towers, offer a future for the area as a new version of Canary Wharf to the north. The days of the Arctic traders who brought back blubber to be boiled in warehouses alongside Greenland Dock are long over; the future seems to belong to the financial traders.

272-3 ▷

In common with other parts of London's Docklands, the change in Surrey Quays between 1938 and 2019 is striking. The complex of docks, wharves, canals and other waterways is almost entirely gone, replaced by an entirely new residential suburb with accompanying amenities.

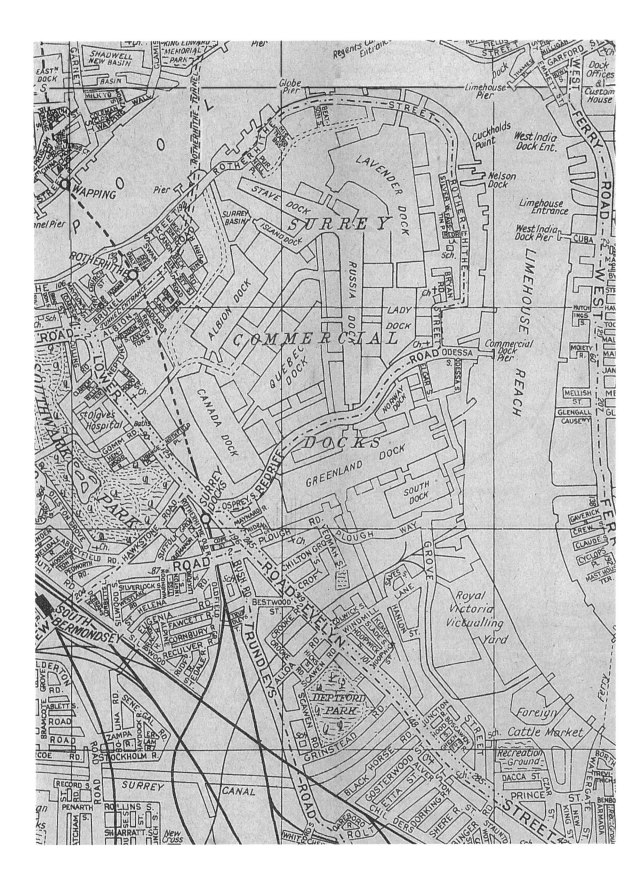

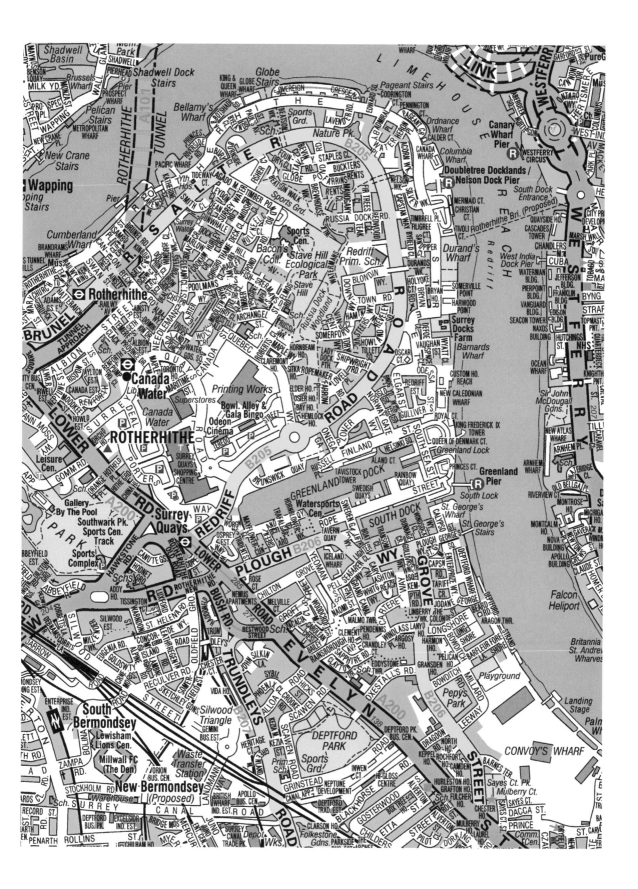

hendon aerodrome AND THE
RAF museum AT colindale

In 1938 a large stretch of land to the north and east of Colindale tube station (opened in 1924 as part of an extension to what was then the Hampstead and Highgate Line) is an almost unbroken blank patch on the map, punctuated by a few buildings. This expanse, Hendon Aerodrome, appears in today's map split into three: a great section to the west built over with the streets and houses of the Grahame Park estate, the south given over to the Hendon Police College, and part of the north retaining the old hangars that now house the RAF Museum.

Hendon's fate could have been very different. The area had lived and breathed aviation ever since Henry Coxwell and James Glaisher, luminaries of the British Association for the Advancement of Science, had made a pioneering flight in a balloon named the *Mammoth* from a local field in 1862. Already by 1909 a powered flight, one of the first in Britain, had taken off from the Welsh Harp Reservoir. The eighty-foot-long airship, built and piloted by Henry Spencer, had as its sole passenger the Australian suffragette Muriel Matters, who took with her a pile of leaflets calling for votes for women, which she intended dropping on a procession led by King Edward VII as he went to the state opening of Parliament at Westminster. Unfortunately, the airship blew off course in bad weather and crash-landed in Coulsden, depriving the suffragette cause of a stunning coup de theatre.

In 1910 the pioneer aviator Claude Grahame-White took off from a field near Hendon in a bid to win a challenge prize offered by the *Daily Mail* newspaper for the first continuous flight from London to Manchester. He only got as far as Lichfield, but returned, bought 200 acres of land, and established an airfield there as the headquarters for his Grahame-White aviation company. He began assembling Burgess Baby planes and watched with satisfaction as the first air mail flights took off from there in 1911.

Grahame-White's plans for Hendon to become 'the Charing Cross of aviation', with all planes to and from London landing on his airfield, were stymied by the First World War. The war retarded the development of civil aviation, including by the requisitioning of the

1944
the year a v-1 rocket hit colindale hospital, killing four members of the women's auxiliary air force

air schools that had opened up there for conversion training establishments for the Royal Naval Air Service (RNAS), and then by the abrupt requisitioning of Hendon by the RAF in 1922. The Government offered no compensation and Grahame-White refused to budge until he was finally forced out in 1925. Disillusioned, he turned to property development and abandoned aviation entirely.

His brainchild only prospered modestly under RAF tutelage. It was the site of the RAF Pageants from 1920 (which became the grander RAF Displays from 1925), but during the Second World War the airfield was mainly used for transport flights, having become the home of No. 24 Squadron in 1933. Further runways were built to accommodate larger planes, but Hendon never became an important station during the Battle of Britain (though one of its hangars was destroyed by German bombing in 1940, and in 1944 a V-1 rocket hit Colindale Hospital, killing four members of the Women's Auxiliary Air Force).

After the war, Hendon's runways were too small to act as a major base, and the last operational unit moved out in 1957, leaving just a volunteer gliding school. It was then that it was decided that the hangars could be adapted to become a museum for the RAF's collection of aircraft (one of which, a Blackburn Beverley, became the last plane to land at Hendon in 1968). The museum opened in November 1972 and now includes a Battle of Britain Hall, a hangar dedicated to Milestones of Flight and a rare collection of First World War aircraft housed in one of Grahame-White's original hangars.

Parts of the land were sold off by the RAF, one section to become the Grahame-Park estate – with its brick-built houses and low-rise flats – another, based around the aerodrome's clubhouse, had been converted to become a police training college in 1934. That project was inspired by Hugh Trenchard, Commissioner of the Metropolitan Police, who ironically had been the first Chief of the Air Staff in 1918, and had been instrumental in the founding of the RAF. Briefly closed during the Second World War, it was reopened as the main training college for Metropolitan Police cadets once peace returned, and experienced major redevelopment in the 1960s when a new Peel Centre was opened, and also in 2016, when many of the older buildings were demolished.

Together, the police, a local community of over 1,700 houses, and one of London's premier museums have breathed life into Hendon. Yet, but for the RAF's requisitioning and the aerodrome's subsequent decline, we could all have been landing at Terminal 4 Hendon, instead of Heathrow, and Colindale's tranquillity could have been regularly shattered by super jumbo jets. In hindsight, today's residents are probably heartily grateful.

◁ 275
This London Transport poster reflects the excitement of early aviation, advertising a series
of aerial races to be held at Hendon in the spring of 1913, including one to celebrate
'Empire Day', a celebration inaugurated in 1902 to promote Britain's imperial heritage,
which gradually fell out of favour and was rebadged as Commonwealth Day in 1958.

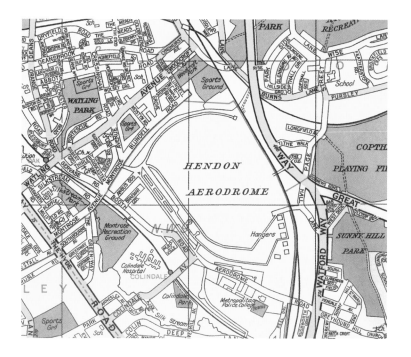

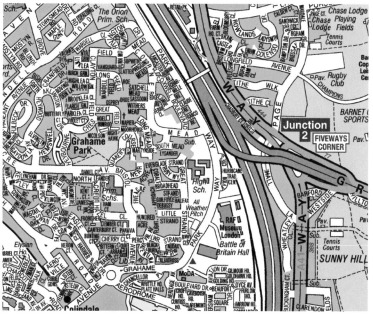

△

The pre-war Hendon aerodrome has now largely been built over, with only the RAF Museum preserving the area's aviation heritage. However, but for the First World War and the subsequent requisitioning of the airfield by the Government, Hendon might have become the site of London's main airport and its map in 2019 would have looked very different.

king's cross

 King's Cross Station long formed the terminus of one of London's principal transport conduits to the north, carrying travellers on lines along the east coast, and ultimately to Edinburgh. Its name pre-dates even the station, and came from a short-lived and much-unloved statue of King George IV that was erected nearby in 1830.

Yet if King's Cross, the largest station in the country when it opened in 1852, was kind – or at least convenient – to travellers, it blighted its immediate surroundings. The map in 1948 shows a concentration of goods yards and sidings in an oval patch of land just to the north of the station; by 2019 this had been transformed, as new roads cut through the industrial wasteland, sprinkled with parks and new public buildings. On the ground the transformation is even more stark. What had been an unlovely and half-abandoned series of warehouses and former railway buildings is undergoing a metamorphosis – not yet complete – into an entirely new residential, retail, business and cultural quarter.

The site's sixty-seven acres presented an enormous challenge and despite an awareness that the environs of the station left a great deal to be desired, decisions were put off for decades. It was the prospect of the transfer of the Channel Tunnel Rail Link from Waterloo to St Pancras in 2007 that provided a catalyst to the owners of the site, London and Continental Railways, to finally decide to redevelop it. Planning permission was received in 2006 and the King's Cross Central Limited Partnership was formed in 2008 to push through a programme that involved the laying of twenty new streets, the construction of ten new public parks and squares and the building of fifty new buildings, with 1,900 new housing units.

The early work focused on the area around the former Victorian Goods Yard, where the Granary formerly used to store wheat for much of London's bakeries became home

9¾
the departure platform for the hogwarts express!

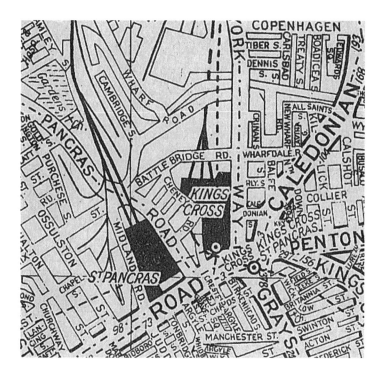

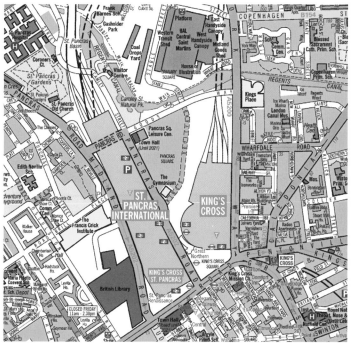

to Central Saint Martin's School of Art and Design in 2011. The Midland Goods Shed, used by the Great Northern Railway as a temporary passenger terminal in the station's early days and from which Queen Victoria departed for Scotland in 1851, has become a supermarket. The German Gymnasium, built in 1864–5 to provide exercise facilities for the capital's German community, has metamorphosed into a restaurant, and the giant frame of Gasholder 8, constructed in 1850, was converted to form a striking frame around a public park in 2012. New cultural venues have opened up, too, including the House of Illustration, a museum of graphic art, which moved into the main Good Yards Offices in July 2014.

The redevelopment also allowed the restoration of some areas to their original state: the façade of the main station, designed by Lewis Cubitt, was stripped of accretions and returned to its original appearance in 2012, while the Great Northern, of which he was also the architect, received a £40 million facelift, restoring the venerable old hotel (which first opened its doors in 1854, but which had lain derelict for over a decade) to use.

The makeover of the area north of King's Cross, which at eight million square feet of flats, offices and restaurants makes it the largest such redevelopment for 150 years, has proven that the centre of the city has surprising scope to reinvent itself. If some of the buildings are not to everybody's taste – the architect Peter Cook described them as resembling 'old biscuits' – this only goes to show that while London lives, it criticizes.

◁ 279
The redevelopment of a comparatively small area behind King's Cross, which had long been an expanse of increasingly derelict goods yards, shows the possibilities of imaginative regeneration even of areas at the heart of London.

paddington basin

Nestled between the Westway and Paddington Station, a small stretch of waterway known as Paddington Basin has undergone a startling transformation over the last decade. In the late 1940s the map shows the area as sparsely labelled, a near wasteland of half-abandoned wharves and old canal buildings, but by 2019 it has sprouted high-rise offices, residential blocks, new bridges and a grassed amphitheatre fringed with cafés and restaurants.

The historic borough of Paddington has origins that stretch deep into the Middle Ages (the tenth-century Anglo-Saxon king Edgar granted the manor there to the monks from Westminster Abbey), but it really came into its own during the great Victorian transport revolution. Paddington Station to the south first opened as a terminus for the Great Western Railway in 1838, though the current grand station building, designed by Isambard Kingdom Brunel, was only completed in 1854. The canal pre-dated even this. Construction began in 1793 on the Grand Junction, intended to link London to the rest of the canal network. The arm leading to Paddington finally opened on 10 July 1801, with its terminus at a basin around 400 yards wide, surrounded by wharves and a hay market. Industry soon colonized the areas, as the canal offered the fastest means of transporting freight (and people too: there was a passenger service, the Paddington Packet, which travelled as far as Uxbridge).

The coming of the railways slowly strangled canal traffic. The land-based system was far more flexible and could run straight to factories, quarries and large towns. Over the decades less and less freight went by canal and in 1928 the Regent's Canal Company amalgamated with the Grand Junction. The new Grand Union claimed that over a million tons of freight were still passing up the Regent's and Paddington Canals in 1945 and some new investment improved locks and brought a fresh fleet of sleeker boats to the waterways. Yet it was not

1854
isambard kingdom brunel's grand station opened in this year

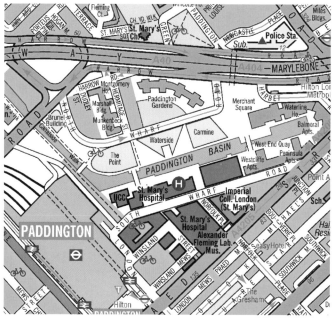

enough. In 1948 the canals were nationalized and by the early 1960s almost no freight was being carried. The canal boats were scuttled on a lake in the Midlands and the canals were left to a few pleasure cruisers and private boats.

Paddington Basin went into a decline. Wharves were abandoned, buildings became derelict and those with a penchant for a riverside existence chose the more glamorous setting of Little Venice to the northwest. A plan to revitalize the area in the 1960s, by moving Church Street market there from north of Edgware Road, and building new offices and restaurants, came to nothing, and the deserted yards continued to decay. Then in 1988, a new plan was developed by Trafalgar House and the British Waterways Board to invest over £350 million in regenerating the basin. It was to be linked to Little Venice as a hub of a waterway system that would attract tourists, new residents and businesses alike. This, too, failed, as a recession struck soon after, and investment in such large-scale building projects became unattractive.

Yet prime land right in the heart of London could never lie undeveloped for long, especially as the city's growth resumed in the 1990s and pressure on housing and office space became ever more intense. In 1999, a new plan was devised to drain the basin and create a new mixed office-residential -retail quarter. A height limit imposed by Westminster Council of 100 metres for the tallest buildings allayed fears among nearby residents that the area was about to become Manhattan-by-the-Canal, and building was soon underway. When finished, the plan envisages two million square feet of offices, houses and shops, with Merchant Square, already completed with a grass amphitheatre, acting as a central focus for the district. The imminent completion of the Elizabeth Line (formerly known as Crossrail) will bring additional traffic into the area, with twenty-four trains an hour scheduled to stop at Paddington and bring new life into a district only now emerging from a deep Victorian slumber. London, as ever, shows a surprising capacity to change, even close to two thousand years after its foundation.

◁

Ever since Victorian times, Paddington has been an important transport hub, and the 1938 map of the area shows it dominated by the railway station and Paddington Basin at the end of the Grand Junction Canal. In 2019, Paddington retains this heritage, and the arrival of the Elizabeth Line will reinforce it, but the basin itself has been redeveloped with new offices, housing and leisure facilities, breathing life into a district which had become moribund.

conclusion

In 2019, London's population reached around 8.8 million. If the city were an independent country, it would rate in the hundred most populous in the world, a touch above Australia, with almost twice as many people as New Zealand and twenty times as many citizens as Malta, the smallest country (in population terms) in the European Union. As London enters the 2020s, one thing is almost guaranteed for the capital's future: these nearly nine million people will face (and create) surprises. And they will equally adapt to and overcome them. London's genius, its ability to thrive and to achieve a position as a world city (from an unlikely perch on a modest-sized island on the northwest tip of Europe), is rooted in this very mutability, an ability to throw up political, social and economic experiments, and yet to provide some stability amidst the chaos of its periodic reinventions.

London now faces the challenge of the – possibly turbulent – unwinding of Britain's relationship with the European Union and the struggle to retain its position as a premier financial centre in the face of stiffening competition from traditional rivals like Frankfurt and New York and the growing economies of newer challenges such as India and China. London finds itself out of sorts with large parts of the rest of the country, its politics and people more internationalist in outlook than those in smaller towns and rural regions, and must balance its needs against the demands of others. And London's politicians must cope with a population that continues to grow, through migration both from elsewhere in Britain and abroad, and the need to invest and plan to prevent its infrastructure collapsing, at a time when, though there is an elected mayor, its city-wide executive authority is weak.

Yet London has always faced such challenges. If the trading competition is from China today, it came from the Hanseatic League in the fifteenth century; if London is receiving waves of Syrian migrant refugees in the 2010s, in the 1680s it played host to an influx of

French Huguenot Protestants fleeing persecution; and if London finds itself at odds with other parts of Britain over voting patterns in the 2016 Referendum or differential levels of investment, it is not a novel experience – the strength of pro-Parliamentary feeling in London during the Civil Wars of the 1640s are but one example. It is almost an inevitable result of a population that at nearly a seventh of the total of Britain as a whole carries a weight and makes demands that create resentment elsewhere.

If there is one lesson to be drawn from London's past it is that change will come, and London and Londoners will accommodate themselves to it. Some precious icons will fall from favour – though they will not perhaps be as readily bulldozed as in the past – and some previously unloved or overlooked areas and buildings will be elevated in their place. London's politicians will declare the capital's problems insoluble and then set about to solve them; London's inhabitants will despair of their city, with all its frustrations and intensity, and yet declare themselves in love with it.

In writing this book, the most surprising – and pleasant – discovery was how much a city even as mature as London can change, adding yet more layers of experience to the complex strata of its history. Those Londoners alive when Phyllis Pearsall delivered her first A-Z street atlas in 1936 would have been amazed at the transformations which overcame their city, and we can be equally sure that those looking back in eighty more years, at the dawn of the twenty-second century, will do so with equal wonder.

index

Like London's history itself, much lies beneath the surface of a book as complex as this. I would like to thank the staff at the Geographers' A-Z Map Company, in particular: Steve Berger, Steve Egleton, Jennie Fraser, Mark McConnell and Mike Waller, for access to their archive and assistance in providing a wealth of A-Z mapping. Jethro Lennox and Keith Moore at HarperCollins steered the project firmly from commissioning to conclusion and Mark Steward has done a wonderful job in editorial management and in designing the book.

Thanks also to Karen Midgley for her able copy-editing, Jill Paterson for her additional editorial services and Lisa Footitt for the index. A final mention must go to the staff at the London Library, a haven for book-lovers and authors, in which almost every word of *The A to Z History of London* was written.

Philip Parker

Map and Image Credits
© A-Z unless indicated

p11 ©Cotton MS Nero D 1 f.187v Roman military roads, from 'Liber Additamen- torum', c.1250-54 (vellum), Paris, Matthew (*c.*1200-59) / British Library, London, UK / Bridgeman Images; **p16** The Agas Woodcut map of London, from the reproduction of 1874. Wikimedia Creative Commons (commons.wikimedia.org); **p20** John Rocque's map of the Environs of London 1744–6 ©N/A; **p24** Map Descriptive of London Poverty, 1898-9 (Sheet 7) ©2016 London School of Economics & Political Science; **p29** A-Z London Atlas & Guide, 1936; **p32** A-Z London Atlas & Guide, 1938; **p34** Pictorial Map of London, 1938; **p41** ©Lordprice Collection / Alamy Stock Photo; **p42** War Map No 8, 1940s; **p45** All in One War Map No 5, 1940s; **p47** Bomb Damage Maps of London ©London Metropolitan Archives; **p50** Geographers' London Atlas, 1948; **p53** A-Z London Atlas & Guide, 1957; **p56** Master Atlas of Greater London, 1967; **p60** Master Atlas of Greater London, 1971; **p63** Master Atlas of Greater London, 1988; **p66** Master Atlas of Greater London, 2000; **p67** Master Atlas of Greater London, 2000; **p70** London Super Scale Street Map 2019; **p76** London Postcode Map 2019; **p80** A-Z London Atlas & Guide, 1938 (top); **p80** Master Atlas of Greater London, 2019 (bottom); **p83** Geographers' London Atlas, 1963; **p85** Master Atlas of Greater London, 2019; **p89** A-Z London Atlas & Guide, 1938 (left); **p89** Master Atlas of Greater London, 1968 (right); **p91** A-Z London Atlas & Guide, 1938 (top); **p91** Master Atlas of Greater London, 2019 (bottom); **p97** Master Atlas of Greater London, 1967; **p103** ©The Advertising Archives / Alamy Stock Photo; **p105** A-Z London Atlas & Guide, 1938; **p106** London Super Scale Street Map 1990; **p110** A-Z London Atlas & Guide, 1938 (top); **p110** Geographers' London Atlas, 1953 (bottom); **p113** A-Z London Atlas & Guide, 1938; **p115** London Super Scale Street Map 2019; **p120** A-Z London Atlas & Guide, 1938; **p121** London Super Scale Street Map 2019; **p126** A-Z London Atlas & Guide, 1938; **p128** Master Atlas of Greater London, 2019; **p132** A-Z London Atlas & Guide, 1938 (top); **p132** Master Atlas of Greater London, 2019 (bottom); **p135** A-Z London Atlas & Guide, 1938; **p136** Master Atlas of Greater London, 2019; **p139** A-Z London Atlas & Guide, 1938; **p140** ©Iconographic Archive / Alamy Stock Photo; **p142** A-Z Information London Guide, 1975; **p143** London Super Scale Street Map 2019; **p147** Handy Map of Central London, 1930s; **p150** A-Z London Atlas & Guide, 1938 (top); **p150** Geographers' London Atlas, 1970 (bottom); **p153** ©Redrick Photo Archive / Alamy Stock Photo; **p154** London Super Scale Street Map 2019; **p157** Geographers' London Atlas, 1948 (top); **p157** Master Atlas of Greater London, 2019 (bottom); **p161** London Sight-Seeing Map 1971; **p162** ©INTERFOTO / Alamy Stock Photo; **p165** A-Z London Atlas & Guide, 1938;

p166 Master Atlas of Greater London, 2019; **p170** A-Z Motorists' Map of Inner London, 1969; **p171** Master Atlas of Greater London, 2009; **p175** London 2012 National Venues Atlas & Guide; **p177** A-Z London Atlas & Guide, 1938; **p178** ©The Advertising Archives / Alamy Stock Photo (top); **p178** ©Shawshots / Alamy Stock Photo (bottom); **p182** Geographers' Guide to London, 1949; **p185** ©Lordprice Collection / Alamy Stock Photo; **p187** A-Z London Atlas & Guide, 1938; **p189** A-Z Information London Guide, 1986; **p190** London Super Scale Street Map 2019; **p193** Handy Map of Central London, 1959; **p194** Iconographic Archive / Alamy Stock Photo; **p198** London 2012 National Venues Atlas & Guide; **p204** A-Z London Atlas & Guide, 1938; **p207** A-Z London Atlas & Guide, 1938 (left); **p207** Geographers' London Atlas, 1964 (right); **p209** Master Atlas of Greater London, 1967; **p212** Master Atlas of Greater London, 1979 (top); **p212** Master Atlas of Greater London, 2001 (bottom); **p218** ©Allstar Picture Library / Alamy Stock Photo; **p219** Geographers' London Atlas, 1953 (top); **p219** Master Atlas of Greater London, 1999 (bottom); **p221** Geographers' London Atlas, 1964 (top); **p221** Geographers' London Atlas, 1964 (bottom); **p223** ©Joe Bird / Alamy Stock Photo; **p225** Geographers' London Atlas, 1968; **p228** A-Z London Atlas & Guide, 1938; **p231** A-Z London Atlas & Guide, 1938; **p234** Master Atlas of Greater London, 1981; **p237** Master Atlas of Greater London, 2019; **p238** London Super Scale Street Map 2019; **p240** London Super Scale Street Map 2019; **p242** London Super Scale Street Map 2019; **p247** A-Z London Atlas & Guide, 1938 (top); **p247** London Super Scale Street Map 2019 (bottom); **p250** Master Atlas of Greater London, 1948; **p251** Master Atlas of Greater London, 2019; **p255** A-Z London Atlas & Guide, 1938 (top); **p255** London Super Scale Street Map 2019 (bottom); **p258** A-Z London Atlas & Guide, 1938 (top); **p258** Master Atlas of Greater London, 2019 (bottom); **p262** A-Z Great Britain Road Atlas, 2019; **p265** Master Atlas of Greater London, 1967 (top); **p265** Master Atlas of Greater London, 2019 (bottom); **p268** A-Z London Atlas & Guide, 1938 (top); **p268** London Super Scale Street Map 2019 (bottom); **p272** A-Z London Atlas & Guide, 1938; **p273** Master Atlas of Greater London, 2019; **p275** ©Shawshots / Alamy Stock Photo; **p277** Geographers' London Atlas, 1951 (top); **p277** Master Atlas of Greater London, 2019 (bottom); **p279** A-Z London Atlas & Guide, 1938 (top); **p279** London Super Scale Street Map, 2019 (bottom); **p282** A-Z London Atlas & Guide, 1938 (top); **p282** London Super Scale Street Map 2019 (bottom); **Endpapers** A-Z London Atlas & Guide, 1938.

1. City of London
2. Kensington and Chelsea
3. Hammersmith and Fulham